THE LUCIANO STORY

THE LUCIANO STORY

By Sid Feder and
Joachim Joesten

DA CAPO PRESS

Library of Congress Cataloging in Publication Data

Feder, Sid.
    The Luciano story / by Sid Feder and Joachim Joesten.—1st Da
Capo Press ed.
        p.   cm.
    Originally published: New York: David McKay Co., 1954.
    ISBN 0-306-80592-8
    1. Luciano, Lucky, 1897–1962. 2. Criminals—United States—Biog-
raphy. I. Joesten, Joachim, 1907–   . II. Title.
HV6248.L92F4 1994
364.1'092—dc20
[B]   94-20522
                                                                 CIP

First Da Capo Press edition 1994

This Da Capo Press paperback edition of *The Luciano Story* is an
unabridged republication of the edition published in
New York in 1954.

CONTENTS

To

Bertha Klausner

a good friend who listens patiently
to writers' troubles

FOREWORD

FOLLOWING THE TRAIL of a man who intentionally leaves none—or carefully covers up any he makes by accident—is a long, dark hunt. The authors of this book spent more than a year, both in the United States and in Italy, piecing together bits of information on Lucky Luciano. Mob men, those on the fringe of the underworld, law-enforcement officials, even some of Lucky's old pals were sought out and questioned, in a plain job of newspaperman's leg work. Lucky, himself, was thoroughly interviewed. A scrap was unearthed here, an incident there. We feel the completed picture to be the most thorough and factual roundup to date on the fabulous felon, member of the board of Crime International.

SID FEDER
JOACHIM JOESTEN

THE LUCIANO STORY

PUT UP OR SHUT UP

The mobster and his cover-up; no one ever did it like Lucky.... Crime, like chop suey, has gone international.... Fairy tales and fables of Luciano; the name fits a headline, or a political football.... Narcotics agents charge much; prove little.... Slow murder, Rome to Paris to U.S.A.... Songbird in a gutter.

MORE THAN political connection, police protection, graft, and pay-off, the "cover-up" is the one sure method by which the mob grows fat in crime. Only so long as the dealer in lawlessness is not talked about, only so long as his name does not get into the papers, can he remain anonymous to flit from racket to racket. Once the disguise is ripped away and the spotlight turned on, it is the beginning of the end.

It is remarkable how few have appreciated this vital gimmick for success, particularly during the wild, alcohol-corrupt days of the twenties. Those who didn't—the flamboyant Legs Diamonds, the Mad Dog Vincent Colls, and all their gaudy breed—were wiped from the scene. Those who did—the Costellos, the Longy Zwillmans, the Joe Adonises—survived, and are still with us.

And in all organized gangsterdom, through the entire run of the mobs, there never has been a cover-up like

3

the one that cloaked Lucky Luciano in almost total anonymity for all except the very end of his American career. As one who was close to the scene put it, "Everybody knows *about* Lucky—but no one knows anything *specific* about him."

If the identity of Lucky Luciano requires any additional pin-pointing at this date, suffice it to say he is perhaps the most vicious of all the criminals in the cartel that has governed American crime for more than two decades. He started life as Salvatore Lucania, became better known as Lucky Luciano, after he came back alive from a gangland ride, and he adopted the label, Charlie Lucky, as a fitting trade-mark for a fellow to whom gambling was—and is—practically a religion. Charlie Lucky remains his underworld tag.

This sleek-tailored, wavy-haired thug with a yen for silk underwear, big bets, and show girls, learned early the value of keeping out of the public eye. As he grew in stature, from skinny, short-pants street punk to associate of the powerful Arnold Rothstein, to mogul of the Italian Crime Society and a director-trustee of the Crime Syndicate, Lucky concentrated pointedly on the cover-up.

The closer he got to the top, the harder he had to work at it. Take his appetite for romance. And in amour, Lucky had quite an appetite. Before he was the big boss of Unione Siciliano, Luciano's activities in this direction were on what might, paradoxically, be called a temporary permanency. He would live with one girl as long as he was interested. Then, when the novelty faded, he would move on to a new temptress. When he hit the top, however, he realized that no matter how he sought to avoid it, a corner of the rug would most certainly be lifted on some business secret or connection by having a young lady *en domicile.* So, Lucky changed. Now he played the field and kept on the move romantically. Few lady friends even knew his phone number or where to locate lover boy. When he was of a mind for play, he would contact one of the lacquered lovelies.

He played the town pretty good, as the boys say. He was at the hottest spots, the best restaurants—especially those boasting the finer Italian cuisine—and the novelty places, like Jimmy Dykes's uninhibited Bowery joint, where café society sought a change of pace and no one raised an eyebrow if your girl danced on the table. But where the general mob mogul on the town tried to take a place apart with hell-raising, Lucky remained discreetly aloof from any and all exhibitionism.

You might see him in this place or that—even sit at the next table and exchange a word—but never have an inkling that here was a kingpin of the underworld. It happened to many.

Once on top, he made it plain to his boys—from punk to torpedo to aide-de-camp—that he was not to be talked about. He was so particular about it that on one occasion he summoned his chief lieutenants to a meeting in a cellar restaurant in Chinatown to lay down the law.

"I'm tired of hearing my name getting used around," he stated.

It seems that several brothel madams had been sending their pimps or business managers around to thugs of his acquaintance, to ask favors in his name. Lucky was irked.

"I don't wanta hear it no more," he commanded.

During the gaudier Prohibition era, the size of a mobster's bodyguard was considered a measure of power by

5

many of the self-glorifying hoodlums. The underworld prince, inflated with his own importance, believed that the more conspicuously he was surrounded by blue-jowled mugs in light snap-brim hats and box-cut blue overcoats, the higher his authority would be regarded.

Not Lucky. He generally had friends around him, but they gave off the respectable aura of clothing salesmen or insurance agents. Shoulder holsters never bulged.

As a result of this unremitting campaign against notoriety, Luciano reigned through a career longer (1919–36) than almost any other gang chief, before the lid was blown off. He was arrested twenty-five times in twenty years, for crimes ranging from dope peddling to assault, from gambling and larceny to bootlegging, fencing stolen goods, and prostitution. He beat every rap except the first and the last. And until he was nailed for the monopoly of vice in 1936, his name had appeared in the newspapers no more than a dozen times. Even when it did, the crime reporters (and police) knew so little about him they spelled it wrong as often as not.

As late as 1929—thirteen years after his first arrest—when he was taken for a mysterious ride, the usually accurate New York *Times,* in its full-column story, called him "Charles Luciania."

When Arnold Rothstein was murdered the previous year, Lucky was one of three suspects picked up. The careers of the other two were minutely detailed. "Charles Lucania" was passed off without any portrayal except his name.

He "made" a Tammany boss whose power was unchallenged. Mafia was purged in a country-wide series of murders, and Luciano headed the resulting Unione Siciliano as the dominant power in national crime. Yet investigative bodies to this day refuse to accept his role.

He had a big interest in the Chicago gang massacres that put first Johnny Torrio, then Al Capone, and more recently Capone's heirs at the helm. He was a key to Lepke's grab of the multimillion-dollar clothing industry, which opened the door to the current labor-industry racketeering. But Lucky is rarely, if ever, mentioned in connection with these operations.

Naturally, Luciano himself denies any part of them, as he sits in the sun of Naples and piously issues endless proclamations of innocence and persecution these days.

Small wonder, then, that even the sharpest sleuths are baffled and bounce along blind alleys, tracking him. Or that, for the better part of a decade now, as many myths have been built around Lucky as Hans Christian Andersen ever dreamed up in all his fairy tales.

There is no intention here of placing Luciano anywhere but in his exact category—a vicious felon who comes closest of all characters in the Crime Syndicate to being No. 1 in world lawlessness today. The authors of this book spent too long in research on both sides of the Atlantic not to have that hammered home. The trail went all the way back to when Papa Antonio Lucania brought his brood out of the Sicilian sulphur mines to America, nearly half a century ago. It followed through to the life and times of the exiled Lucky in Italy today. There is no mistaking where the sleek beetle-browed mobster fits.

During most of the era from 1921 to 1936, the "O.K. from Charlie Lucky" was an important factor in any individual enterprise in the far-flung realm of lawlessness. In murder, the numbers racket, the Italian lottery, compulsory prostitution, and a large portion of industrial extortion, the name of Lucky loomed ominously.

That's how it was then; that's how it may still remain. In 1946 Lucky was exiled to Italy for the rest of his life. Yet, today, with an ocean between him and the really big racket money in this country, he still seems to have the last word in many things.

This points to a devastating development in organized crime, which today confronts every law-enforcement agency and every honest citizen as well. The Syndicate—the crime organization that for two decades has been a government-within-government—no longer rules only from New York to Los Angeles, from Minnesota to Florida. Like chop suey, veal scallopini, and the parakeet, crime has gone international. The mob that operated from rock-bound coast to sun-kissed shore, now skips oceans and Federal boundaries with the same unhampered ease that it formerly crossed state lines.

There is evidence, incontrovertible, that the tentacles that have slithered into every city and town of any size in the United States are no longer restricted to the national Syndicate. The cartel is *international* now. And there is further evidence that Lucky was not far away when it was carried across the ocean to new headquarters on a foreign shore. Only one man wields such terrible authority that a word from him in Europe becomes a command here in America.

However, in that same research, it became glaringly apparent that too many of the fables being passed around these days never are backed up with any kind of evidence. Too often the most casual coincidence or circumstance ... even the flat contradiction is dusted off and made to look

8

like fact, until you get the idea that Lucky frequently may be a most convenient peg on which a law-enforcement man of one sort or another can hang his hat.

Many of the myths have sprung up as a result of statements by the United States Bureau of Narcotics or its agents, who have been shrieking accusations since 1947—but unfortunately have failed, as of this writing, to come up with any solid evidence against him. It is hard to say whether—or if—the reasons for the shrieks may be politics, publicity, or misguided zeal. Or something else.

It seems that every time an election year rolls round—Presidential, New York State gubernatorial, or New York City mayoralty—it becomes stylish to inflate the name of Luciano to football proportions (political football, that is). In the years between, it is rarely mentioned. Some of the contradictions this fashion has developed have produced the neatest about-face maneuvers seen anywhere outside a military marching formation. Maybe it is for the sake of the hard-working newspaper headline writer. *LUCIANO* fits exceptionally well into a head—and the reading public eats it up.

The prime example, perhaps, centers around a pair of gangland shotgun slayings some years back: Ignazio Antinori, who was wiped out in Tampa, Florida, in 1940, and Carl Carramusa, who received the treatment in Chicago five years later. Both were narcotics traffickers.

In February, 1947, Lucky was discovered in Cuba, where he had no right to be, since he had been deported to Italy the year before. Promptly came the proclamation from George White, a much-publicized Narcotics agent, that Luciano had hired the killers of Antinori and Carramusa as part of a plan to establish a nation-wide operation in vice and drugs, with headquarters in Chicago. White was quoted at length on the matter in dispatches by the accurate United Press. What's more, the agent averred, he had "evidence" that could be produced at the "proper time," a shocking statement in itself, inasmuch as any policeman or prosecutor will tell you that the sooner-the-better is the proper time to produce evidence on murder.

Some time afterward, the Narcotics Bureau furnished information on the shotgun erasures to the Kefauver Crime Investigating Committee of the United States Senate. Any resemblance to its previous picture (as painted by Agent White) was purely coincidental. The Committee's Third Interim Report, in 1951, quotes the "following comments from the Narcotics Bureau":

"Antinori, in return for $25,000, delivered a poor grade of narcotic [to a Midwest gang]. . . . Having failed to make good, he was killed. . . . Evidently, the middle western group ordered the Tampa leader to do this job. . . . We arrested [Joseph] DeLuca [leader of the mob] and . . . many others involved. The testimony of one of the defendants, Carl Carramusa, served to assure conviction of all defendants. . . . Carramusa moved to Chicago to escape vengeance. . . . His murder . . . unquestionably was the work of the Chicago members of the combine, on orders from the Kansas City, group."

It would be easier to pair up pickles and ice cream than to reconcile the Narcotics officials' own two pronouncements. The first story (via Agent White) is that the two dope peddlers were exterminated—five years apart, mind you—to further Lucky's new vice-drug racket; the second (from the Bureau) states one was knocked off because he cheated, the other because he turned stool pigeon. The first claims Lucky directed the rub-outs; the second, making no mention at all of Luciano, holds that the orders came from "the middle western group" to "the Tampa leader" for Antinori, and from "the Kansas City group" to the "Chicago members" for Carramusa.

Utterly confusing, at times, is the manner in which officialdom insists on placing Luciano in the throne room of the insidious illicit narcotics domain, yet neither backs up its charges nor is even consistent as to just where he does belong in the traffic.

On February 25, 1947, the *New York Journal-American,* in a copyright story from Washington, asserted that Federal Narcotics Commissioner Henry J. Anslinger "officially" revealed that: "The biggest, richest, deadliest narcotics ring in the nation's history is operating in a huge revival of the 150-year old Sicilian Black Hand Society, the Mafia, headed by the Mafia world chief, Charles (Lucky) Luciano." But in July, 1954, testifying before a United States Senate Foreign Relations Subcommittee, the Commissioner was not nearly so positive when asked flatly if Lucky headed an international drug ring.

"I'd like to decline to comment," he hedged. The reason, he explained, was that even then the Italian Government was "engaged in a very serious investigation" of Lucky's position.

In the light of apparent contradiction, regard Commissioner Anslinger's testimony before the Kefauver Committee, behind closed doors, on June 6, 1950. His statements have never before been made public. The authors have learned, however, that in discussing heroin, the opium derivative most popular with the pitiful addict, the Commissioner vowed:

"Its chief source of supply is abroad, particularly Istanbul, Turkey. . . . It is smuggled in here from Turkey."

This hardly places Lucky at the faucet of the pipeline flooding the United States with the white death. Yet, the official report of Anslinger's Federal Narcotics Bureau for that same year—1950—had this to say:

"It is considered that Italy is now the major source of supply of heroin which is being smuggled into the United States."

Istanbul . . . Italy; what next? Well, in July, 1954, Mr. Anslinger testified before the subcommittee of the Senate Foreign Relations Committee, and this time he reported that the principal sources of the illicit tide are Iran, India, and Communist China, as well as Turkey. A notable omission from his list on this occasion was Italy.

Sometimes the charges leveled against Lucky have been so lacking in solid backing as to shock the more legal mind. One Kefauver Committee session was graced by Charles A. Siragusa, a Narcotics agent only a shade less publicized than Agent White. He went through generality after unsupported generality: "We had indications" about Luciano, or "I feel" so-and-so about Luciano, etc. and etc. Finally, Senator Alexander Wiley of Wisconsin could stand it no longer.

"We want the facts," he broke in. "We don't want just guesswork."

In the summer of '51, one Joseph Dentico was captured after a hunt that spread through various parts of the world over six years, four months, and two weeks. He had been among seventeen indicted in a dope-peddling ring on March 5, 1945, and had fled. At that time, U.S. Attorney John F. X. McGohey said the group had its source of supply in Mexican poppy fields. When Dentico was nabbed, Assistant U.S. Attorney Louis Kaplan told the court the fugitive was "tied up" with Lucky's "mob," trafficking in narcotics. Somehow, in the six years Dentico was out of sight, from 1945 to '51, those peaceful poppies nodding sleepy heads in Mexico's sunny fields had managed to become Lucky's supposed stockpile in Italy.

Again, when a twenty-three-man gang hustling the "junk" was rounded up in San Francisco in 1952, George W. Cunningham, Assistant Chief of the Narcotics Bureau, insisted that Luciano was "definitely" behind it, that he was controlling "all drug smuggling from Italy."

Promptly, the highest Italian law-enforcement officials pleaded for this "definite" information, or any evidence to back up the statements. They watch the tricky felon twenty-four hours a day, the Italian police pointed out; and he had been under close surveillance, too, by the feared International Police, and even by American agents who drop over to Italy. But this time, Assistant U.S. Chief Cunningham had said Luciano's connection was "definitely" established. So far as has been disclosed, though, the appeal produced nothing firm from this side of the Atlantic.

Whether the Narcotics Agents know it or not, the law here still holds a menacing weapon over Lucky. It is not publicly known that the "Terms and Conditions of Parole," which he signed before leaving these shores, states:

"If I should be arrested in another State during the period of my parole, I will waive extradition.

"I will not indulge in the use or the sale of narcotics."

Thus, with Mr. Cunningham's "definite" knowledge, all

13

that had to be done was to obtain an indictment against Lucky, as was done against the other twenty-three in the ring. The Italian Government, informed of the terms of parole, would hardly have hesitated a moment in shipping him back for trial and—assuming the "definite" knowledge was just that—for imprisonment for a long, long time.

The same, of course, might apply to any of a number of cases of dope or murder in which the finger has been pointed at Lucky over here. Somehow, it never has been done.

Now, all this by no means even implies that Luciano is not up to his dark eyeballs in the devilish dope business. As a matter of fact, our research developed—as will be detailed later—that he is particularly chummy with certain high-level drug manufacturers in northern Italy who boast solid fronts of legitimacy. Which may or may not be a key to his connection. Nor is there any intent here to detract from the dangerous ferreting work of the Narcotics Bureau.

True, Lucky's cunning at keeping out of sight in any dirty work is a legend in crime. But the flow of heroin and opium and cocaine has become acute under a vastly stepped-up smuggling traffic—not only across the Atlantic, but even more pronouncedly from the Far East.

Thousands of Americans are helplessly addicted to the slow murder—60,000, the Narcotics Bureau estimated, as of the summer of 1954—and among them are increasing thousands of schoolchildren. The stepped-up supply meant new demands had to be created, and the sadists who deal in dope turned to kids to open hitherto untouched markets. In New York alone, it has been estimated 6,000 school-children are already either confirmed addicts or on the way to enslavement. More than cancer, more than polio, more than the reckless motorists, the dope traffic is the most dangerous disease on the American scene today.

So, if this slippery master of crime really is at the heart of the evil, pouring deadly menace from across the seas, then it plainly calls for Narcotics officials to produce their "definite" information, their evidence, and have him indicted, so that he may be put out of the way. And if he is not the brain and the body of the awful octopus, then these same officials should stop painting contradictory and unfactual pictures for public consumption and should concentrate on the real setup.

Serious criticism, in fact, already has been leveled by official quarters at Federal Narcotics operatives and operations. Last summer (1954), John M. Murtagh, Chief Magistrate of the City of New York, took occasion to blast their methods.

"The Federal Government is failing miserably in dealing with both the public health and the enforcement aspects of the [narcotics] problem," he asserted flatly. "Federal authorities take a rather indifferent attitude."

Obviously, then, the time has come to put up or shut up. With concrete evidence, that is. After all, it is not reasonable to believe that the cover-up—even one as sly and cunning as Lucky's—can forever stand off the combined forces of law with their modern crime-fighting techniques. But it will take cold, hard fact—not myth, fable, or the story that makes a good headline. And it must be admitted that there has been some toying with the facts going on in any number of cases where Luciano has been concerned. Even in murder.

Gene Giannini was nothing if not a tough guy. He'd been in robbery, gambling, dope, and murder since he was twenty. Once he'd been caught, with confederates, operating a string of illicit poppy plantations in Mexico. The poppies were not intended for floral decoration; the outfit did $4,000,000 worth of opium business before it was shut down. And Giannini had beaten any number of raps the law had against him.

But then, Gene was a graduate of a very tough school—that part of east Harlem in New York that is the home of the 107th Street mob of dope peddlers and killers—the same neighborhood where, years before, the American branch of Mafia had been spawned by the sadist, Ignazio Saietta.

Of late, Giannini had embarked on a caper that for sheer illegitimacy omitted practically nothing. He and his pal, Salvatore Shillitani, had been a couple of bookies in New York, when the capable George Monaghan, taking over as commissioner, had started running the gambling gentry out of town. Putting their evil heads together, the partners came up with a scheme for selling American vitamins and other prepared medicines on the Italian black market. The proceeds they would use to buy narcotics, which would be smuggled into the U.S.A.

Eventually, the enterprise expanded to new fields, with new allies. It progressed to printing batches of counterfeit dollars, to be peddled in both America and Europe—more funds to purchase heroin and opium for U.S. consumption. A transatlantic organization sprang up, and to it flocked a number of the slickest operatives known to the law here and in Europe to take charge of the new setup.

This almost unbelievable operation was carried on from Rome to Paris to New York, and thence across the nation. It involved such top-level international gangsters as François Paoleschi, the notorious French smuggler who is known in half the nations of the world. And it was directed by one Joseph Orsini, a pudgy Frenchman, while he was actually in a cell on Ellis Island in New York Harbor, awaiting deportation for Nazi collaboration and treason!

In the States they could get $22,000 in legitimate money for $100,000 of the phony. In Europe, the deal would be much more profitable. American dollars have been the most valuable commodity there since the war. What ordinary Italian or Frenchman or Luxembourger would know whether the black-market dollars he was buying were bona fide or just so much green face tissue?

Giannini's dealings necessitated several hops to Italy. On his third trip, in April, 1951, he was in Milan with Dominick Petrelli, an old east Harlem acquaintance—and a deportee from America. They did some business there, and shortly thereafter, Italian authorities caught up with them. The old Harlem pals were no end embarrassed to be nabbed cavorting around with phony American dollars.

"You got nothing on me; I'm with this guy," Petrelli quickly shrugged, aiming a thumb toward his friend. "He brought forty thousand of the phony into Italy and asked me to take a ride to Milan with him."

Giannini was shocked at such a fairy tale, he said. Why, he made the astonishing disclosure, he worked for the United States Bureau of Narcotics!

"I was only hanging around to see who was in this thing," he explained. The way it happened, his story went,

17

it was Petrelli who started out for Milan, and Gene accompanied him. There they met two Swiss gentlemen.

"I seen Petrelli give them ten thousand of the phony for four kilos of heroin," Giannini insisted. The four kilos, it might be added, were nowhere in sight when the pair was picked up.

Italian authorities did not know which to believe. So, they tossed both into the Rome prison to meditate on their misdeeds.

Not too many weeks afterward, misfortune befell the counterfeit-for-narcotics combination. More than a dozen members of the fantastic ring were collared in New York and Baltimore. Information was at hand that the outfit, financing its dope dealings with counterfeit money, had smuggled into the United States drugs with a retail value of close to $30,000,000 in just two years (1949–51). And into the roundup net, along with the rest, went Giannini's partner in bookmaking, vitamins, and heroin, Salvatore Shillitani.

Immediately officials let out the old cry. "There's no doubt in my mind," proclaimed James C. Ryan, New York District Supervisor of the Narcotics Bureau, "that this mob has functioned with Luciano's sanction. It is an established fact that illicit drugs in any appreciable quantity cannot move out of Italy without Luciano's approval. How direct the tie between Luciano and this French-Italian combine is, is still to be ascertained."

Hanging in mid-air, as usual, was the "established fact" concerning Luciano's position, on the one hand, and on the other, the hedging remark that his "tie" with the ring still had to be ascertained. And, as usual, no evidence ever was produced to back up the allegation.

Identity of the source of information that had put the law on the track did not emerge. It was revealed that a Narcotics Bureau operative, Jean Labadie, had masqueraded as a mobster, wangled his way into Orsini's confidence on Ellis Island, and secured the evidence. But how had the finger pointed to Orsini and his co-workers in the first place? How had the roundup reached into all the dark corners—to a tiny upstate New York restaurant, where three persons were nabbed, and to other spots? The roster of the ring had to come from inside. It was half a year before the secret was to come out.

In one respect, at least, Giannini had told the truth. He really did work for Federal Narcotics officials! For several years—perhaps as long as a decade—he had been an informer. And all the time he worked for the Federal men, he, himself, was able to carry on his own business as a dope purveyor—smuggler, seller, dealer! In fact, he has been ranked, at times, as one of the ten biggest illicit drug operators in America during that period!

And in his role of informer, it was Giannini who had supplied the tip-off on the Orsini mob—the very mob he, himself, was in business with. Actually, he told Narcotics Agent Arthur Giuliana (now with Army Intelligence) about it in 1950, nearly a year and a half before the gang was rounded up, All about it, in fact—and not once did he mention the name of Luciano.

The jailhouse in Rome, Italy, is no place to spend a vacation, as Giannini soon found out.

"It's murder," he wailed. "The rats . . . and the dirt . . . and the chow! Geez . . . it stinks!"

In July, 1951, while bemoaning the ten weeks he already

had suffered in the Roman prison, Gene had a visitor—a dark-haired young man, with a particularly sharp, alert attitude. The young man introduced himself—Roy Cohn, from the Federal Attorney's office in New York. This, incidentally, is the same Roy Cohn who has since won considerable notoriety as counsel to Senator Joseph McCarthy's investigating subcommittee.

At that time, as an assistant Federal Attorney, Cohn was on the Orsini case. Since Giannini had supplied the first tip-off on the mob, Cohn was dispatched to Italy to talk to him, in preparation for the trial ahead.

Afterward, the young attorney reported to his office on the interview. He said the informer outlined all the details of the devious deal, even to the fact that the mastermind behind the counterfeiting end of the business was one Joe Petrone, just then doing a fifteen-year bit in prison. Cohn's report was unusual in one other detail: It remarked that Giannini's information was favorable to Lucky.

As the days went by after Cohn's visit, and Giannini still stewed in durance vile, he felt more and more that his old associates among the Narcotics agents should get him out of his rat-infested incarceration. To the shifty-eyed thug, one jail was definitely not as good as another. Not when it was the Roman "clink-O" as compared, say, with the new Tombs on Centre Street or even Manhattan's Federal House of Detention.

Finally, he penned a letter and bribed a jail guard with fifty dollars to smuggle the missive out for him. It was addressed to Narcotics Agent Irwin I. Greenfeld, who is now in charge of the Bureau's Baltimore office. In it, he reminded Agent Greenfeld of past favors, such as the two dope smugglers who had been arrested some months before "on information I gave you." He reported on Roy Cohn's visit, but added that because the prison keepers might have overheard, he could not tell the young Federal Attorney what he was now about to disclose. And this was that he had information to give on Lucky Luciano.

The hoodlum must have been suffering from a severe case of amnesia. He had talked at length about the Orsini ring to Agent Giuliana in 1950 and again to Cohn in '51. And only now did he recall that he had completely forgotten to mention the man who is labeled No. 1 in the business!

Whether his letter had anything to do with it or not, some weeks later, Giannini entertained another visitor— U.S. Agent Charles Siragusa, who was just then roaming around Italy for the Bureau. By then, Giannini undoubtedly had grasped his predicament—that if he did not produce on Lucky, he stood a very good chance of rotting in Rome, in jail. So he produced.

"In August, 1950," he related, "I went to Palermo in Sicily, and had a meet with Lucky and some other guys who were deported . . . Pici and Callace and Petrelli. . . ."

Siragusa's report to the Narcotics Bureau in Washington quoted Giannini on one startling bit of information picked up at the Sicilian "meet":

"Lucky told me that he [Lucky] and Pici were in the narcotics business together."

This, mind you, was information that had slipped his mind in a year and a half of previous squealing to enforcement officials. And which he suddenly recalled only when he was desperate to get out of his Italian prison. Of course, it couldn't have been that in his anxiety to get away from the rough rats and the rougher rations, he figured he would need an exceptionally good story; and a story on Lucky would be a sure-fire sales talk. It would not have been the first time that the cunning mind of an informer had slid around a crooked corner to gain a point.

Meantime, back in the United States, indictments had been handed down by a Federal Grand Jury against the characters in the Orsini ring. And by ironical justice, Giannini was one of those charged—in the very conspiracy on which he had squealed.

The information he had provided on Luciano was very hot, naturally—but still he languished in the Rome jailhouse. A Federal warrant was issued for him in the States, and still he remained.

In February, 1952, those in the Orsini ring who had maintained their innocence were placed on trial. The proceedings lasted a month or more, and one name was notable by its complete absence from the sworn record—that of Luciano.

Agent Giuliana took the witness stand and testified to the working of the nefarious network, naming each defendant and his function. He was on the stand for several days, but he did not mention Lucky. And he swore it had all been told him by Gene Giannini, a year and a half before.

Giannini should have been one of the defendants, of course, but he was not present. The defense attorneys were no end incensed over Giuliana's testimony. This was strictly hearsay information. Objections were piled on the court against such flagrant violation of the rules of evidence.

"Where," they demanded, "is Giannini? Produce him to testify to all this!"

Remarkably, the record shows no explanation of Giannini's whereabouts. Narcotics agents knew it; the Federal prosecutor's office knew it. Representatives of each had visited the hard-faced felon at his current address in the Roman cell. But no one let on. Of course, if he had been at the trial, there was a reasonably good chance that Narcotics officials would have seen one of their own informers sentenced to years in prison for the very crime he had informed on.

There seems little doubt that he could have been obtained from Italian officials. Less than two months after the trial ended, a deal was made, and Gene finally got away from the jailhouse rats that had been his only playmates for nearly a year.

Later, Narcotics officials were to claim that they brought Giannini back to the United States, a prisoner. A check, however, shows only that Siragusa escorted him to the plane in Rome—and from there on, Gene was strictly on his own. Although he was under indictment in this country, with a warrant out for him, he not only came back alone, but even bought and paid for his own plane ticket. And before he took off, he cabled his New York attorney to meet him at the airport.

The flight set down at LaGuardia field at 12:30 A.M., and waiting to greet the returned wanderer were his lawyer and Narcotics Agent Giuliana. The agent suggested that because of the hour, it would be a far better idea if attorney and client postponed any conference until the following morning. It was pointed out that Giannini would be taken to the Federal House of Detention overnight, and after a brief court arraignment early the next day, the lawyer could have a nice long talk with him.

As they stood there, Giuliana excused himself and went to a telephone booth. He called Agent George White and was told to bring the prisoner to White's apartment. There, Giannini was questioned through the night. Who else sat in on that session or a subsequent interrogation five days afterward is not known. Among those present may have been Rudolph Halley, who had been counsel for the Kefauver Committee, but just then was interested in running for mayor of New York. At any rate, Halley was to announce later that he obtained from Giannini certain information concerning an individual with underworld connections who, said Halley, had taken over command of U.S. crime, including Lucky's interests, because Frank Costello, the Prime Minister of the mob, had encountered difficulties with the law. It was only coincidental, of course, that the man Halley named was alleged to be friendly with another mayoralty candidate.

Later Agents George White and Joseph Amato were to add that this same individual was designated by Lucky as his over-all contact man and co-ordinator for dope distribution in the United States. He shall remain nameless here, because neither White nor Halley ever came up with a single bit of proof to back up the charges. New York police files are bare of even the slightest syllable that he is hooked up with the drug trade in any way.

It was even more far-fetched to insinuate that Costello may have been in the illicit traffic. The mere mention of the name of the Prime Minister is always good for a head-line—as ambitious prosecutors and publicity-minded law enforcers well know. But anyone cognizant of even the rudiments of crime and its personnel is aware that Mr. C. does not lean to dope. Alcohol? Yes. Gambling? To be sure—from New York to Miami to New Orleans to Las Vegas. Political connections? Positively. But dope? No!

In fact, the underworld recalls that in all the years Lucky and Frank C. have been friends—and that goes back to their teen-age running with kid gangs—the one trait Costello didn't approve in his old *paisan* was Luciano's dealing in drugs in his young days.

"It's no good, Charlie," he deplored time and time again.

Halley's presence at the interrogation of Giannini was no more irregular than anything else that went on in this strange case. How come a man under indictment, for instance, was permitted to travel across the ocean with no custodian? Or, by what authority did Agent White give orders to have a prisoner, who should have been taken to a suitable jail or detention house, brought to his (White's) apartment? And finally, do Federal Narcotics Bureau files contain a report on White's actions and Giannini's remarks that night?

In due time, Giannini was arraigned on the narcotics charges, was admitted to bail of $10,000, and walked out onto the streets. He pointed like a bird dog for uptown and his old hangouts in Harlem. His only subsequent contact with the law, as far as can be ascertained, occurred on June 14, 1952, when FBI agents questioned him.

The chances are he hadn't the slightest idea that Narcotics Agent Giuliana had publicly, in open court, labeled him a stool pigeon only two months before he came back from Italy. Had he known, he hardly would have shown his face in the very haunts where his betrayed gangland buddies and their friends still played.

Here was the one man who—according to the agents' own admitted knowledge—had all the evidence (and the only evidence) to put the finger on the mob lord they claim is the biggest dope figure in the world: Lucky, himself. He was the only one who ever hung something definite on Lucky about narcotics—very, very definite: Lucky's own words, he said. And with this priceless knowledge, he had been publicly named only two months before as a stool pigeon. Any law-enforcement man must realize his death warrant was signed.

There is no secret about the mob penalty for singing. The Crime Syndicate's unrecorded annals list not one, not a dozen, but hundreds who paid it.

Who could forget Kid Twist Reles? He sang, back in the Murder, Inc., investigations of the early forties—the loudest song any informer ever warbled on organized crime. He put seven members of the Syndicate into the electric chair—including the infamous extortion czar, Lepke—and went right on singing. To keep the crime cartel from silencing him, eighteen policemen were assigned to the exclusive task of guarding him, every minute of the day, behind a steel door, in a secret, inaccessible hide-out.

Yet Kid Twist had been hurled from a sixth-story window and silenced forever!

Giannini left custody unattended. No guard was placed on him; no effort made to put him and his invaluable information on ice. He was a sitting duck. And five months later, the duck was potted.

Thomas J. Steo, a nondescript person to whom life has offered little excitement, stirred in his sleep. He grunted and opened his eyes. A sharp report—several sharp reports—like balloons pricked with pins, had penetrated his subconscious and brought him awake.

It was customary for Mr. Steo to take a nap during the early-morning hours on his job as caretaker in the Major Athletic Club, a social gathering place of sorts on Second Avenue, above 111th Street, in east Harlem.

On this September morning in 1952, he muttered in protest as he stumbled to the front door, and peered sleepily into the 5:00 A.M. darkness. The street was deserted.

"Car musta backfired," he muttered and turned back inside.

An hour later and five blocks away, on East 107th Street, Anthony Santora put the key in the lock of his delicatessen shop, swung open the door, and was ready for the day's business.

He surveyed the street, which, in a few hours, would be teeming with the melting-pot population of the neighborhood. His eyes fell on two garbage pails overflowing with refuse at the curb, awaiting the Department of Sanitation trucks.

Suddenly, Mr. Santora's eyes strained from their sockets. His jaw dropped. His throat muscles sent up a yell, but no sound came. For perhaps seven seconds, the delicatessen man stood frozen.

The dead eyes stared blindly up at him from the gutter. The swarthy skin had the flat white color of a fish's under belly. A neat round hole, rimmed with crusted blood, punctured the forehead.

Obviously, this was no bum. A neatly tailored tan sports jacket and brown slacks covered the figure. The shoes had the soft look of expensive leather.

Mr. Santora dashed back toward his store, to notify the police. Before he could reach the door, however, a squad car careened to a stop alongside the corpse. Two uniformed

27

occupants bounced out. It was not a chance appearance. Minutes earlier, a telephone call had come into the 126th Street Precinct.

"I heard something like shots on Second Avenue, around 110th, 111th Streets," the unidentified caller reported. Then he hung up.

The patrol car arrived just in time to save Mr. Santora the expense of a phone call.

The killer had taken no chance on a miss. He must have stood inches away from the chunky man in the sports coat and fired. The .38-caliber bullet had entered the back of the victim's head, drilled clear through the skull, and come out through the forehead.

It was not robbery. The dead man's watch still ticked on his wrist, and the wad of bills—$140—in his pocket was untouched. A driver's license bore the name "Gene Telagrino," which meant nothing to the officers.

Obviously, the killing had not been done here on 107th Street. No blood stained the pavement. The garbage cans were erect. A dying man could hardly have fallen so close without upending them.

The mysterious telephone caller had mentioned shots at Second Avenue near 110th or 111th Streets. There the answer awaited the officers.

Outside the Major A.C., Thomas Steo was just sweeping the walk. One glance at the rubbish told the story. Red spots stained the filth—and they were not from paint. The caretaker recalled the noises of an hour or so earlier, the sharp reports he had dismissed as the backfire of a passing car.

Fresh pockmarks on the wall of the nearby building added more evidence. Bursting balloons or automobile backfires do not dig holes in brick. Two spent bullets were picked up across the street from the club.

Here were all the earmarks of gang murder. As the police reconstructed the crime, the man evidently had been standing in front of the building. Perhaps he was pinioned there, perhaps merely talking with someone he knew, his back to the street. A car drove up. A gunman placed the muzzle of his .38 inches from the man's dark hair and squeezed the trigger.

Quickly, the killer and aides shoved the body into the automobile and fled. Five blocks away, the driver slowed down enough for his confederates to swing open the rear door and kick the body into the gutter in front of the delicatessen.

At the station house, the contents of the dead man's pockets were combed for further identification. Tucked in a corner of the crammed wallet, was a card reading:

"GENE GIANNINI, KINGSDALE FUEL OIL COMPANY."

That put an altogether different light on the matter. Narcotics agents revealed that Giannini had done some singing in White's apartment. And what singing he did that night, the agents said! He had actually uncovered, name by name, the upper-level table of organization on the dope trade across the United States. No one had ever ferreted this out from behind the wall of silence and the dread threat of death to the informer.

According to Giannini, Agent White disclosed, this big business—a business that runs well over one hundred million dollars a year—had been organized internationally, and in America was placed under a general manager with four regional directors to cover the country. The sectional bosses in this top drawer set were four characters whose police records were strong recommendations for their positions. And the man at the top—the general manager in charge of the works in America—the singing gangster vowed, is a figure who has always been able to keep himself in the shadow of legitimacy as a businessman; a man who is uncommonly chummy with well-placed political officials as well as ranking mob men across the country. All in all, here were more priceless gems than the agents could have hoped to scrape together in a year of prodding ordinary informers.

Again, however, we must point out that the Narcotics agents are the exclusive source for the details of Giannini's astounding revelations. And they revealed the shockers he provided only after he was dead. In fact, the top man they say Giannini named has never been picked up to this day for dope connections.

Only then, too—after he was exterminated—was it revealed for the first time that Giannini had also chirped about Luciano, himself. Mostly, the implication was that because he had talked of Lucky, the source of the bullet that had brought the songbird down could be no mystery.

Did this reconcile with what was known, however? Agent Giuliana, in his testimony the previous February, had stated only that Giannini told him about figures in the Orsini counterfeit-dope combination. He had not mentioned Luciano. Certainly, those who had been convicted had considerably more reason for revenge. Besides, no one knew of the references to Luciano until *after* the squealer was dead. How could Lucky have found out?

No difference, it was declared. Why, at Agent White's

apartment, that night, he had voiced mortal fear of the boss.

"In God's name, don't let Lucky know," he was said to have implored, "or I'll wind up in the gutter!"

Didn't that make it look especially convincing? Particularly since it is acknowledged fact that the tentacles of organized crime now reach across oceans and international boundaries. Under those circumstances, then, would this situation be impossible: That a terror-stricken informer babbles, "If Lucky finds out, I'll wind up in a gutter!"—and a comparatively few weeks later, the informer's corpse *does* wind up in a gutter, five thousand miles from Lucky?

However, there is one omitted point, one enlightening incident, which is disclosed here for the first time. In fact, it would come as no surprise if the New York police, whose investigation of Giannini's assassination has run into one barren frustration after another, have not been informed of this even yet.

Some time after his release on bail, unguarded and unattended, Giannini looked up a certain Joe Anderson, with whom he had been in one jail or another, during one of the less fortunate periods in his career. Giannini had a proposition for his old jailmate: he had four kilos of dope stashed away in a safe place in Italy, and he wanted to get it to the States.

Now, if reference to four kilos of dope rings a bell, recall that this was precisely the amount that was missing when Giannini was jailed in Italy for the counterfeiting caper. He had said then that he saw his friend, Dominick Petrelli, give two Swiss men a bundle of counterfeit money in return for four kilos of heroin. Search as they might, Italian authorities had never been able to turn it up.

31

Giannini's proposition to Anderson was not complicated. "I'm out on bail, so I can't get out of the country,"
he related. "How about you and your wife going to Italy,
getting the junk from my connection there, and bring it
back? There's a G-note in it for you for each kilo, plus
expenses."

Anderson conceded the offer was generous, but he
wanted time to think it over. What Giannini did not
know was that Anderson, like himself, was a stool pigeon
for Federal Narcotics men!

Like a good little pigeon, Joe flew at once to report on
the proposition he had been offered. The Narcotics men
wanted the four kilos, and they wanted Giannini's connection in Italy. They did not, however, want to place too
much temptation in Anderson's path.

Go back to Giannini, he was directed, and tell him you
can't make the trip, because you can't get the good-conduct
pass required for a passport. But tell him you have a
nephew who could make the trip with Mrs. Anderson to
get the junk.

Giannini fell for it. "If you put the O.K. on the nephew,"
he agreed, "he's O.K. with me."

Anderson brought his "nephew" around. Giannini took
a dollar bill from his pocket, tore it in half, and gave one
piece to the nephew.

"You go to this town south of Naples," he outlined,
"and make contact with a certain guy. Don't do anything
until he shows the other half of this bill. He'll have the
stuff."

Giannini, of course, did not have the slightest idea that
Anderson's "nephew," to whom he was revealing the entire
conspiracy, was really Anthony Zirilli—and that Anthony

Zirilli was an undercover operative of the Federal Narcotics Bureau.

Gene, himself, bought the plane tickets for Anderson's "nephew" and Anderson's wife. In fact, when the tickets were turned over to the two travelers, Narcotics officials snapped photostats of them for future reference.

In due time, the "nephew" and his fair companion reached the appointed spot in southern Italy. There, they made contact with Giuseppe (Joe) Pellagrino, who had been deported from the United States after a narcotics arrest in 1942. The Italian press calls Pellagrino "one of the most important traffickers." No one to date has ever linked him with Luciano. He was, however, close to Giannini. In fact, he was Gene's own brother-in-law.

He showed half of a torn dollar bill, and Anderson's "nephew" showed his half. They matched. Proper identification thus established, the trail led to a meeting in the Piacarello Restaurant in Salerno, on August 27. Pellagrino came along, accompanied by one Genaro Rizzo. That day he turned over a package to the "nephew," and Italian authorities, apprised of the situation, broke up the party.

The package contained precisely four kilos of purest "snow"—worth well up in the hundreds of thousands. Italian authorities estimated the value, even on the market there, at 55,000,000 lire. The powder was all carefully wrapped in small packets, for easier transporting.

Thus, Giannini had unconsciously put the finger on his own brother-in-law and drew a new stamp of stool pigeon to himself—unwitting as it was. With all the vendetta-minded victims of his singing around the premises, it is astonishing, indeed, that no one held target practice on him even earlier.

33

The Orsini mob men had good reason (according to mob ethics) to take aim at him. And now Pellagrino's relatives must certainly feel that he had done wrong by their *paisano;* even more horrendous, his very own brother-in-law.

With any number of suspects to pick from, there still seemed a concentrated campaign to "sell" Lucky Luciano as suspect-in-chief. But Giannini's murmuring about Lucky had never been made public until after he stopped a bullet. The Narcotics men did not tell Lucky. And if they didn't, then who could have? No one else knew.

It is odd, indeed, that with evidence of the smuggling conspiracy in its lap, and with Joe Anderson to corroborate it, Narcotics officials did not seek to indict Giannini. He was not even arrested for plotting to bring in enough illicit dope to wreck countless lives. Yet, no one can deny that if he had been arrested for the dope conspiracy after his brother-in-law was nabbed, he would very likely be alive today—to uncover more of the covered trail hiding the core of the rotten drug evil.

With Giannini, the counterfeiting, and the four kilos of heroin accounted for, there remains but one loose end. What of Dominick Petrelli? He and Giannini, remember, were thrown into jail together in Italy when they pointed accusing fingers at each other about that embarrassing counterfeit money.

Petrelli had been deported in 1947, after being nailed at Tucson, Arizona, with a load of narcotics in 1942. He did five years for that. They called him "Gyp the Gap"— "Gyp" for obvious reasons; "the Gap" because of an adenoid condition that forced him to breathe through open mouth, thereby giving him the look of an entrance to the Holland Tunnel, in miniature.

The Gap was a character of some importance in the crime set. "Bigger than you think" was the cryptic description offered by one of his friends. Big enough, certainly, so that when the American Government sought to deport him, he was able to fight it off for three years. His battery of attorneys in such tiffs with the law numbered a former judge and an ex-congressman. For several years, he lived in a seventeen-room mansion at Newburgh, New York, complete with swimming pool and tennis courts.

Narcotics agents assert that, in Italy, he was among Luciano's buddies in exile—socially and businesswise. Aside from the uncorroborated statement of a dead man—Giannini—no alliance has been definitely proved, however.

He had a police record dating back to 1914, and he must have worked hard at compiling it. It included arrests for homicide, rape, burglary, and extortion, as well as dope, and it covers four single-spaced typewritten pages.

When last heard from, after his interrupted travels, the Gap was still sweating it out with the rats of the Roman jailhouse. He stayed there two years before the doors sprang open for him—long after his erstwhile companion, Giannini, had sung his way out.

Although in exile and presumably—with his record as a drug dealer—under surveillance of the U.S. Narcotics Agents who spend time in Italy for that purpose, Petrelli nevertheless managed to sneak back into this country late in 1953. His well-covered route lay by way of South America.

"I'm back in legal," he told a surprised acquaintance

who bumped into him shortly afterward. Needless to say, he was not even flirting with the truth.

He stopped off to ask his wife, Julia, about $2,500 he'd left with her when he was shipped out of this country, supposedly forever. Julia, stripped of financial support, had tried to make ends meet by sinking the fund into a costume-jewelry shop, and it had gone broke. The Gap was displeased. "I'll cut up your face," he snarled. Julia fled in terror.

Unlike Giannini, Petrelli did not take to looking in on the old east Harlem hangouts. Rather, he flitted about spots well up in the Bronx, off the beaten path of the mob boys on their socializing rounds. It was plain that the Gap did not want to see—or be seen by—his old chums and business associates.

The reason became obvious two weeks before Christmas of 1953. He was having a brandy nightcap at 3:50 A.M. in a Bronx tavern when three well-dressed young men strolled in. All wore glasses, and all were equipped with .38-caliber pistols. They may have been former business associates with whom Petrelli traded in past years—and not to mutual satisfaction. They were definitely an extermination committee. Seven bullets buried in the Gap's head, chest, and back, and blew him out of this world. The only advantage he could boast over Giannini was that he wound up on a saloon floor and not in a gutter.

The rub-out had many earmarks of reprisal for a double cross. It is reasonable to theorize that he had come back to deal in narcotics by individual enterprise, instead of for his mob. Even more likely, however, is the possibility that his playmates suspected him of the same songbird tendencies Giannini displayed. To them, it may have seemed peculiar that he had managed to get out of the same Rome jail from which Giannini had been "sprung" for squealing. The boys had had nothing but trouble ever since the two of them had been tossed into that jailhouse. Since they were already certain one had turned informer, what more likely suspicion, then, that the other, too, had blown the whistle? Guilty or innocent, Petrelli received the same treatment.

Yet, with all signs pointing otherwise, up popped the old headline name once more: Luciano. The story supplied to newsmen on this one was positively hilarious. Some time before the Gap slinked back into the States, it went, he and Lucky had had an argument over mob policy. In the heated controversy, Petrelli, enraged, had slapped the Boss's face. For this, the insulted Lucky ordered his extermination five thousand miles away.

This was a brand-new switch. Any law-enforcement officer who has been on the scene since Luciano appeared as the fancy-tailored titan of crime knows better than this. Lucky is of the modern-day school of gangland directors who resort to the trigger only when all mediation fails. These are the moguls of lawlessness who realized, after Prohibition was repealed, that the era of depositing corpses promiscuously about the landscape was ended. Crime, like anything else, had to be put on a businesslike basis to survive, especially because the mob was now faced with the necessity of worming into more-or-less legitimate circles to reap its rotten dollar. The lush rumrunning racket, in which mobster killed mobster and the average citizen felt only a good riddance, was gone.

Besides, even if the slap-in-the-face were true, which is unlikely, Lucky could have found any number of ways to get even without having a finger pointed toward himself by something as obvious as having Petrelli knocked off. After all, as the head man in the Syndicate's multisided operations, he could dictate who got the cream and who the leftovers when pay-off time came round.

Long and deep delving into this swarthy gang lord's past and present leads only to the conviction that there is more than enough factual paint in the can to get the picture of Lucky in his true colors. With all he has done and is doing—as will be related in these pages—no fictional touch-up job is necessary to make the portrait any gaudier. As the acknowledged No. 1 man in international lawlessness, he has his manicured fingers dipped up to the elbows in all manner of business matters that do not smell of Chanel No. 5. Just as he has had for the past three decades—almost from the beginning, back in the Sicilian hills.

2 LUCKY DISCOVERS AMERICA

The Lucanias leave the Sicilian sulphur mines. . . . Life in the jungle of New York. . . . Lucky, the dope-pusher, graduates from prison. . . . Salvatore from Fourteenth Street. . . . Mafia initiates a new member.

LERCARA FRIDDI is a Sicilian sulphur-mining town of some thirteen thousand souls. It squats, drab and squalid, malodorous with the smell of sulphur, among the rugged bandit-infested hills southeast of Palermo.

In this sordid poverty, on November 24, 1897, Rosalia Lucania presented her husband, Antonio, with a dark, handsome son. They named him Salvatore—and if ever the label did not fit the package, this was it. Pinning the tag meaning "Savior" on the boy who grew up to become an international symbol for lawlessness was like calling the city dump a garden of roses.

Like most of his poor *compadres* sweating in the sulphur pits, Papa Lucania scraped and saved and dreamed of escape. When Salvatore was nine, the great day came. Early in 1907, Rosalia and Antonio gathered their progeny, turned their backs on the unlovely Sicilian squalor, and set out for the new world.

The Lucanias found no gold paving the New York streets when they emerged from the sweaty steerage of the slow boat. Like most immigrants of the day, they gravitated to the slums—to a cold-water, railroad flat on First Avenue, just below Fourteenth Street, on the upper rim of the teeming lower East Side.

The lower East Side of New York is a mile-square human jungle, stretching from Fourteenth southward, through Chinatown, to the Brooklyn Bridge, and eastward from Centre Street almost to the East River.

Life on the East Side is raw. When young Salvatore Lucania was thrown into it, it was even rawer. There are no secrets—and little privacy—in the slums. In the tottering tenements, ratholed with undersized flats, families of ten crowd into space four would overflow. Women nurse babies openly, as they sit on worn tenement steps seeking the breath of fresh air that is never there. A child looks from his window into the next apartment and sees a baby born or an old man dying. The boy in puberty needs only to glance across a narrow alley to watch a man and woman undress and go to bed.

The streets teem with pushcarts and people. Children by the hundreds have no other playroom. Alley crap games are a popular local sport. Street fights are endless. A boy serves his apprenticeship with brick and broken bottle and baseball bat and matriculates soon to knife and gun.

Each sector has had its boy gangs and its older crime mobs through the years. Almost every youth considers the policeman his hereditary enemy, from the moment he is old enough to hit the street.

You are told that the slums have bred the famous as well as the infamous. So they have—jurists and princes of industry, men high in elective office and the professions.

40

But for every great doctor, for every respected judge, three or four or more names are on the police books.

From this area—and its opposite number in Brooklyn just across the East River—came Johnny Torrio and Al Capone and the shock troops that made their Chicago reign possible. It heaved up Buggsy Siegel for the role of crime organizer in California. Lepke sprang from the filth to rule an industrial-labor-extortion empire. The slums gave Joey Adonis and Frank Costello to the billion-dollar gambling octopus that grips a nation. Jack Dragna and Mickey Cohen, Buggsy's heirs in California; the rulers of gambling hot spots and hotels in Las Vegas, Miami, and New Orleans; the Fischettis, Capone's heirs in Chicago— all had their beginnings here.

It was into this unsavory maelstrom that nine-year-old Salvatore Lucania was dumped in 1907.

The Lucanias must have had their signals crossed when they bedded down on First Avenue. This is east of the Bowery, several blocks from Little Italy's borders, in what is predominantly the Jewish and Slavic section.

It is likely that here, among people of different creed and custom, Lucky acquired the qualities of diplomacy so evident in his later role of organizer and peacemaker among mobs of varied interests and diverse nationalities. Still another trait must have been developed here. Young Lucania was small for his age. In this jungle he had to depend for survival on something more than sheer muscle.

The probation report on Salvatore, written into court records much later, revealed in one all-enlightening sentence his stand on schooling:

"He was a chronic truant," it said.

Until he was fourteen, he went to P.S. 19. His former

schoolmates recall he had little to say in class. They remember a skinny, serious kid with a mop of unruly black hair that kept dropping over one eye. His eyes sparkled darkly, and he spoke with a low hesitant hoarseness that he has never lost.

The pattern young Salvatore followed as he grew up was no different from that of maybe seven of every ten boys bred in the slums. The streets are their real classrooms, the lessons ruthlessly practical. First comes shoplifting from neighborhood stores—cigarettes and candy and then, as the boy grows more experienced, loot that can be "fenced." The street pushcarts, with wares ranging from a shoelace or toothpick to a table or side of beef, are early prey. The embryo mobsters swoop down in packs on these portable stores, overturn them, grab what they can, and disappear with all the swiftness and surprise of an Indian attack.

There is, too, for boys like the growing Lucania, an annual payday from rival political forces for breaking up election meetings in the neighborhood by the dropping of prepared balls of chemicals, aptly called stink bombs.

In the Bowery area, rolling drunks who have passed out in hallways provides both entertainment and remuneration. A boy can pick up small change running errands for the frowsy females of the neighborhood disorderly houses. The take here is doubly rewarding. The lipstick or prepared hair-wave lotion can be pilfered, and thus the errand yields both a tip and the cash the prostitute gave him for the article.

The older hoodlums, who have graduated from the penny-and-nickel thievery of the short-pants punk to the mob's lusher larcenies, keep an eye on the kids. The more promising are tapped, and their education stepped up.

In due course of time, this opportunity came to Salvatore. But not until he had taken one whirl at honest toil. Fired with shiny-eyed ambition, he accepted employment in a downtown hat plant. For the munificent sum of seven dollars, he labored six days a week, ten hours a day, as combination errand boy and shipping clerk. To his credit, let it be said that most of his earnings went into the family pot. Because of economic necessity, first of all. But, over and above this, Lucky was, and always has been, thoughtful of his family—his parents, while they lived; his two brothers and sister, to this day.

Young Salvatore's honest endeavor was, however, brief— a matter of months. Then, one evening, on his way home from the hat factory, his path crossed an alley crap game.

All his life, Lucky has been an inveterate gambler. In his frequent arrests, when he was asked his occupation, more often than not his answer was "gambler." (He also described himself as chauffeur, fruit dealer, and salesman. Which may have been within reasonable distance of the truth, when you consider the piloting of getaway cars, the lucrative artichoke racket, and the salesmanship involved in persuading a reluctant businessman he'd better pay up for "protection.") When the easy money rolled in later, Luciano's bets on a single horse race ran into four figures— and that was the rule, not the exception.

Sixteen-year-old Salvatore hesitated only momentarily that evening on his way home. Then, weekly pay in hand, he advanced on the crap game. When it broke up, late that night, the dice had rolled $244 his way—a fortune to a seven-dollar-a-week slum boy.

More important than his winnings, though, was the conviction left by the hot dice that he was Lady Luck's own private darling. In the credo of the gambler—where the hunch is a religion—what else could have guided his steps by that particular alley, at that particular moment?

Salvatore never went back to the hat factory.

"Who wants to wind up being a crum?" he remarked to a friend. "I'd rather drop dead."

This creed governed his life forever after. To Luciano, a "crum" is anyone who works for an honest dollar, who has the decency and initiative to play it straight. For in his world, the guys with the flashy clothes, the big cars, and folding money never work.

Lucky and an honest day's toil were never again on speaking terms. In fact, years later, his memory had to be prodded hard before he could recall having owned a piece of a restaurant at Fifty-second Street and Broadway. The matter came up during his vice trial.

"So the one legitimate enterprise in which you were engaged in twenty years, you forget?" the prosecutor pointed out.

"Yeah . . . I guess so," Lucky grudgingly admitted.

Naturally, young Salvatore returned to the alley. Just as naturally, the dice never got that hot again.

Now, these regular nightly crap games are infested with usurious Shylocks, ready and willing to lend to the player who has "tapped out." In repayment, the lender only demands interest of one dollar a week per five dollars borrowed—a rate of 80 per cent a month! And payment had better be on time. The Brooklyn chapter of Murder, Inc., perfected a technique for delinquents that was almost universally adopted in the underworld's usury department.

They called it "schlammin." It consists of a beating with lead pipe wrapped in newspaper. It has resulted in more than one unsolved murder.

Before long, Lucania was also borrowing from the loan sharks. Soon he was in over his head and getting further and further from his immediate ambition—to be one of the sharply dressed street-corner hoods, with the big cars to drive and the lacquered ladies to loll with. Young Salvatore was ripe for picking when he was approached one day by a neighborhood hoodlum, known as Cherry Nose.

Cherry Nose had eyed his subject well through the street gang wars, the pushcart raids, and the rest of the growing-up period. He was satisfied the Lucania kid would do.

"How'd you like to make a few bucks doin' errands for me?" he asked.

"What kind of errands?"

"Deliverin' my stuff."

"Stuff," of course, could only mean "horse," "powder," "snow," "junk," or if it was heroin, "H." The use of boys in short pants for drug deliveries is shrewd business. A small, flat envelope about the size of three postage stamps, containing one shot of prepared heroin, is easily hidden inside the buckle holding up a boy's knee breeches. Law-enforcement officers do not readily suspect a boy in knee pants or think of searching the fold at the bottom of his trousers.

Salvatore was told there would be ten, twenty, possibly thirty dollars a day for "delivering the stuff" for Cherry Nose. It was a deal. Thus did young Lucania graduate into higher education.

In the making of a professional criminal, two experiences are said to be essential: a slum upbringing and a stretch in prison. Salvatore had the first; he soon acquired the second.

He stepped into a bar one night to deliver a small packet of narcotics, and the customer turned out to be a law man. The judge gave Lucky a year, which meant he would have to serve at least six months.

If the streets are a slum kid's grade school, prison is his postgraduate course. The educational value of a semester among hardened thugs, in an environment of discipline softened up with corruption, is priceless to an eighteen-year-old on the lookout for new ways of acquiring a quick buck.

To begin with, the young punk's arrest and prosecution offer a close-up study of law-enforcement routine—for future use in evading, avoiding, and outwitting the police.

In jail he gets another firsthand course in corrupt officialdom. Too frequently, the prison keeper or guard is willing to grant special favors—for a consideration. The bribe may be money. It may be goods. It may be as little as a pack of cigarettes.

Salvatore served only six months behind bars. But he was blessed with a quick, absorptive mind. When he was spewed back into society, he was a confirmed, unregenerate criminal. He returned to the slums with new ideas, as well as new standing in the community.

One of the angles he had learned was that no man planning a career in crime could be a "loner"; to succeed, he must run with a mob. Without assistants in a lucrative illegal enterprise, he too easily falls afoul of the law.

Lucky, free again, began making operational associations. In this respect, however, he left his First Avenue friends. More and more he sought out the fellowship of his own kind. He drifted west and south, to Mulberry Bend and Little Italy.

When the Civil War was still a coming event, the East Side was already a gang battleground. At the time the Lucanias arrived, the dominant mob where Mulberry Street bends toward Chatham Square was named the Five Pointers, from the intersection of streets at the bend.

The wars between the Five Pointers and the Eastmans, a gang east of the Bowery—for racket and protection territory, for gang supremacy, or just for the fun of fighting— are legendary in downtown lore. The Eastmans took their title from their leader, Monk Eastman, a bullet-scarred killer (and pigeon fancier). Probably the bloodiest gang battle in police annals exploded on overcrowded Allen Street the day in 1902 when the two sets smashed head on, in full strength. One hundred young thugs, all armed, waged a war up and down the pavement for hours. A lot of them did not walk home.

In drifting over to Little Italy, young Lucania hooked up with the Five Pointers. This was his first real mob connection, excluding the kid gangs with which he had foraged during his elementary education. He continued to peddle dope; he continued to gamble. But now the flashy clothes were added, the car and money. Standard equipment included a gun. The kid who wouldn't be a "crum" was branching out.

The Five Pointers connection was only temporary. There came a day, along about 1920, when his specialized skills as a native Sicilian attracted the attention of a more powerful set—the most powerful in the realm of illegitimacy: the secret Sicilian society of Mafia.

47

Mafia, during its heyday, was complete with cloak-and-dagger trimmings, even to the deadly code of *Omerta,* or silence by assassination, and the scratched-wrist-to-scratched-wrist initiation rite as a token of blood brotherhood. Only native-born Sicilians were admitted. In Sicily the activities of this society of bums had begun with the terrorizing of the simple natives. Before the end of the nineteenth century, the same brand of extortion-through-fear was exported to this country.

In the less than sixty years since Mafia hit New York, the books show murders by the hundred across the country, and crime in every known category: nickel-and-dime extortion from street-corner peddlers, millions a year in narcotics, billions in gambling, and even more in labor-industry rackets.

Most insidious of all has been the corruption of government. In this, Mafia specialized. So awful and mighty has been the evil invasion that mayors and governors and national representatives have been involved. The trail has even led up Pennsylvania Avenue to the very door of the white building that stands as a symbol of Democracy.

Mafia in its original form has passed from the scene, purged and succeeded by Unione Siciliano, which, under Lucky's leadership, came to dominate organized crime. "Owning" officials in high places, Unione does as much to wreck the republic as any fifth column digging at the nation's vitals under direct orders from the Kremlin!

The New York invasion of Mafia was launched by one Ignazio Saietta, a greedy sadist widely known as Lupo the Wolf—or just plain Lupo (which means "wolf" in his native tongue). He lit out for America in 1899 after murdering a man in his homeland, and settled in that east

Harlem which today is regarded as the dope mob's national distribution headquarters.

Lupo and his brother-in-law, Giuseppe Morello, put the program in motion. The center of operations was the deadly "Murder Stable" on East 125th Street—a stable that housed far more homicide than horses.

Silence, always, was demanded of the membership, since silence supplied the power to make it go. Morello's own stepson was tortured and murdered merely on suspicion of having violated the code!

In those early years, the mob preyed mostly on uninformed immigrants of their own blood, who were slow to learn that relief was as close as the nearest police station. Bombing, blackmail, and killing piled up, as tribute was exacted from the artichoke dealer, the olive oil and cheese peddler, and the *pasticceria.*

Now, if Lupo the Wolf had remained in his own racket, he might have prospered indefinitely. But delusions of grandeur tempted him from extortions against his immigrant countrymen to a real-estate swindle. Then, to pay off, he began printing up money in a neat little counterfeiting plant in the Catskill Mountains. He was sent away for thirty years.

The removal of the Wolf from the scene left a vacancy in the command echelon that suddenly blew the lid off the inner peace in the family of Mafia. Ciro Terranova, the "Artichoke King," was securely ensconced as uptown boss, but in downtown Manhattan and Brooklyn, around 1920, the chair was unoccupied.

It was at about this time that young Salvatore Lucania's eligibility for membership, as a son of Sicily, was noted. Quite frequently the novice was required to commit a mur-

49

der under orders of the high council, as a requisite for membership in the inner circle of Mafia—a token of good faith, so to speak. Lucky made the inner circle—that is definite. But whether the condition of homicide was imposed on him cannot be established with certainty.

Lucky himself has a natural reticence about discussing the matter. Suffice it to say that for the next fifteen or sixteen years, he was close enough to any number of killings for the blood to have spattered all over his custom-tailored worsteds, if he hadn't been careful.

As "Salvatore from Fourteenth Street," he had acquired a considerable reputation in the downtown set by 1920. He kept his mouth shut; he carried through on any enterprise he undertook. There was practically nothing he wouldn't try. He always used his head—and stayed out of trouble. These talents had not gone unnoticed by his elders.

Certainly, Salvatore's popularity enjoyed a sudden marked upsurge. Members of Mafia stopped around for a casual chat.

"There's trouble in the family," he was informed by these delegates. To Mafiosi, it was never "the club" or "our mob" or anything but "the family." That blood-brother initiation razzmatazz was taken very seriously.

Salvatore was careful not to get drawn into any real discussion or exchange of views. "Yeah," he would reply, "I hear things. . . ." He remained noncommittal until he had thoroughly cased the situation.

He knew various self-nominated candidates had already launched campaigns to take over the downtown-Brooklyn chairmanship. He realized that the one who came up with the most votes, in the form of guns and muscle, was going to wind up winner. He looked over the field, weighing carefully the potential of each candidate, and decided the one most likely to succeed was Giuseppe Masseria.

Joe Masseria was short and chunky, and a gunman dating back to 1907. He was especially clever at organizing his campaign for this bitter struggle. He did not move until he had put his army together. As soon as he did round up a suitable staff of ambitious sons of Sicily, who did not grow faint at the sight of blood, things began to hum.

3 LUCKY GROWS UP

*Joe the Boss, of Mafia. . . . Repertoire of
a racketeer. . . . Lucky turns stool pigeon.
. . . Enter (and exit) Arnold Rothstein.
. . . The Big Seven of the rumrunners. . . . Lucky walks back from a ride—
and gets a nickname.*

MASSERIA HELD a strong hand as he launched his drive.
He had assembled a first-class firing squad and a number
of astute advisers like Lucky. What's more, his candidacy
had the blessing of Ciro Terranova, the big man uptown.
A lot of men were killed before he made it stick, however.

Power in Mafia was not the only burning incentive
goading the various hopefuls who sought Lupo's vacant
chair. Prohibition was just arriving, bringing with it
golden opportunity in the control of the bootleg industry.
Leadership of the "family" would give the holder a long
head start.

Before rumrunning and the importation of new merchandise were firmly established, much of the illicit liquor
stock was stolen from bonded government warehouses.
The problem was a sufficient variety to satisfy all markets.
The audacious assassins organized a "curb exchange"
under the arbitration of silent Tommy the Bull Pennocchio, an old hand at such operations as prostitution
and illegal liquor. Here the bootleggers traded for needed

stocks. A dealer with too much Scotch but no bourbon to meet his customers' orders simply turned to the next curb tradesman and swapped his surplus Scotch for the other fellow's extra bourbon.

And where did these uninhibited thugs pick to set up their exchange? Only the streets facing Police Headquarters!

Much of Masseria's *putsch* to establish his claim as head of the family centered about the curb exchange.

Salvatore Mauro was one of the early contenders for the post. Masseria met him on Chrystie Street and wiped him out. Next, Mauro's speak-easy partner, Umberto Valenti, proclaimed his bid. He put together a band just as tough as Masseria's mob.

Valenti's torpedoes murdered Ciro Terranova's younger brother, Vincent. Masseria and his picked gunmen ambushed Valenti the same evening in a doorway a few steps from Police Headquarters. When Valenti and his bodyguard, Silva Tagliagamba, appeared, the shooting started. Two men and two women who happened to be passing were felled. Valenti fled, but his aide was mortally wounded.

Police streamed out of Headquarters. Masseria's gunmen melted into the tenement doorways. Giuseppe, however, chose open flight through the curb exchange. Detective Sergeant Ed Tracey caught up and brought him down with his blackjack.

Tagliagamba died, and Masseria was charged with the killing. Police had the weapon and more than enough evidence. But the trial was postponed and postponed—and finally tossed out altogether! Such was (and is) the power of the Italian crime society—Mafia and its bastard son, Unione.

Masseria even had a legal permit to carry a gun, although he had been a known mobster for fifteen years. The license was signed by State Supreme Court Justice Selah B. Strong in January, 1922—in the middle of the gun battle for Mafia leadership. What's more, the Justice had written *"Unlimited"* in red ink across it, which meant the permit was good anywhere in New York State. Later, when the gangster's target practice could no longer be ignored, it turned out the papers on the permit were missing from official files!

All the shooting, of course, took time. It was well into 1922 before Valenti was finally disposed of, on the sidewalk outside an East Side spaghetti house.

Lucky had guessed right about the war for control. Giuseppe Masseria was now established, unqualified and undisputed, as commander of all Mafia, to be known henceforth as "Joe the Boss." (The head of Mafia is always "the Boss." It was the same when Lucky succeeded to the top later.)

Joe chose wisely for his regional general managers. Brooklyn operations were placed under Frankie Uale, an underworld Beau Brummel who altered his name to the more academic Yale. Frankie is generally credited with killing Big Jim Colosimo in Chicago in 1920 (to pave the way for his old school chum, Johnny Torrio, as commander of the Loop), and with murdering Dion O'Bannion, four years later, to set the stage for Scarface Al Capone as Torrio's successor.

For the Manhattan district, Joe chose, as operations

chief, the hard-eyed, soft-voiced young hoodlum, Salvatore Lucania.

Young Lucania demonstrated such talent for organization that the Boss made him right-hand man and personal counselor. Masseria rarely went anywhere or did anything without his able young aide.

A girl who knew him in that era recalled that he was at the bottom of the ladder about 1921. "And he looked it," she said. When she saw him again, two years later, during a party at Masseria's house, he had blossomed out as first assistant to the headman.

"I could hardly tell it was the same fellow," she confessed. "He was going up fast—the closest man to Masseria. The first time I didn't give him a tumble. The next time I was more friendly." The lady, clearly, was ambitious.

Mafia and Unione have never restricted members in business operations—provided outside activity does not violate the regulations of the code. Mafia, remember, was a society of Sicilian brothers who belonged to many gangs. Thus, a member might extend his sphere of operations at any time, just so long as the extension did not infringe on a fellow member.

A wide-awake brother like young Lucania could climb high in the society, exercising his business talents to the full. He was perhaps the most gregarious of all the thugs. As right-hand man to Joe the Boss, he made the acquaintance of many businessmen—large and small—in trades allied with his own, not excluding politicians who could be useful. And he had his finger in more pies than any of them.

During the next few years his repertoire spread all over the map. As downtown director of Mafia, he took over the

Italian lottery, along with a variety of gambling operations. He had to see to the society's "in" at the produce markets, as well as to the concessions it granted for the importation of olive oil—source of rich revenue to Mafiosi because of its great demand among their people.

Soon, too, Lucania was up to his black hair in alcohol—on the curb exchange, in rumrunning, and in domestic production. He and one Manfrede operated a distribution outfit behind the front of "The Downtown Realty Corp." There were also rumors that he organized neighborhood residents, providing sugar and other ingredients, as well as the tubing and material requisite for home distilleries. This would give him priority in purchasing the output from the kitchens and parlors of the slum hovels. It was a most dependable reservoir. Federal agents and city police combined could never have dried up every overcrowded cold-water flat.

His deal for fencing stolen goods may have been one reason Salvatore took to spending time uptown—much of it around Moe Ducore's drugstore at Seventh Avenue and Forty-ninth Street. Ducore later went to jail as a fence. Joe Bendix, a common burglar who could never remember how many times he'd been in prison, got to know Lucky well. He had especial use for a market where he could dispose of a sparkling gem or other merchandise—at a fraction of its legitimate price, of course. Bendix insisted Lucky had a "piece" of three drugstores. A drugstore could be an admirable outlet for dealing in narcotics and disposing of articles such as stolen perfume and cigarettes.

Another little-known facet of the expanding thug's progress may have been the application of muscle to the profits of other lawbreakers. On one occasion, at least, he and his men were heard discussing their "cut" of the take on a big holdup they didn't commit. The inference is that Lucky's boys simply demanded a slice of the loot—with guns and brawn to back up the demands. Talk about thieving thieves!

Along about the same time as Masseria's assumption of Mafia leadership, the Diamond brothers—Jack, who was infamous as Legs, and Eddie, an even more ruthless desperado—appeared on the West Side with a nondescript mob that practically advertised its willingness to handle any line. It is historic as the first of the really modern gangs. Its specialties were bootlegging, fur and silk robberies, and hijacking, plus a side line of narcotics when the price was right.

About a year after Lucky moved in with Joe the Boss, he turned up in Legs Diamond's mob. This was a picked crew, including, besides Lucania, the climbing Dutch Schultz Flegenheimer and the jewel burglar, Eugene Moran. All later came to despise Legs. In those days, though, there existed a free-and-easy camaraderie, and sometimes even an afternoon in the country at the Diamond estate.

It was along about this time that an incident occurred that has perplexed students of crime, psychologists, and other experts.

Lucky was still handling a considerable amount of his narcotics business personally—that is, making his own distributions. One day contact was made with a potential customer who turned up with excellent references.

"I don't know what we can do," the client was informed, in the usual cautious manner. "Be around tomorrow, in the joint on Fourteenth Street."

The next day, in the appointed saloon, Lucky sold the

man two ounces of morphine. Three days later the buyer was back for more. Only this time, when he accepted a one-ounce packet, he pulled a gun and a badge. A confederate popped out of a nearby booth.

"I'm a Federal agent," the supposed customer announced. "You're under arrest, Lucania."

Secret Service man John Lyons and his companion, Agent Coyle of the Narcotics Bureau, hauled Lucky in. In his rooms, they found another two or three ounces of the drug. Salvatore was nailed—but good!

"Who's your supplier?" they demanded. "Where are your pushers? Who's in this with you?"

As the interrogation continued, Lucky's mind raced ahead. This arrest made him a second offender. Two-time losers can expect the state to pay all living expenses for quite a while.

Lucky kept answering, "I don't know, I don't know." Then suddenly he changed his tune.

"You guys are wasting your time. You can't make this stick. But there's more of this stuff around—plenty more. What's it worth to you to get it?"

The agents were rocked back on their heels. An offer to squeal from a dope man was surprising enough. From a peddler who was also a known member of the Italian society, it was practically unheard of.

"How much more?" Agent Joe Van Bransky wanted to know.

"A whole lot."

To a man experienced in narcotics, "a whole lot" means important quantities. A deal was made. Lucky would go free, if the cache was all he claimed.

"Go to one-sixty-three Mulberry Street—" Lucky filled

in the directions. The agents went. As Lucky had promised, they found an entire trunkful of dope. Even at the un-inflated prices of 1923, this load was valued up to six figures.

Lucky's squeal has puzzled crime psychologists and law-enforcement men ever since. Why did he turn informer? He has faithfully upheld the code of silence through his entire lawless life otherwise. And how did he escape wind-ing up in a bag on a vacant lot, with the penny on the forehead that marks the stool pigeon?

The explanation is not complicated. On the lower East Side, racial delineations were subdivided along caste lines. In Little Italy, the Sicilian looked down his nose at the Neapolitan. Both sneered at the Calabrian.

It is significant that Lucky did no talking about his own suppliers and peddlers, who were very likely Mafia men. But to inform on dope dealers not connected with the society—perhaps "Napolitano" or Calabrian—would not upset his own mates, especially if it was the price of freedom of one of their leaders. Lucky has never looked on it as squealing.

"What were you, a stool pigeon?" he was asked later.

"No," he scoffed. "I only told them what I knew."

As for reprisal—it wasn't till twelve years later that the owners of the drug-filled trunk even discovered who had reported their treasure to the law and put them in prison. Anyway, no outsider would have dared knock off one of Mafia during the iron-handed rule of Joe the Boss.

After this narrow squeak in 1923, Luciano seemed to exert a mysterious (?) spell over the law. Though arrested frequently, his position in Mafia seemed to render him immune to the punishment handed out to ordinary criminals.

He was picked up across the Hudson, in Jersey City, with a gun in his pocket. Case dismissed.

He was brought in when trigger-happy Legs Diamond shot up that notorious Prohibition trap, the Hotsy Totsy Club, and was promptly released.

He and a buddy, Joe Scalise, were stopped for passing a traffic light on Fifth Avenue. The policeman on duty looked over their car and spotted two pistols, a shotgun, and forty-five rounds of ammunition. But the only charge Lucky had to answer for was driving without a license!

"What was the arsenal doing in the back seat?" he was asked.

"We just come back from hunting," was his easy explanation.

"What were you hunting?"

"Oh, peasants."

"Pheasants?"

"Yeah—that's right—*peasants*."

It was only a question of time before Luciano came to the attention of the very top man. Arnold Rothstein had started out as a salesman in his father's thriving clothing establishment. By the mid-twenties, he was overlord of much of the crime of the period. A self-styled gambler, he once had a hand in a $250,000 betting coup at Jamaica Race Track and was the most prominent suspect in the infamous World Series fix of 1919, the Black Sox scandal.

Not that he ever took an open hand in illegitimacy, mind you. He was far too cute ever to get close enough to be burned. But setting up almost any illegal enterprise requires cash. Arnold had the necessary capital to invest—

at inflated profits. He was described as the financier of the underworld. Since he was never involved directly in any of the nefarious goings on, he was in an irreproachable position to make good connections. Thus he could offer protection as well as financial backing.

Lending money to gangland is a ticklish business. Such deals cannot be put down on paper, for obvious reasons. The occupational hazards make a mobster susceptible to sudden death, thus rendering meaningless all verbal pledges. Rothstein, however, couldn't miss. He simply held insurance policies on the lives of those with whom he did business! If the borrower died at his work, Arnold was protected. And if the operative got the mad idea of welching, the insurance became the price on his head.

Much of Rothstein's narcotics investments centered about George Uffner (sometimes Hoffman), onetime forger and graduate of the Diamond Brothers finishing school. (The name of Uffner has popped up again recently in unusual society. Oil leases on several hundred acres in Texas and Oklahoma in 1950 list one George Uffner as a partner of Frank Erickson, New York's biggest bookmaker, and Erickson's close friend, Frank Costello. What's more, a telephone at Frank Costello's swank Sands Point (Long Island) estate was in the name of a George Uffner. Uffner took out two policies totaling $28,000 on his life, and Rothstein held both as collateral.

Being in the same line, Luciano and Uffner naturally ran into each other. Some say it was under Uffner that Lucky won his master's degree in narcotics manipulation. At any rate, the associations they soon formed had the effect of moving Lucky in as an operative for Rothstein.

Rothstein was murdered immediately before Election

Day in 1928, in the gangland affair that caused more gaudy explosions, in both crime and political circles, than New York ever has enjoyed before or since. And the first boys to be picked up in connection with it were Uffner, Arnold's bodyguard Fats Walsh, and Charles Lucania. (This is the first time a change in Lucky's name is formally noted. The Sicilian Salvatore was supplanted by the Anglo-Saxon Charles.) Lucky and his two companions were nabbed in a fancy apartment overlooking Central Park, not far from Masseria's penthouse.

Now, a suspect can be held for questioning for little longer than forty-eight hours without a formal charge. That was hardly sufficient for the police to find out all they wanted to know from and about this trio. That same afternoon, however, holdup men had stopped Arthur Davey, a contractor, and relieved him of an $8,300 payroll. To keep Lucky, Uffner, and Walsh in custody, the police named them as suspects in the stick-up. Eventually, though, they were released. Though Uffner and Walsh were among the known Rothstein cohorts, the police knew very little about Lucania. Consequently, he was written off by both law and newspapers with a bare mention of his name.

As the mad twenties roared toward their close, the more important operatives in illegal alcohol changed their ways. They had always been "loners." Now, though, they were beginning to realize that some form of co-operation was necessary in the hazardous and highly competitive business of liquor importation.

Lucky was the inspiration, if not actually the prime mover, in the new trend. If the major importers got together, he pointed out, they could control supplies, and thus maintain high prices.

A meeting was held, and a group was formed that became the notorious "Big Seven" of bootlegging. In the table of organization, Mafia was one member, with Lucky as its delegate, aided by Johnny Torrio and Joey Adonis, whose political connections were the best. Irving Bitz and Salvatore Spitale, the underworld characters who later acted as go-betweens in the fruitless hunt for the kidnaped Lindbergh baby, represented the New York "independents." The Buggsy Siegel–Meyer Lansky partnership was the Philadelphia member. For Newark, New Jersey, it was Abner (Longy) Zwillman, who insists on his respectability even to this day. For Boston, it was King Solomon; for Providence, Rhode Island, Danny Walsh; and for Atlantic City, Cy Nathanson.

This was still far from the "Syndicate," but it did cast a faint shadow of the organization to come.

The Big Seven was monopoly in its purest sense. It controlled all rumrunning of any consequence on the Atlantic seaboard. And since the East was the major importing area, this meant just about the entire United States.

The ring operated its own ships, lined up its own protection, established loading bases in the Bahamas and Canada, and set up its own radio communications. Prices were firmly fixed. The labels to be used—even the shape of the bottles after the liquor was cut—were decreed. The volume to be imported was rigidly regulated.

It was a business partnership, and the nominal head was the rapidly rising Charles Lucania. Not only had he the organizing talent, but only Lepke, of all the gang lords, ranked with him in ability to keep peace among mono-maniac mob leaders.

Headquarters were set up in a midtown hotel. The radio would send word to Saint Pierre and Miquelon off Newfoundland or to Nassau in the Bahamas, detailing time of arrival, method of importation, and the precise number of cases in the shipment.

No deviation from the set quotas was allowed. Once Johnny Torrio planned a two-thousand-case load without the necessary clearance. Because the inventories showed more than enough in the country to meet demand, Johnny was ordered to cease and desist until business warranted.

"So, the next day," one of the ring's hired hands related afterward, "he turns up with orders for two thousand cases from Chicago and Minneapolis and St. Paul. Then he got the O.K. to bring in the load."

Although Lucky was policy-setting leader of the Big Seven, when exposure came, his name was not even mentioned. Here again was evidence of that fantastic success at keeping the spotlight off himself—that same old cover-up.

For a full decade after he climbed to the position of managing director of Manhattan lawlessness, Salvatore, or Charlie, Lucania was a mere name in the few news stories that even mentioned him. And then, one day in October, 1929 . . .

On a glorious Indian summer morning, Charlie Lucania woke up on tiny Huguenot Beach, on Staten Island, and thought he was dreaming—or having a nightmare, anyway.

The downtown manager of Mafia was not just any run-of-the-mill beachcomber, in need of a shave and a bath, that morning. He looked like a cross between an over-worked chopping block and something out of an abattoir.

Lumps and bruises covered his head. His eyes were swollen almost shut. A jagged wound, evidently from a knife, cleft his chin. His back was pocked with pricks, as if jabbed repeatedly with a sharp skewer. Blood caked his expensive tweeds. His mouth was sealed with adhesive.

As he staggered painfully to his feet and picked the tape from his lips, Luciano stared meditatively at the wavelets of Prince's Bay, lapping at the beach, and tried to recollect. His shoulders lifted in a gesture of futility. The last thing he remembered was being mauled by some unfriendly individuals in the rear of an automobile.

Staten Island is a body of land across New York Harbor from Manhattan and Brooklyn. It is connected to the rest of the city by the longest nickel ferry ride in the world. A policeman, assigned to pounding a beat on Staten Island, shudders as if it were Siberia. And Huguenot Beach is at the outer reaches of this Siberia.

Luciano set out haltingly to return to civilization. As he limped along broad Hylan Boulevard, he glanced back frequently over his shoulder, hoping some means of transportation would come along. None did. He had gone less than a mile when he stumbled onto a police booth.

For a startled moment, Officer Blanke, on duty, could only gasp at the bloody specter that, by all the laws of nature, should have been horizontal in the morgue instead of ambulatory. Lucky broke in on his shock.

"I need a taxi. Call me one, will you?"

"Cab, is it?" said the officer. "It's an ambulance you need. What happened?"

65

"Never mind what happened," Luciano snapped. "I just want to get back to town. Get me a cab and forget all about this—and there'll be fifty in it for you."

Officer Blanke, a conscientious minion, put the arm on the blood-spattered figure and hustled him to a hospital. Then he called the precinct.

Detective Charles Schley sped over, followed by other detectives. They asked questions.

"I'm Charlie Luciana," the well-walloped patient insisted. (Note that here Lucania is gone. Luciano was still to come. For the moment it was Luciana.)

Aside from identifying himself, however, Lucky gave only the barest facts concerning his "accident."

"I'm standing on the corner of Fiftieth and Sixth Avenue," he reluctantly offered, "waiting for a girl, when this car pulls up. The curtains are down on the windows.

"Three men get out and put guns on me. They shove me in the car, and take off."

As he lay on the car floor, the mysterious abductors taped his hands and his lips. Then, while the curtained sedan drove aimlessly for hours, its occupants gave him as fancy and thorough a going over as any "schlammin" administered for nonpayment of a Shylock debt. They used feet, fists, and knives, he related.

From the looks of him, the full treatment had been administered. Some of the marks offered evidence suspiciously like the more savage tricks of the mobster—such as lighted cigarettes applied to tender parts of the anatomy, and hanging by the thumbs.

Somewhere along the way, Luciana said, he passed out. The captors must have figured he was dead, or near enough to it so no further push from them was needed. They

66

dumped him. The next thing he knew, said Charlie, he was lying there on the beach, wondering what happened.

"Who were these guys?" the detectives demanded.

"Like I told you, I never saw them in my life."

"What did they want?"

The victim's memory seemed to improve with time. His next recollection made the interrogators even more skeptical.

"They said for ten thousand dollars they'd let me go," he asserted. "I told them I'd get it. Maybe that's why they let me out."

"Don't give us that," the officers prodded. "You must have known at least one of them, or seen them around, anyway."

"I'm telling you, I don't know them."

"Well, who might be after you? Anybody got a grudge?"

"Nobody's after me. I'm pals with everybody; everybody likes me." He said it proudly, bragging.

"Look—we want to straighten this out," the detectives pursued patiently. "But you've got to co-operate. Now, who were they?"

"How many times I gotta tell you? I never saw them in my life. And you guys don't have to lose any sleep over this," he brushed them off. "I can attend to it myself."

"Don't give us that. There'll be no new gang wars around here if we know it."

That was as far as Luciana would go. "Why don't you let me outa here?" he asked. "I'm O.K., and I wanta go home."

The detectives didn't give up so easily. Once he was patched up, they took him to Police Headquarters and stood him in the daily line-up.

"I had bandages all over my head, just like one of them Egyptian mummies," he told a chum later. "Felt like one, too."

No requests for further detention came from the other side of the line-up lights. Nevertheless, further effort was made to keep Luciano on ice. An old stolen-car case, in which he and Eddie Diamond had been suspect, was dusted off. Bail was set at a substantial $25,000. In less than no time, Lucky was sprung and on his way again.

The stories are legion as to just what astonishing underworld upheaval could have resulted in the seizure of an untouchable of Mafia for treatment usually reserved for the two-bit punk. Lucky's own version—that he was taken for a gangland ride—is laughable on the face of it, if for no other reason than that he came back alive. Ride victims do not. They are generally found in a bag, carved up like a beef steer.

Examine Luciano's story:

He is standing on a busy street corner, a step from Broadway, where he is well known. Along comes a suspicious automobile with curtains mysteriously drawn. It stops inches away, and three thugs dismount, drawing guns. This is the preconvertible era, remember, when it took more than a fleeting moment for three men to get out of a car. Yet Lucky claims not to have noticed this play, though he was admittedly alert for the arrival of his lady of the evening.

Then, says Luciano, he is thrown into the car and driven around the city for several hours while he is clobbered out of shape. New York is not exactly Hotchkins' Corners. People are afoot; police are on duty in every section. Yet, not once did this suspicious, curtained vehicle

68

or the violent goings on inside draw anyone's attention. Haw!

Or take the bit about the demand for $10,000 ransom. No kidnaper—mob breed or otherwise—let's a victim slip out of his hands until the ransom is in his pocket. Once let a mob boss loose before the money is forthcoming, and he'll barricade himself behind a wall of bodyguards that not even his wife can penetrate.

Another conjecture is that Luciano had a cache of narcotics, and that his captors were rival mobsters who sought to beat the whereabouts of this supply out of him. Just as ridiculous. Lucky was the big boss of dope. He knew everyone in the business. No hoodlum would have risked his own neck by moving against the headman. Even had he dared, where could he dispose of the powder without being traced through it and hunted down?

Another popular fable of his abduction has to do with his notorious reputation as a ladies' man. Luciano collected girls like a philatelist adds stamps to his album. In the course of his romantic wanderings, this fable proposes, the Don Juan of the dope peddlers met a young lady who, unluckily, was a policeman's daughter!

No amount of remonstrance on the part of her family did any good, this popular theory goes. Lucky's charm was fatal. So the policeman papa and a couple of his pals stowed the straying Romeo into a car and proceeded to impress on him the wisdom of leaving the lady alone!

This makes about as much sense as if Luciano had confessed to beating himself up out there on the beach—just for publicity. No policeman would have to risk being mistaken for a mobster doing a gangland ride job. Any two (or two dozen) fellow officers would have been eager to join him in meting out just deserts to a hoodlum of Luciano's stripe. And the method could easily have been made to appear above reproach—such as the charge of resisting arrest. Nor would anyone with Luciano's astuteness have risked getting himself mixed up with a policeman's daughter, wife, or fifth-cousin-on-the-mother's-side. Especially not when he already had to fight off some of the most gorgeous girls on the Main Stem, panting to share his bed with no strings attached.

There is, however, one rarely heard whisper that could be close to the truth. This one stems from a sick call that a former friend of Lucky's claimed to have paid the gangster while his face was still swathed in bandages.

"Lemme know if there's anybody you want taken care of for this, Salvatore," the friend offered.

"Thanks, pal, but it won't pay to take care of these guys," Lucky was quoted as replying.

"What you mean?"

Then the friend heard this story:

The highest executives of Mafia had been advised of a way to bring in a substantial shipment of narcotics from the Near East, probably from Greece. They had put up the necessary financing, amounting to several tens of thousands of dollars.

With the Greek ship en route, however, disturbing word was heard that news of the cargo had leaked. Lucky was dispatched to the Staten Island dock, where the freighter was to tie up, to plot security for the investment.

But the advance whisper had also fallen on the ears of Federal Narcotics authorities. The very night Lucky went to the Staten Island pier, Federal agents were also there, trying to pin down the rumors. Imagine their elation when they spotted an old playmate—one who had once told them where to find a trunkful of dope and had since become a recognized top man in the crime society. The Federal men needed no abacus to put two and two together. They seized this known narcotics dealer. And when he would not tell what they wanted to hear, they resorted to the persuasion that usually guarantees results.

Luciano himself gave some hint as to the authenticity of this version during an interview in Naples in 1953.

"Do you know who did it?" he was asked by one of the authors of this book.

"Sure—the cops," he answered immediately. "They were just trying to find out things."

(To Luciano, as to all mob men, any law-enforcement man, local or Federal, is a cop.)

The authors believe this explanation of Luciano's famous ride is the only one that holds water. It is the only one that explains why he was able to come back alive. It clears up the mystery of how he got to Staten Island without attracting the attention of commuters, ferry attendants, and police on duty at corners where a car would have to stop for traffic signals. And why he was dumped in the outer reaches of the island, instead of being tossed, very dead, onto any convenient pier along the Hudson River.

From this incident, Luciano made a headline for the first time. Actually, it wasn't much of a headline as far as his illicit enterprises were concerned. Gang rides were common enough by 1929, so that news type for them was not too much larger than for church socials. This one was unusual only because it was a two-way ride. The victim came back.

However, Luciano brought home from it a couple of items that stayed with him. The beating left him with a permanent droop of the right eyelid, as well as a number of scars.

And then there was the matter of a name. He can thank the boys for that. After hearing the story, their immediate reaction was: "Geez—you're a real lucky guy!"

From that moment he became "Lucky"—to police, to the newspapers, and to his pals along gangland trail.

At first it was "Lucky Luciano." Gradually, he tried other combinations. Finally, he had it: "Charlie Lucky."

And that's how it remains to this day in mobdom: Lucky—Charlie Lucky.

4 LUCKY THE BOSS

The impeachment of Joe the Boss. . . .
A new kind of crime is born. . . . Lucky
and Lepke take over the clothing in-
dustry. . . . Mafia is purged; Unione
Siciliano comes of age. . . . "Lucky is
the Boss" . . . . Strange bedmates at a
Presidential nominating convention. . . .
Enter the National Syndicate. . . . A
gang lord is erased—to save a D.A.

It is hard to tell just when Charlie Lucky got growing pains. Maybe he mapped out his whole campaign way back there at the end of World War I, when Salvatore from Fourteenth Street first felt that he was a man of destiny. Or maybe he got the idea, along the way somewhere, that he was better equipped than Joe the Boss.

Nevertheless, as the thirties dawned, Lucky's growing pains took definite form and direction. Charlie knew what to do about them.

The qualities that lift a hoodlum from hired hand to boss mobster cannot be listed, A-B-C, like a prospectus for selling oil stock. In Lucky's case, two factors are apparent. He knew the right people, from coast to coast. And his boss, Giuseppe Masseria, was falling behind the times in crime.

The seed of a new outlook had been planted in the

outlaw world—an outlook based on co-operation among mobs. Neither Joe the Boss nor his associate directors in Mafia realized, however, that it was here to stay. They were of the Old World isolationist school that shunned progress and refused to associate with any but their own Sicilian-born *paisani.*

A new generation had grown up that resented this narrow-mindedness. The boys who had migrated with their elders or who were born after their families' arrival had gone to American schools and learned American ways. These fledgling felons felt it was possible and profitable to work with fellow hoods not of the same blood.

The crack between the generations widened into a schism of hatred. The elders were referred to contemptuously as "Handlebar Guys" and "Mustache Petes," because of their customary flowing facial adornments, resembling coat hangers.

The new-generation crime boss was nothing if not realistic. Lucky saw the growing danger of indiscriminate gang warfare. Clannish, every-man-for-himself business competition would, in the end, be suicidal.

"Muscle is only good so long," was his approach. "Comes a time another outfit with more guns than you got shows up—and you're out. Y'gotta have brains and money to stay on top."

Lucky never overcame his disgust at the maniacal goings on in Chicago, where crime development was far bloodier than in New York. "A real God-damned crazy place," he would say. "Nobody's safe on the streets."

He was all for seeking ententes between outfits. After all, their interests were interlocking. And the Big Seven of

74

alcohol, more or less his brain child, had worked admirably.

Joe the Boss couldn't see it. And Masseria was, in fact, more liberal than the other immovable Mustache Petes in the inner circle. Joe wasn't against friendships—he merely opposed combination. His credo was: "An outfit runs on its own and knocks off anybody in the way."

No imagination—that was Joe.

Masseria should have had a glimmer that something was wrong the night in 1930, when pistols started popping all over the place as he and two bodyguards left an apartment where he'd been attending a meeting of Mafia. The two guards were dropped in their tracks. Evidently soft living and kicking the gong around in his swank Central Park penthouse hadn't impaired Joe's bullet-dodging agility. He wasn't even nicked.

As far as anyone knew, Joe had no suspicion of his downtown manager. Charlie continued to be invited to the parties at the Boss's penthouse—the class parties, with glamour girls and bonded liquor, as well as the strictly stag, opium-pipe frolics for tired gang lords.

However, a report in the New York law-enforcement files, revealed here for the first time, is definite evidence that Masseria was feeling, at least, a certain resentment toward his powerful lieutenant. Apparently Joe thought Lucky was "getting too big."

"He called in Joe Adonis," the hitherto-undisclosed report adds.

Joey A.—real name, Joseph Doto—is the one thug who looks like the movie version of a big-shot mobster: handsome in a sinister way, hair graying at the temples, dangerous gleam of eye. When the film bad man, Humphrey

Bogart, saw Joey A., his immediate reaction was: "That's the fellow I'd like to play in a movie."

"Mr. A." was (and is) a buddy and associate of Albert Anastasia, boss of the killers of Murder, Inc. He used to run a popular restaurant in Brooklyn. Through his clientele, he made very big political connections. He became a gambling impresario in Brooklyn, New Jersey, Florida, and Saratoga. For many years he was a major figure in a trucking company that had an exclusive license from the Interstate Commerce Commission—the Federal Government, mind you—to haul cars from the Ford Motor Company's plant at Edgewater, New Jersey.

What Masseria wanted the sinister gambling mogul to do about Lucky is not on the record. However, the Boss committed a costly error in selecting Joey A. Adonis was both associate and good friend of Luciano.

"Joey A. double-crossed the Boss," the report continues, "and told Luciano of the Boss's intentions."

In the ensuing weeks, Masseria's smooth front would have convinced any observer that nothing had changed in the ideal relationship with his downtown manager. On the other hand, neither did the droopy-eyed thug ever let on that he had the vaguest suspicion of his boss.

One unseasonably warm April day in 1931, Lucky invited Joe to dinner. When Charlie planned a dinner, it invariably was one to taunt the taste buds of the true gourmet. Modern in his taste for crime, Lucky had an Old World flair for living. He still has. Anyone who has ever been in Naples sits, sooner or later, at a table in Zi Teresa and comes away raving over the victuals. Lucky is a regular there, these days. Also at Alfredo's, in Rome—when he's allowed in Rome, that is.

"We'll go over to Scarpato's in Coney Island," Lucky suggested to Masseria that April day. "I'll pick you up."

Scarpato's was every bit as good as Charlie had promised. Joe the Boss pushed back his chair, glanced around the emptying restaurant, and lazily wiped his chin. From *antipasto* to *zabaglione,* everything had been as delicious as the Old Country.

"A little cards, Giusepp'?" Lucky proposed pleasantly. "Some three sevens, maybe, or *brisco?*"

Masseria didn't want to move. "Good," he agreed. "For an hour or so. Then I must go."

A deck was obtained from the house, and for some forty-five minutes they played and talked. Except for the help sweeping up in the kitchen, Scarpato's was now completely empty. Lucky glanced at his watch and excused himself. Slowly he walked away among the white-clothed tables and disappeared into the men's room.

The finale of that dinner party is reported in the book, *Murder, Inc.,** written a couple of years ago, by one of the authors of this volume:

It is too bad Lucky took so long washing his hands, he explained. He missed it when impeachment proceedings were carried out against Joe the Boss. It seemed there must have been three voters. They came in while Lucky was away washing his hands—as he explained—and he missed it all. More than twenty bullets were sprayed around the premises. The passing years must have robbed Joe of his agility, for five of them were buried in him.

The Boss (ex) was slumped over. His right arm was pushed out straight, as if it had been his play with the cards. His hand

* By Sid Feder and Burton Turkus (New York: Farrar, Straus and Young, 1951).

lay frozen on the gleaming cloth. The lone bright spot of the ace of diamonds sparkled up from his lifeless palm. Ever since that night, it has not been considered good manners to mention the ace of diamonds in certain circles—such as Mafia.

Lucky said sure, he heard the shooting.

"As soon as I finished drying my hands, I hurried out and walked back to see what it was about," he related.

He was too late to see who the impeachers were. Thus he is unable to comment on the report, as mentioned in Case No. 133-31 of New York law-enforcement files, that among those present may have been such stalwarts as Albert Anastasia, Joey Adonis, and Buggsy Siegel.

With the extermination of Masseria, the younger element was dominant in "the family" for the first time. Unione Siciliano, born with the Americanized generation, had reached adolescence.

There still remained, however, some unfinished business. The Mustache Petes whom Masseria left behind were not yet ready to yield their long-rooted authority. They retired to a spot in Brooklyn to lay plans for the long-simmering war that was in the open at last. As their captain they elected one Salvatore Marrizano, or Maranzano.

The new leader hadn't been in this country very long, but he had already demonstrated remarkable aptitude for self-advancement. He had a suite of modern offices high in the New York Central Building, a-straddle Park Avenue and towering over Grand Central Station. The sign on the door announced his business as real estate. Very likely, Maranzano wouldn't have known a land title from *smörgåsbord*. His real line consisted of smuggling in aliens from Sicily and lower Italy, especially criminals whose guns were ready for hire.

Now, at about this time, civil war broke out in the clothing industry. Dissension ripped at the vast Amalgamated Clothing Workers of America—the parent labor organization that produces some 75 per cent of all the men's clothing in the nation.

Hovering in the background was the greatest organizational conniver crime ever saw. He was a small, nondescript man. His name was Louis Buchalter, but so widespread was his infamy that, like Bluebeard, he was known by a single alias—Lepke. Just as Frank Costello was the "Prime Minister" and Lucky became "the Boss," Lepke was "Judge Louis" in the underworld.

In many ways, Lucky and Lepke were cut from the same pattern. Luciano's father was a poor, honest mechanic. His brothers went into trades—tailoring and tonsorial. Lucky landed in the most vile and violent lawlessness.

Lepke's father, industrious and decent, worked day and night for his family. One son became a leading clergyman, another a highly respected pharmacist, a third a successful dentist. The only daughter, a teacher, headed the English Department of her school. Then there was Lepke.

"The most dangerous criminal in America," F.B.I. director J. Edgar Hoover called him. He ordered at least seventy murders—very likely a hundred or more.

He chose as his prey ordinary people and their ordinary needs. From the prosaic realms of labor and industry, he extorted five to ten million dollars a year for a decade—from more than half the states in the Union.

He virtually owned the clothing industry. From this one gold mine extortion alone, his take-home pay was a gaudy million-a-year—after settling all protection and operational costs. On top of that was the plunder he exacted from the hundred-million-dollar rabbit-fur industry, the bakery industry (from which, it was estimated, his outfit seized a penny a loaf tribute—on all the bread eaten in a city of over seven million, mind you), motion-picture theaters, leather workers, milliners, handbag makers, shoe manufacturers, the taxicab racket, the poultry-market racket, the restaurant racket, ad infinitum. And his gimmick was captive labor unions and captive trade associations.

He introduced Luciano to this brand of illegitimacy, and they worked a couple of industries on a co-operative basis—the cleaning and dyeing trade and the motion-picture-theater business.

The latter was a matter of cheating cheaters, inspired by the theater owners themselves. To break the powerful camera operators' union, they asked Lepke to form a rival labor organization. From this experience, Lucky absorbed a valuable lesson applicable to almost any line of criminal endeavor.

"Y'see," Lepke pointed out, "we're doing somebody else's dirty work."

"But what happens if the new union takes over?" Lucky inquired.

"That's easy—then we take them over."

Lepke became interested in the clothing industry through supplying strong arms for both labor and management in their frequent strife. Each of the many crafts in clothing manufacture had its own union, but all were gathered under the sprawling wing of the Amalgamated Clothing Workers. It numbers close to half a million workers today. When Lepke arrived on the scene, it already comprised an army of some fifty thousand.

He made the remarkable discovery that the heart of this

labor Goliath was the Cloth Cutters' Union of about eighteen hundred men. If they stopped work, the entire business had to shut down. Thus, the continued employment of some fifty thousand workers could be controlled by the manipulation of less than two thousand.

Lepke quietly inched his way inside the door of the Cutters' Union by obtaining the assignment as the local's staff strong arm. Not long afterward, Philip Orlofsky, the union's business agent, was elevated to the top spot as manager. Without warning, the well-knit Amalgamated organization was blasted by factional rebellion that appeared entirely spontaneous. Orlofsky's group launched a rival parent organization to grab control from the administration of Amalgamated's president, Sidney Hillman. A key man in the Hillman organization was Bruno Belea, Hillman's efficient expediter.

The imminent danger of Lepke's presence as Svengali for the rebels was realized at once. Counterenforcement—meaning strong-arm—measures obviously were imperative.

Calling in Luciano, however, would amount to the same grave error Masseria had committed when he asked Joe Adonis to do something about Lucky's getting "too big." Lucky and Lepke had had dealings. From mutual satisfaction, had grown mutual respect. Their outlooks on mob co-operation were identical. They had found complete agreement as regards the muscle-conscious tough guys who worked for them.

"Too many prima donnas," Lucky had said once in discussing some of the boys, who had strongly urged a new enterprise, unattractive to the skeptical leaders.

"Sure, Charlie," nodded Lepke. "But they wouldn't be

working for us otherwise. Smarten 'em up, and they'd be out on their own."

Lucky was approached as a counter strong arm to Lepke in the civil war. He shook his head.

"They're friends of mine," he explained. "I can't handle this."

As a result, other allies were sought. And the eyes of the seekers fell on the Mustache Petes, the remnants of Mafia. They were still a formidable force, under their aggressive new commander, Salvatore Maranzano. The alien smuggler was sufficiently astute, however, to look up Lucky before committing himself.

"I'm taking the contract, Charlie," he explained. "But there's nothing to worry about. We're just going for the payday. We won't make trouble."

"O.K.," Lucky conceded. "Just remember—those guys are my pals."

What Maranzano did not appreciate was that he was bucking the mob mogul who practically wrote the book on labor-industry racketeering. In no time at all, the trouble he had promised wouldn't happen, did. Some of Maranzano's sluggers threw rocks at the window of a clothing district shop. John Ferrari, a clothing manufacturer who happened to be in the place, led a charge outside to do battle. An Amalgamated business agent was shot.

"That Ferrari," the enraged Maranzano charged. "He made this trouble, coming out like that, when it wasn't even his window. Take care of him," he directed.

The inexperience of a leader is reflected in his men. Maranzano's torpedoes "took care of" the wrong man. They murdered Ferrari's brother, Guido, by mistake!

The undue publicity attendant on the murder of a noncombatant represented, to Lepke, a menace to his plans. He dropped in on his old chum and suggested that Lucky get his head down out of the clouds.

"You think this is a clothing business fight only? It ain't. Maranzano is out to take over the 'family' again. He knows you and me are pals—right? He figures hitting me is the same as hitting you."

Lucky was convinced. The ultimate and decisive purge of Mafia was decreed. The word went out that all Mustache Petes of any consequence had to go, not only in New York, but clear across the country. All the mob bosses pledged their co-operation.

Almost simultaneously, on September 11, 1931, and within forty-eight hours thereafter, some thirty to forty Mafia executives were wiped out from coast to coast. So remarkable a feat of planning and execution was it that these thirty-odd homicides have never been linked, one with another, as organized mass murder.

And the first to get it was Maranzano.

Five men strode through the door marked "REAL ESTATE" in the New York Central Building that September 11. They flashed what appeared to be police badges, and mumbled something about a raid. The leader was Bo Weinberg, ace of Dutch Schultz's crack crew of killers. The group also included two trigger men from the Newark mob and two Bug & Meyer hoods. None of the quintet was a Unione man. That obviated possible identification when they barged into Maranzano's suite.

There were twelve visitors in the outer office. Confronted with the badges, they lined up against the wall. Two of the raiding party crashed into the inner room and disposed of Maranzano by shooting and knifing.

83

One of the dozen bystanders was Tommy Brown. Tommy—or Three-Finger—Brown is the most familiar alias of Lucky's long-time friend, Gaetano (Tommy) Luchese. Many law-enforcement men claim that Luchese-Brown stands high in the gangland hierarchy to this day. Some even say he is top man. If he is, no one has even come close to proving it. He operates as a legitimate garment manufacturer. He has been chummy with almost every ranking mob man across the country and uncommonly (for a man of his background) friendly with well-placed political figures and with officials in the office of the United States Attorney. He has been on social home-and-home visiting terms with Federal Judge Thomas Murphy (former New York City Police Commissioner) and has shared hotel quarters with a recent U.S. Attorney. Not too long ago, when he needed a Certificate of Good Conduct from the Parole Board (to regain the right to vote, which he lost on his imprisonment for car-stealing back in the twenties), those who went to bat for him included State Senator Arthur H. Wicks, recent Lieutenant Governor of the State, and Armand Chankalian, who was Administrative Assistant to the U.S. Attorney. In contrast—name almost any gang lord, from Costello and the late Lepke in the East to the insidious Dragna brothers in California—and Three-Finger Tommy is sure to be acquainted, at least. His clothing business interests are reported to extend considerably beyond simple manufacturing, although here again no law-enforcement arm—Federal, state, or municipal—has ever produced one bit of evidence to prove he is anything but what he claims to be. Aside from his one stretch for automobile theft thirty years ago, the law has pinned nothing on him that it could back up with proof.

His presence in Maranzano's office that day has never been explained. No one has ever pointed to Tommy as the "finger man" and "caser" on the job. There is no doubt that two roles so vital to a successful gangland rub-out, in a contract as important as this, would have required an expert hand.

The day of the purge was the end of the line for the Mustache Petes. Mafia, as it had been known, was wiped out as the Italian crime society. Unione Siciliano had come of age.

Many investigative agencies, especially interested in headlines, have made a habit of lumping Italian crime groups in one pot, with interchangeable names. The Kefauver Senate Crime Investigating Committee, when it staged its TV circus in 1951, spread the misconception by declaring that Mafia is "also known as Black Hand and Unione Siciliano." The Senators should have taken the trouble to examine police files. Some four decades ago, the Black Hand was exposed, once and for all, by Lieutenant Joe Petrosino, one of New York's all-time great police officers, as having *no* connection with *any* organization.

Ever since the purge of '31, Unione has been no more Mafia than a processed shot of heroin is the original poppy. This has even been a matter of sworn testimony from various underworld sources. J. Richard (Dixie) Davis, notorious attorney for Dutch Schultz and many other mob lords, turned state's evidence not long afterward and told under oath of the purge that left Unione and Lucky as the surviving power.

In 1944, eagle-beaked Ernest Ruppolo, a one-eyed assassin known as the Hawk, pleaded guilty to performing a homicide for $500, and began to sing to save himself from a life sentence. Unione, the Hawk swore, is the successor to, but not the continuation of, Mafia.

As events progressed, the Hillman faction was not in a comfortable position in the internal war in the clothing industry. Lepke, eager for the kill, talked with Lucky about the situation.

"Bruno Belea's as much to blame as anybody," the soft-spoken extortion czar emphasized. "He should be taken care of too."

The threat to Belea's life was the key move. A man marked for sudden death—and aware of it—will hardly quibble over a proffered reprieve. Belea saw Lucky. Bargaining time had come.

Shortly afterward, Lepke summoned his top expert on labor manipulation, Max Rubin.

"I just had a meet with Charlie Lucky," Lepke advised. "We made a deal."

"Good," the aide nodded. "What was it, Louis?"

"Orlofsky gives up his union—he is out," Lepke stated. "We'll see he gets a year's pay."

Thus Lepke topped off his connivance with treachery. He took charge himself after that. His men said he even used Belea's rooms for his staff meeting.

"I," he proclaimed, "am Amalgamated now!"

Such disclosures must leave a decidedly unpleasant taste with the average citizen. Remember that Amalgamated's president was the same Sidney Hillman who, as director of the Office of Production Management during World War II, was one of the half-dozen most important men in the United States. His position was emphasized in 1944, when President Roosevelt was questioned about the acceptability of Harry S. Truman as his running mate for re-election.

"Clear it with Sidney," the President commanded.

The clothing revolt had achieved many things: Lepke had the industry in his pocket, to hold until he was eliminated and Amalgamated cleaned house some years later. Mafia was purged. Unione spread like a high tide of scum across the country. And sitting at the head of the Italian crime society was Charlie Lucky—who might have been a "crum."

The title emblematic of undisputed chieftain of the society was Luciano's now. The word went out:

"Lucky is the Boss!"

As the Boss, Luciano was power with a capital "P." The next step was to get a man of his own in the driver's seat politically. Albert C. Marinelli was picked for the job.

Marinelli had been born on the lower East Side; he grew up with its leading citizens. He had been an election district captain under Big Tim Foley, the Tammany leader from downtown who is still reverentially remembered, and he'd been port warden of New York in the early twenties, when rumrunning made a boulevard of gold out of the harbor. His trucking business office in Little Italy was at Kenmare and Mulberry Streets, in the middle of the bootleggers' curb exchange.

The candidacy of Albert C. Marinelli as Tammany District leader downtown was announced in opposition to the incumbent, Harry C. Perry. Although confident, the boys took no chances that the party's election organization would upset their plans. The underworld story is that a couple of Lucky's hands walked into Perry's office, laid a pair of mean-looking pistols on his desk, and advised him to resign before the election.

"You got a wife and kids, ain't you?" they demanded. Perry made no response to the obvious. "You wouldn't want to see them in the river, would you?" the hoods went on. "Well, just remember, Marinelli gets the job. And the boss says no slip-ups. Get it?"

The next day, Perry resigned. He wouldn't discuss the rumors concerning his abdication. He did, however, let drop one short, significant sentence:

"I got out of the district because I was afraid to stay."

Marinelli became the district leader. Within five months of his accession as supreme boss of the society, Lucky's man was in the councils of Tammany!

In 1932, the rival candidacies of Al Smith and Franklin D. Roosevelt for the Democratic Presidential nomination provided an inside peek at just how powerful Lucky had become. In Tammany Hall, loyalty to Smith was almost a religion. But Jimmy Hines, the Hall's nominal head, had his eyes on the patronage plums, should the twelve-year drought since the last Democratic President finally end. He threw his support to F.D.R.

In Hines's betrayal of the Hall's old warrior lay a chance for Marinelli to consolidate his increasing strength inside the Tammany Wigwam. He stayed with Smith.

Hines and Marinelli headed rival delegations to the Democratic National Convention in Chicago that summer. Some of the roommate combinations in the Drake Hotel for the conclave were truly wonderful. New York's top political leader, Hines, shared quarters with gangland's czar of gambling, Frank Costello. Marinelli, number-two man in city politics, had, as a roomie, his old buddy, Lucky

Luciano, supreme boss of the Italian crime society in America!

There is no record that Lucky exerted influence on any delegate. He would be far too cute for that. But some of the delegates had lacked the foresight to make sure of adequate thirst quenchers for the duration of the convention —which occurred during Prohibition, of course. Lucky did not fail a single one of them in their hour of need.

The remarkable pairings at the conclave that nominated President Roosevelt for the first of his four terms exposed to public view the insidious gimmick by which modern organized crime ticks. It made no difference to gangdom that Hines and Marinelli were at each other's throats politically. Lucky and Frank C. were both "members of the same club"—the Mob. The important fact was that two politicians, representing the voting power of the world's biggest city, were backing rival candidates. To the one on the right horse would come the patronage plums—especially in the U.S. Attorney's office, where trouble for the crime moguls was cooked up in spite of corruptive efforts.

The Mob was simply making sure it was going to be on the right side, no matter which side won!

That's how gangdom has done it ever since Lucky took charge. In crime, one miss can be fatal. The lifelong gambler takes no gamble at all in the field of protective insurance.

The new Boss now zoomed crime to a position where it was no longer the servant of politicians, but their master. His man, Marinelli, soon took over the power in Tammany. The underworld had ceased buying political protection from elected leaders. It was now putting up its own candidates—and owning them. And Lucky, who never became a citizen or earned the right to vote in this country, was pulling the strings!

In the 1933 municipal elections, for instance, a landslide in the other boroughs of the city put Fiorello La Guardia into the mayor's chair. Manhattan, under the grip of Marinelli (and Lucky), not only stood off La Guardia's boom, but elected Tammany's district attorney and borough president.

The New York Democratic County Committee, which served Marinelli, was charged by Thomas E. Dewey with having twenty-five members either convicted or accused of such felonies as burglary, homicide, assault, fencing stolen goods, and narcotics. And eight of the twenty-two election inspectors—or more than one-third of those assigned to ensure honest elections—were ex-convicts or charged with criminal acts!

As late as 1935, with La Guardia screaming death to gangsters in radio broadcasts, there were shakedowns of thousands a week in industrial rackets. Lucky, and later Frank Costello, who learned from his cunning Sicilian *paisan,* dictated the appointment of judges and prosecutors, even state legislators.

As the scope of crime widened, the corrupting fingers even poked into national office. Many things that affected his business, Lucky discovered, were done in the halls of Congress. Congress could hamstring trade between mobs when it crossed state lines. Income tax was handled on the national level. So was deportation.

As a matter of fact, the Mob could even put a Presidential candidate across, simply by dictating the vote of key delegations—not merely in New York, but in dozens of cities and states.

And make no mistake about this: Republican, Democratic, or independent—the underworld moved in on all parties.

So firmly did Lucky and his associates entrench themselves that they withstood—barring minor bruises—the shock of investigation after investigation. The ironical truth is that the very probes aimed at cleaning out corruption were turned into steppingstones toward greater power by America's criminal empire. Fighting the inquiries sapped Tammany's treasury. And with the great business depression of the early thirties cutting its swath, gangland plunderers were almost the only businessmen with cash to let out.

As recently as 1952, irked at being labeled head of the international dope ring by various official bodies and individuals, Lucky announced that, from far-off Italy, he could—and would—still blow the lid off.

"I'll tell certain stories," he threatened, "which will make everybody in the U.S. take notice."

The protection that clears a killer of murder in New York cannot get Mr. Milquetoast out of a traffic ticket in Kansas City. But Lucky had the key to transform local crime into a national menace that would make the Borgias look like Sunday-school teachers and the Medicis angels of mercy.

And this key was syndication.

With the doom of Prohibition, the thugs grown fat on profits from beer and alcohol had no intention of turning to anything so peasantlike as earning an honest dollar.

Some, aware of Lepke's gold mine, got into labor and industry extortion. Dutch Schultz gave it a switch with a restaurant-protection proposition that quickly became a million-dollar piracy. Narcotics traffic quickened, too, as the deposed bootleggers turned to new fields.

By far the major conversion was to gambling. Frank Erickson, the East's biggest bookie, had shown them the light. The moon-faced odds man, who started out as a busboy in a Coney Island eatery, has admitted paying a man $20,000 a year just to tote his gambling take to the bank!

As a result, bookmaking, slot machines, plush gambling joints—any enterprise of chance to take the sucker's money —became the biggest of all postrepeal operations. A recent official report put the yearly national take from slot machines alone at $2,000,000,000—of which $400,000,000 goes for protection. Erickson's records disclosed that he banked over $30,000,000 in twelve years. Dutch Schultz's Harlem numbers banks were a $20,000,000 business.

Lucky was right in there with the rest. He had a piece of a horse-room outfit that Fred Bachman, a well-known character of the day, was handling. Lucky's Chicago Club at Saratoga Springs, New York, ranked with the famed Piping Rock and Arrowhead at the Spa. Like so many of the mob moguls across the country, he also cut in some Florida clubs.

These were the gambling gold mines—the swank saloons, plush eating places, and roadhouses—with craps, roulette, or name-your-game behind the velvet drapes in the back room or upstairs. They had to be, with the investments involved. Costello's Beverly Club, not far from downtown New Orleans, cost $1,000,000. The flamboyant Flamingo Club in Las Vegas was a $6,000,000 investment for Buggsy

Siegel and several others—including Costello—who bailed him out before it was finished.

The new executive line-up was already posted by the time Prohibition was interred. In the East, the leading establishments were headed by Lucky, Costello, Adonis, Lepke, Longy Zwillman (in New Jersey), Dutch Schultz, and the Buggsy Siegel—Meyer Lansky partnership, a notorious gang of cutthroats known as the Bug & Meyer Mob. The top executives, with the exception of Schultz—who was considered an insane individualist having little in common with the others—were known loosely as the "Big Six." But the entire setup was still more or less horse-and-buggy stuff. Each individual boss or partnership lined up its own protection and declared mob war indiscriminately.

By the end of '32, the conversion from alcohol was already so spectacular a success that the bosses sought insurance against any interruption in the boom. The top moguls got together in a plush Park Avenue hotel suite to see what could be done.

The gimmick was so obvious it is hard to believe the gang lords had missed it before. True, Lucky had had the general idea for years. It was the kind of thinking that had made him the Boss. Lepke, too, had been a believer. But despite their persuasive authority, the one who put it over finally was chunky Johnny Torrio. The round little man started out as a Brooklyn water-front saloonkeeper, went west to take over Chicago—and then turned it over to Al Capone, because it got so a fellow could hardly sit down to tea without a gun going off.

At that famous hotel meeting, Torrio called for the floor as the first order of new business.

"See what you think of this," he began. And he proceeded to tell the crime moguls of the East how they could have power and a guarantee of personal security by cooperative effort. Mumbled protests greeted the suggestion from the individualistic, egoistic mob lords.

"You don't have to throw everything in one pot," they were counseled. "Each guy keeps what he's got now, but we make one big combination to work with."

Pooling of certain resources only—connections, for instance—that was the idea. With repeal, a lot of contacts were disappearing. Those that remained should be tossed into the pot, for every mob's common use.

There were still plenty of protests from those present. Then Lucky and Lepke threw in their ideas. The first requisite was the elimination of fighting among themselves.

"A guy gets hit—his troop goes after the outfit that did it. First thing you know, a war's on."

These fellows knew how great had been the toll of intermob conflicts. This new suggestion snapped up their attention.

But not one of them would ever forgo his cherished overlordship sufficiently to agree to a single ruling chairman or president of any combination.

Once more the protests were met and satisfied. Let all the bosses sit as a panel, a board of directors, to run things. No sacrifices would have to be made by any boss; all would be on the same authoritative level. The board could arbitrate intermob disputes, dictate policy, and rule on anything requiring intergang negotiation.

Enthusiasm now replaced hostility. This new-style crime that Lucky had sponsored for so long sounded like gilt-edged insurance. The moguls could not help but approve.

94

Further details were ironed out, chiefly under the sage counsel of Lucky and Lepke, and it was put into operation.

Each mob leader still operated his own business affairs, but he was backed now by the combined strength of all the mobs in the organization. The territory of each, his rackets and his authority, were inviolate. No killings were allowed in his domain unless he gave the nod. In fact, the only gang crime that could occur in his bailiwick without his blessing was that in which the board of directors overruled him. And that step could never be taken until he had presented his side. Democracy had hit crime!

This was more than a corporation. It was a cartel. If any of them knew the meaning, he would have called it state's rights in crime!

Quickly, the word spread through the underworld. Before long, a second meeting was called, in Kansas City. The Capone crowd came from Chicago; the Mayfield Road Gang and the Purple Mob had delegates from Cleveland and Detroit. Miami, New Orleans, Baltimore, St. Louis, and St. Paul were represented, in person or by proxy. All jumped on the bandwagon. The confederation of crime had become nation-wide. The National Syndicate was in business!

That the cartel worked is proved conclusively by the fact that the same system, the same government, still rules organized crime today, two decades later, in spite of periodic attack from the most august agencies of the law—up to and including the United States Senate. A lot of the founding personnel have disappeared, but the Syndicate remains and puts its evil touch on the everyday life of nearly every citizen in the nation.

The Mob works like an army replacing falling men.

No matter how many bosses or underlings are nabbed, there are always new troops moving up to fill the holes. Worst of all, in any operation of the Crime Syndicate, you follow a trail up from echelon to echelon only so far. Then you hit a road block. The twisting, devious chase always comes to a dead end short of the top.

"So what?" you shrug. "It hasn't touched me."

Well, if Lucky and Lepke hadn't exacted enormous tribute from baking and clothing and a dozen other industries, your cost of living wouldn't be as high as it is today.

If Lucky and Costello and the Capone Mob, the Jack Dragnas and Buggsy Siegels of California, the Adonises and Lanskys and Purple Mobsters who worked Miami as a team hadn't piled up huge gambling profits, they couldn't have corrupted your elected or appointed officials.

And Federal Narcotics authorities would have you believe that if Lucky hadn't put together a narcotics empire halfway round the world, thousands of your children would not be on the way to slow death this very minute.

When the boss mobsters voted the national Syndicate into existence, Dutch Schultz was not present. He had taken off running, a short time before, about a step and a half in front of the income-tax men. And no one expected he would be back, ever. In any case, he would not have been invited into the cartel. The Syndicate organizers were convinced that the twitching trigger finger of the Mad Dog mobster spelled only trouble for all.

There always has been more than a suspicion, though, that other considerations dictated the blackball of the Dutchman. His Harlem numbers banks and restaurant racket were lush operations, doing business in the millions.

They appealed to the extortionate appetites of Luciano and Lepke. It would be no violation of Syndicate muscling law to grab these plums—if Dutch were left out of the cartel. So, left out he was. Lucky simply reached over and snatched the numbers banks. Lepke took the restaurant enterprise.

Nor was that all the other mob magnates annexed. The Dutchman had one of the most efficient crews of killers in the business. Bo Weinberg, acting commander-in-chief in Dutch's absence, was summoned.

"Deliver the mob to us," the moguls directed.

Bo needed no blueprint to appreciate what was happening. Dutch's return was doubtful, at best. Besides, these mob lords took what they wanted anyway. He turned the troop over.

And then Dutch beat the rap!

When he returned, cleared of his tax difficulties through some amazing juridical manipulations, New York still wanted him for certain matters. So he settled in Newark, New Jersey. He discovered what Bo Weinberg had done. Bo was never heard of again—except in gangland legend. Underworld lore has it that Bo received an overcoat that he is still wearing—at the bottom of the East River. Seems the overcoat was tailored of cement.

Schultz was, of course, insane over his lost rackets. Mad Dog though he was, however, he realized that, with the Syndicate in operation, he could not take on every mob singlehanded. He managed to recoup some of the numbers trade, and he opened a business or two in Jersey, without drawing rude stares from Longy Zwillman. And he still had millions stashed away from palmier days.

But more trouble was in store. Early in 1935, a grand

jury investigating the numbers racket demanded the removal of Manhattan District Attorney William Dodge for not supplying the evidence it wanted. At the suggestion of the runaway jury, Governor (now U.S. Senator) Herbert Lehman appointed a young lawyer with an excellent record as an assistant Federal attorney. His name was Thomas E. Dewey.

One of Dewey's accomplishments had been the income-tax indictment from which all of Schultz's trouble had sprouted. And now he was dipping into the numbers racket, one of Dutch's few remaining enterprises.

"That Dewey," mourned the Dutchman dolefully. "He is my nemesis."

For days, he slowly steamed. Then one night he boiled over.

"Dewey's gotta go," he bellowed. "He's gotta be hit."

By this time some of the other Syndicate executives also had grown uneasy. A few even felt, like Schultz, that Dewey should be "hit"—which is mobese for gang murder. The Syndicate governors were called in emergency session in New York, to consider the murder of a prosecutor. Dutch risked arrest to attend—as a nonmember, of course, but as an interested party in an allied trade.

Mostly, the gang lords were cool and methodical in their debate. Opinion was split, and with the argument dragging endlessly, the board voted to adjourn the question for one week, to allow further thought.

"But what if we vote to hit him next week?" inquired the impatient Schultz. "We should be ready to move quick."

Good idea, it was decided. If the ultimate verdict were

thumbs down, speed would be essential. The smart thing would be to have all the delicate details mapped out. (Just what many of these details consisted of was outlined in the aforementioned book, *Murder, Inc.*)

A man was assigned to "case" Dewey during the interim —check and clock his comings and his goings and work out the usual painstaking plan that the Syndicate generally makes for such operations.

For so high-priority a job, the best man must be selected. No less an individual than Albert Anastasia was proposed. Anastasia was (and may still be) the czar of the Brooklyn water front. He bossed the Syndicate's death squad (later labeled "Murder, Inc.") The estimable reputation of this man who once beat the electric chair (because all the key witnesses had been slain) has remained untarnished through the years—right up to the present.

The caser went right to work. Four mornings of uninterrupted observation before Dewey's uptown apartment building was all the expert needed to note a pattern in the prosecutor's daily habits. Dewey and his two constant bodyguards emerged at almost the same minute—8:00 A.M. —each day and strolled to a drugstore two blocks away. Dewey entered, while the guards stood outside the door. The prosecutor reappeared after several minutes, and the trio departed.

A moment or two of casual conversation with the druggist easily disclosed the reason for the stop. From the pharmacy's phone booth, Dewey made the first call of each day to his office.

"I did not want to disturb Mrs. Dewey by using the phone at home so early," he explained later. (He did not mention the possibility of a tapped telephone.)

At the Syndicate meeting the following week, the caser submitted a detailed blueprint of how the hit would be accomplished, if approved:

A few minutes before Dewey's regular arrival time, the trigger man on the job would enter the drugstore. He'd be contemplating some purchase or other until Dewey came along and entered the phone booth.

The torpedo would then whip out his gun, equipped with silencer, and drill the prosecutor, trapped there in the booth. "A sitting duck," the caser noted. The druggist would also have to go, to forestall alarm then or identification later. The flat crack of the silencer would never be heard through the store's closed door by the bodyguards outside.

His mission accomplished, the killer would amble calmly out past the unsuspecting bodyguards and stroll casually around the corner to the getaway car, waiting with driver at the wheel.

Schultz, especially, was practically ecstatic over the simplicity of the plan. In the week's interval, however, the cooler heads of the Syndicate had balanced the potential consequences of so rash a move against any advances to be gained. Lucky and Lepke dominated the discussion.

"Dewey can only go after the business here in New York," it was pointed out. "He can't touch anything anywhere else."

The cartel was in business nationally. Even if the prosecutor succeeded in Manhattan, the damage would not be mortal to the Syndicate.

"But if we knock Dewey off," Lepke maintained, "the Feds will jump in—and we'll be chased right out of the country."

So, in the end, the board voted "no" on the murder of Dewey. Ironical justice was to laugh mightily over this turn before long. Dewey's life was spared by the persuasive oratory of Lucky and Lepke. A year later, Dewey sent Lucky to the penitentiary under a thirty-to-fifty year sentence. And not too long afterward, this same Dewey let Lepke go to the electric chair, when one word from him would have saved the extortion executive.

Schultz was not happy about the decision of the Syndicate directors. "I still say Dewey's gotta be hit," the Mad Dog snarled after the meeting broke up.

Only one friend heard him, but the word was promptly relayed to the executives. Such guilty knowledge was too hot to keep. Schultz was bragging that he would rub out Dewey in the next forty-eight hours!

"And that Dutchman is just crazy enough to do it, too," Lepke warned.

What astonished the gang lords was Schultz's open defiance of Syndicate authority. There could be but one answer. Schultz must die. The Mob ruled that one of its own gang lords must be slain—to save a prosecutor's life!

Two of Lepke's ranking operatives were assigned—curly-haired Charlie (the Bug) Workman and hulking Mendy Weiss. A third man, who knew his way around Newark, where Dutch was headquartered, was furnished by the Jersey outfit. His only formal identification to date is "Piggy."

The trio rode to the Palace Chophouse in downtown Newark a few minutes after ten on the night of October 23, 1935. As the "wheelman," Piggy remained in the car, motor running. Mendy, "cover" for the getaway, took up a post at the door. Charlie the Bug barged right in and strolled past the bar to the rear area.

101

The Bug caught Schultz in the men's room, washing his hands, and shot him where he stood. Then, in the back-room niche where the Dutchman had his "office," Workman disposed of Dutch's two bodyguards, plus Abbadabba Berman, a mathematical genius who rigged the daily winning number in favor of Schultz's numbers banks.

Lucky remained in his swank hotel suite from two days before the shooting until five days afterward. That way, when questions were asked about possible connection with the murder, his "Who, me?" was unchallengeable. He had a seven-day alibi. At the end of this alibi period, he hopped into his private plane and left for Florida, to cavort with Johnny Torrio and several more of his northern buddies.

Now, for the first time, the spotlight was on. Luciano made the headlines—big black ones. He was mentioned as one of the mob magnates back of the Schultz assassination. What bothered him more, though, was that he was also listed as one of the top half-dozen in the underworld, with rackets galore.

Workman had done an excellent night's work, rubbing out four men by himself. Unfortunately for the Bug's artistry, however, the Dutchman lingered almost twenty-four hours, even with the big bullet hole in him. In his conscious moments, he alternately babbled deliriously or blurted out a lucid word or phrase, while detectives and F.B.I. men at his bedside sought to ask questions.

The answers were not very enlightening, until at one point he seemed momentarily aware of what was going on.

"Who did it?" he was asked for the hundredth time. "The Boss himself!" gasped Dutch, through his pain.

Not a law-enforcement man there but knew that, to all in the "family," Lucky was always the Boss.

5 LUCKY ON THE TOWN

"This is three-twelve speaking." ... The Boss shows the boys how: Park Avenue hotel—Fifth Avenue tailor. ... A day in a mob mogul's life: golf course, race track, prize ring, and hot spot. ... Playboy and party thrower; never mistake a play girl for a call girl!

CHARLIE LUCKY really showed them how to maintain the prestige and dignity befitting the title of the Boss.

Installed as head of the "family," he deserted the slums for the grandeur of the swank Barbizon-Plaza (where he was registered as Mr. Charles Lane) and, later, of the plush Waldorf-Astoria (where he was Mr. Charles Ross).

It is an oddity of Luciano's mental make-up that out of town, in Miami or Hot Springs or Chicago, he made no bones about his identity. The hotel register always read "Charles Lucania" or "Luciano," in a tight scrawl, as though the pen were an unaccustomed tool in the hand of the writer. But in New York, he listed himself under some alias almost invariably. Perhaps he had the idea that disguise was important only in his own back yard.

When he spoke on the telephone, through a wire that might be tapped, he was even more mysterious.

"This is three-twelve," he would say.

There was, for instance, the time in Cincinnati, when

Jeannette Lewis, Abbadabba Berman's girl friend, asked him to get her a job in New York.

"I'm sick of this town," she complained.

"If you really want to come," Lucky said, "I can fix it."

He picked up the phone and made long-distance contact with Manhattan. "This is three-twelve," he announced. "I'm sending a girl named Jean Lewis. Take care of her."

Jeannette got the job, all right—in a brothel!

The "three-twelve" represented the letters in the alphabet corresponding to Lucky's initials—3 for "C," 12 for "L."

Luciano rode only in the most powerful and expensive cars. He had a private plane to whisk him about the country. Public facilities were not for the Boss.

He could afford all of it now. Even when he was still taking orders from Joe the Boss, his income had been in the neighborhood of $200,000 a year. Now, with his fingers in practically any kind of pie on the underworld menu, his take was five times that much, or more.

To his long-time partiality to silk underwear, he now added a yen for the cutaway. Someone has said that in this garb, with his swart, sinister features and his droopy eyelid, Lucky looked like Dracula. To the less morbid, he was the personification of the Grade-B movie mobster. His black hair was so thick it grew almost to a widow's peak in front. His square jowls were hard, and the rapid growth of his beard made him envy the man afflicted with merely a five o'clock shadow. Lucky was a three o'clock man, at least.

To many women, Lucky was exciting. To Molly Brown, he was just "different." Molly cleaned the bathrooms on the thirty-ninth and fortieth floors of the Waldorf Towers. She would clean all the other bathrooms before going to 39-C. Partly, this was because Mr. Ross rose so late. Partly, though, it gave her and Hedwig, the chambermaid, a chance to compare notes in the corridor outside his door, and watch the strange visitors who emerged from the elevator to enter Mr. Ross's suite.

The visitors did not always come by elevator. Sometimes the thirty-ninth-floor stairwell door would open slowly, and a head would poke through for a precautionary look. Then the cautious caller would move quickly to Lucky's door and vanish inside. One who periodically put in such unorthodox appearances was a prominent citizen, very high in politics.

Lucky's days and nights were full after the purge of Mafia. He never rose until the sun had passed its peak. While he breakfasted in soft silk pajamas, his department heads would check in personally and report on business progress. The Boss's interests were spread like fertilizer over a cornfield in those days. Narcotics played a part. But that was only one of the many Unione specialties. The Italian lottery was another. So was the corner on many everyday commodities used in the Italian home—olive oil, the succulent artichoke, grapes for wine. The Syndicate, remember, has many businesses—murder and industrial extortion and gambling and rackets by the dozen.

All these have been more or less well advertised through the years. There were, however, others that have never been revealed. Take the time Nancy Presser, the most celebrated play girl on bright-light lane, was visiting one day.

A few of the department heads checked in while she was there.

"Go in the toilet and turn on the water," Lucky directed.

With the water running, Nancy was not supposed to hear what went on. But the play girl, as curious as any other woman, was a little slow twisting the faucet. She paused just long enough to catch a phrase or two:

". . . the cut on the armored-car job . . . the take was four hundred thousand bucks. . . ."

Nancy heard this conversational titbit in the early fall of 1934. And just then the combination of $400,000 and an "armored-car job" was as hot as three feet inside a blast furnace. A few weeks before, ten crack machine-gun bandits had closed in on an armored car at the Rubel Ice Plant on the Brooklyn water front, lifted $427,950, and disappeared in high-powered speedboats waiting at the docks. It was the biggest cash robbery in the history of American lawlessness, and remained so for sixteen years—until in 1950 the Brinks Express Company holdup in Boston netted a million dollars and some change.

Early in 1936, Nancy got around to mentioning the matter to authorities in Manhattan, who had no jurisdiction over a Brooklyn affair. In normal procedure, Manhattan officials would pass the word along to the folks over in Flatbush. There is no record, however, that anyone in Brooklyn knew a thing about the disposal of the Rubel loot until three of the holdup men were finally nailed in 1940, four years after Nancy revealed in Manhattan what she had heard in Lucky's place.

The stick-up men insisted, however, that they hadn't enjoyed much of the money themselves. They told a tale about how some of the town's top racketeers caught wind of their caper and cut themselves in for a large slice of the $427,000—for "protection."

Such were the reports the Boss received from his department heads each noontime. Business and breakfast concluded, the sectional managers took their leave, and Lucky prepared for the pleasures of the afternoon.

Shaved and powdered, he drew back the door to his wardrobe and, with approving eye, selected an ensemble from his imported-worsted suits, custom-fitted by the same fashionable Fifth Avenue tailor who draped the manly forms of many of the leading hoodlums—at $190 per drape.

Chroniclers of the Lucky legend through the years have pictured his daily costume as a cross between a neon sign and a tropical flower bush in full bloom. This is based on the popular fiction that mobsters are commonly supposed to sport clothes that would blind unless viewed through smoked glasses. Lucky's dress actually was the rich, conservative garb of the successful executive.

"He leaned maybe a degree or two to the liberal side of conservative," is the way one gentleman's couturier put it. "But always in the height of style. His suiting was usually gray, black, or brown, with subtle design or stripe. His ties were subdued, with genuine originality in *décor*."

Finished dressing, Lucky descended via the elevator and strode through the Waldorf's famed Peacock Alley, ready for what the day offered. If time permitted before the afternoon's recreation, he headed west, for a stop at the drugstore—Moe Ducore's pharmacy at Forty-ninth and Seventh. There the fashion-plate hoodlum spent a few minutes greeting this or that character. Perhaps one of his business associates, like Joe Bendix, the thief, might be on hand, trying to dispose of a piece of merchandise lately burgled.

The drugstore stop was never lengthy. Post time was fast approaching for the first race at Belmont or Aqueduct or Jamaica, whichever track was running. Or he might have a golf date at one of the expensive clubs in Westchester County, out on Long Island, or over in New Jersey.

The grand and ancient game has been, for years, an occupational disease of the mobster who rises above the pack. Generally he is as serious about it as any duffer. The sport itself, however, is not the prime lure for the thug, so much as the eligibility it offers for membership in exclusive country clubs, and the resultant entree to better social circles.

Famous foursomes have trod the fairways around and about. Lucky, Joey Adonis, Meyer Lansky, and Jimmy Hines, the respected politico who fronted for gangland, got together quite frequently. Frank Costello and Lepke often fitted in. One winter, when the boys were habitués of the links adjacent to the Arlington Hotel in Hot Springs, the Mayor of New Orleans was a simultaneous guest. Where else could thugs mingle with such high-class folk as in the game of which a sage Scot once said, " 'Tis a great leveler"?

After Charlie became the Boss, though, weekday afternoons on the links were the exception. The race track offered a three-way opportunity for business, pleasure, and society.

First, Lucky's social standing and fashion leadership were never more conspicuous than when he placed his custom-tailored figure in a clubhouse pew at the horse park. Before Luciano arrived on the scene, the hoodlum had no pride in appearance. He was a bum; he looked like a bum. His identity was as evident as if he wore a sign. Lucky changed all that.

"Charlie was the guy who put a white shirt and a tie on the hoodlum," the Broadway characters still say. Before he came along, they couldn't be mistaken for anything but mugs. None of the big shots slicked up until Charlie started it.

Remarkable indeed was the deference paid to this bedecked mob man at the track, not only by his fawning followers, but by persons of position in politics and public office, as well. Any number of them came to him for frequent favors!

The track's second reward lay in the advantages it afforded to transact business without arousing curiosity from observers. Like detectives, say. Most of the mob lords were regular customers at the horse park. If two or three Syndicate associates put their heads together in a clubhouse box, who could possibly say whether they were passing the word on a murder contract or merely asking each other, "Whadda ya like in the next race?"

But most of all, the track tickled Lucky's ingrained gambling palate. With all the rackets paying off, he bet a thousand, even five thousand, dollars on a single race. And did it with less hesitation than young Salvatore had exhibited when he invested his entire weekly pay of seven dollars in that alley crap game in the slums.

He won and he lost, but the word was that the percentage was in his favor. There were occasions when the boys might "have something going," as they say concerning a proposition that is synonymous with death and taxes as a certainty.

This could happen in Lucky's heyday, when New York tracks operated under the bookmaking system. Since legalization of pari-mutuel wagering in 1939, the chance for concealment, vital to the betting coup, is gone, and for the fixed race, lessened. What's more, racing has provided itself with an especially capable police force, the Thoroughbred Racing Protective Bureau, manned mostly by former F.B.I. agents and headed by J. Edgar Hoover's onetime deputy, Spencer Drayton.

If Luciano, with his reputation, were to show up at any T.R.P.B. track anywhere in the country today, he not only could not bet, but he would be thrown off the premises on the seat of his imported worsteds. Frank Costello knows, from personal experience.

It was in the evenings that Lucky really spread himself in those palmy days. There was always a party of half a dozen or more for dinner, among them his own date for the evening. She might be the gorgeous show girl, Gay Orlova, a pet Luciano play toy. But since Lucky played the field, it might have been any one of the dozens who did one-night stands in his favor.

Cautious as he was about letting any of them close to his plush parlor, bedroom, and bath, Lucky was surprisingly loose about the chatter he permitted at table—with some lacquered lady of the evening sitting there and taking it all in. It is odd, indeed, that when business was brought up, the Boss didn't order the subject changed, or at least refuse to voice an opinion himself.

Time after time it happened. Once someone reported a recalcitrant contributor to the rackets, and Lucky suggested, "Put the screws on." Another time, it was a complaint about a certain party "making trouble." Lucky said, "Why don't you go ahead and wreck the joint?" Later, when the roof fell in, one after another of the disillusioned damsels popped up to haunt him with his own words.

Luciano may have moved to the upper crust of Park Avenue, but come mealtime, he never left the downtown cuisine on which he grew up. Plus elaborations, naturally. In the old days, for instance, the Lucania fortunes were rarely fluid enough to permit Mama to place lobster *fra diavolo* before her hungry brood. When this was the yen of the evening now, the party would swing over to the upper forties, just off Sixth Avenue, to the Villanova, where the succulent sea food with the "devil sauce" is in a class by itself. In fact, any time he was dining uptown, Lucky was likely to point like a bird dog to the Villanova, long famous among the sporting set. (Most eating houses noted for fine food are.)

Charlie liked spaghetti very much, so frequently the Boss led his fawning party downtown to the old Mulberry Street neighborhood—and Celano's. Here could be found a Neapolitan repast comparable with the old country in flavor and the old days in informality.

There was also the advantage in location. Celano's, on Kenmare Street near Mulberry, is a landmark of the bootleg days and the curb-exchange battleground. It always was a most discreet meeting place, if Lucky had business with any of his hired hands. He could discuss it over the dinner.

Occasionally, for a switch, he chose a certain basement restaurant in Chinatown, or some similar specialty eating house. But his gourmet soul was never long away from the familiar Italian delicacies.

The new hotel residence hampered his style in this respect, for this caliph of crime fancies himself an amateur chef, just like any suburbanite tossing a salad bowl or performing at his back-yard barbecue! What's more, friends who have been favored with an invitation to one of Lucky's personally prepared meals insist he is a right handy man with the skillet and condiment.

"His tomato sauce is as good as you'll get in any Italian restaurant," a friend of those days still insists.

Dinner, Italian style, is never quick. It must be prepared and served slowly, course by countless course, with appropriate wines for each and much small talk. Lucky liked it that way. Except on fight nights. Then the rite was curtailed in order to make the semifinal bout, at least, at Madison Square Garden.

Ranking mob executives always are fight fans. For years, in fact, they have been "buying into" prize fighters or have owned them outright. As a matter of fact, six of the last ten world heavyweight champions have been backed by underworld connection to one degree or another.

In the old days, the mobster got a thrill merely out of owning a winning fighter. Today the hoodlum master is far more money-minded. Syndicate mobsters frequently own *both* fighters in a match and are thus in a position to write the script for a bout in advance. The resultant betting pays high (and sure) dividends. It is, too, slowly strangling the sport.

Back in Lucky's day, the cut of the boxer's purse carried less weight than ownership of a winner. Possession of a pugilist of standing was looked on by the gang lord more as a badge of importance. The Boss felt compelled to acquire a fighter or two for himself. Where other gang lords went about broadcasting the fact that their play toys sported cauliflower ears, however, Charlie as usual did no advertising. He placed his fisticuffers in the hands of legitimate, competent managers. Behind this front, his connection was so anonymous that not even the fighters were aware they were owned by the Boss.

Lou Salica, a capable, smart, little warrior who held the bantamweight championship for a while, never suspected Lucky might have owned a piece of him. A boxing promoter recalls that he was standing in Madison Square Garden lobby one night, when a friend came up and introduced his companion.

"It was this man that's so notorious all over the world—this Lucky Luciano," related the promoter. "He told me he had a fighter by the name of Salica, and he wanted me to manage him. I told him a promoter is not allowed to be a manager."

Lucky is invariably characterized as a hot-spot man, sweeping through the night-club belt evening after evening, from Harlem to the Bowery. Actually, he was not nearly so busy a rounder as he has been depicted, for he fully realized the prominence attendant on playboying. And when he did make the hot spots, it was mostly a quiet stop with his light o' love of the particular evening, and with very few hangers on.

Some readers may be surprised to learn that Luciano was not a drinker. He went moderately for wine, the traditional beverage of his homeland, but touched hard liquor only infrequently. "It was always wine; maybe, once in a while, a beer," recalls one night-club owner with whom he was especially friendly.

The old Paradise and the Hollywood, facing each other across Broadway, were the places to go in those days. They were Lucky's favorite haunts on his nights out. The Paradise boasted a floor show with some of the most beautiful girls a chorus line ever sported. The Hollywood not only had the lovelies, too, but had discovered how to make nudity legal. By the simple expedient of dressing up the well-curved torsos in nothing at all and having them stand perfectly still on the stage long enough to be called "living statues," legitimacy was accomplished. Didn't art museums display nudes with no argument from the law?

Top names of the Social Register, of industry and politics, rubbed elbows nightly with the trash of the underworld at these two high-class saloons. This was the era when society debutantes, who should have been limited to a diet of malted milks, were running loose around half-lit traps, pouring cut whisky into their expensive stomachs. They got their kicks from talking to gangsters and drinking with hoodlums in the saloons. After about four drinks, they would start pitching what they owned all over the place—and then scream righteously of honor when a hood got the wrong idea. It was most confusing to the thugs!

"Y'know," one of Lucky's pals philosophized one evening, "down in Mulberry Bend, a dame's either respectable or she's a tramp—and she gets treated accordingly. But uptown, the society bimbos paint up like bums and act like two-bit broads looking for business. But when you want to give 'em what they're asking for, they holler copper. Them uptown guys oughta straighten their broads out."

In the Paradise and the Hollywood, Lucky discovered that, in spite of all the cover-up, he was not altogether unknown. An occasional whisper drifted over from an adjoining table, where sat some blueblood or stockbroker or lady companion of same.

"There's that Lucky—Lucky Luciano," the whisper would go, as he was recognized.

"The newspaper said. . . ."

Of course, the papers never had said very much, except that Lucky was around, or had been a friend of some hoodlum dumped in a gutter, or the like.

He would never let on by so much as a flicked eyebrow that he had heard the whisper. In fact, in no public place, at any time, would he even acknowledge a friend or associate with anything beyond a slight nod, before the friend sought recognition.

"He never speaks to anybody, unless they speak first," his pals said.

Any number of those who did speak first sought more than social contact. They were after a touch. For all his ruthlessness in crime, Lucky was an easy mark in money matters, where they did not involve business. Perfect strangers could—and did—come up to him and get $100, $200, even $1,000, on the strength of a hard-luck story. Not as a loan either. Lucky never kept books on such outlays.

"It was different, though, if it was a business proposition somebody wanted financed," an associate explained. "Then he'd want to know who was in it and when he'd get it back. But he was always a sucker for anybody who put the bite on him."

In those days the hoodlums owned many of the better-known night clubs, as well as prize fighters. Several of Lucky's *compadres* in crime urged him again and again either to join them in operating a hot spot or to launch one himself. Lucky's sales resistance finally weakened. The incident came to light when an old friend mentioned it to one of the authors of this book.

It seems the Boss and Big French DeMange, who was a partner in probably the biggest of all beer enterprises, and Harry Cannon, a character still on the scene, got to talking one night about plush traps. One word led to another, and pretty soon they were plotting a supercolossal spot that would make all others look like so many telephone booths.

"We each put up five thousand for a starter," Big French proposed. The others agreed.

At that time, dark-haired Helen Morgan was just about the hottest thing in show business. She'd sit on the edge of a piano, wring a tiny bit of handkerchief in her hands, and make with torch songs until there wasn't a dry eye in the house. It packed them in and gave Big French an idea.

"Why don't we build a club for Helen?" he suggested. "Call it 'Chez Morgan' or 'The House of Morgan,' or like that, and star her. It'll draw the suckers like Macy's basement."

Lucky was cured at once. "This is where I get off," he announced to his partners. "I was willing to go along. But if I'm gonna be in on any club named after a dame, it better be my dame—or I won't get any peace. I ain't lookin' for trouble."

Thus ended the Boss's night-club career—before it began. From then on, he was strictly a customer in the saloons.

Actually, Lucky preferred a private party to a night out. He didn't drink; he didn't want to get mixed up with "society broads"; and he only socialized with his own invited group anyway. He preferred to throw the party himself.

Sometimes he would arrange a shindig in the apartment of a lady friend. He would send over the food and beverage, and she played hostess for his guests. More often, he would rent a double suite in a midtown hotel, have wine and whisky and delicacies brought up, invite girls in bunches, like grapes—and then let nature take its course. These soirees were especially successful for entertaining distinguished visitors from out of town—such as the boys from Chicago, Kansas City, or Miami, in for a business conference.

The source of the girls depended on the kind of party. For a strictly social affair, with laughs and liquor and no rough stuff, Lucky knew where to get all the show girls, models, and chorus hoofers he needed. These ladies depended on their salaries for their living, and were delighted to come. They knew there was a fifty-dollar bill in it for each of them at the end of one of the Boss's frolics—and that when Lucky said no rough stuff, the only requirements were light conversation and parlor entertainment exclusively.

On the other hand, if it was to be a no-holds-barred brawl, with bedroom action, there was not a madam in New York Lucky couldn't contact, or one who dared refuse to send over a load of her very best female stock in trade. Nor was there a prostitute who would not accept eagerly. The same fifty-dollar bill was waiting, although the service rendered was somewhat more strenuous.

Occasionally, signals became crossed. That led to confusion. One fete, still bright in underworld memory, was a party Lucky pitched for several of the Purple Mobsters from Detroit. The Boss went all out. He brought in some of the most gorgeous talent on the main stem—all show girls. The western thugs were not quite clear on the line of demarcation, though. Before long, they were making indelicate proposals to the ladies. Things were rapidly getting out of hand when Luciano took the floor to set the record straight.

"Listen, fellas," he explained, "these gals are show gals. They work for a living."

The hot bloods from Detroit showed their disappointment keenly. The host, eager to please, telephoned an S O S to Polly Adler, the nationally known madam. Polly sent over a few of her best girls at once.

"Why, they're better-looking than the show broads!" exclaimed one of the boys.

Then a curious incident developed. The girls were mingling with the guests and joining in the conversation when not otherwise occupied. It was noted that one of the mobsters was keeping his eye on them, wherever they went. As soon as one finished a drink, the watchdog grabbed up the empty glass and smashed it against the artificial fireplace.

"Now, that's a pip!" roared one of the guests. "How can a broad spread more germs on a drinking glass than in bed?"

No matter what the hour when the fun-making wound up, hardly an evening was complete for Lucky without a final nightcap at Dave's Blue Room, on Seventh Avenue, just above Times Square. All strata, from criminal to high society, crowded the place in the hours just before dawn. On the way there, Lucky could stop for a final check with the drugstore, which was just across the street.

Thus ended the little man's day. Now he repaired eastward once more, to the Waldorf. There was, of course, no bride to welcome him home, and Lucky sometimes found it hard to go right to sleep.

When this happened, the Boss would break his house rule against bringing romance into his home. He would telephone one of the favored few, to come up for a visit. Generally, it was 4:00 or 5:00 A.M., but they rarely—if ever—failed to come.

6 LUCKY IN LOVE

The Boss plays the field. . . . Nancy meets the mob, and her price goes up. . . . Nancy gets a call; "Lucky had something wrong". . . . Gay Orlova, the gorgeous Russ. . . . Broadway beauty and underworld beast. . . . Mildred the Madam—and others. . . . Lucky had something the girls wanted.

LUCKY HAD QUITE an appetite for love—despite a certain social affliction from which he suffered. (That, incidentally, was the cause of his rejection for army service in World War I. His probation report to the courts later mentioned a chronic condition that "lighted up" from time to time.)

Before he became the big boss of Unione, Luciano would live with one girl as long as he was interested. Then when the novelty faded, he'd move on to a new temptress.

When he hit the top, however, as previously detailed, he altered his habits to maintain the cover-up he so desired. He started playing the field, taking his dalliance where he found it.

After that, when he was in the mood for play, he'd contact one or another of the damsels and make a date to meet someplace or to visit her. Only a scant few favored dolls were ever invited up for a drink, talk, or whatever he had in mind.

"You wouldn't like me if you knew who I was," he said to one of these hit-and-run mistresses. She didn't know until long afterward, but she did notice that his orders to a henchman produced the same reaction as those of a five-star general to a buck private.

By the time Lucky was installed in the Waldorf as Mr. Ross, the girls who knew him were always ready to jump through a hoop if he called. They realized, of course, that a crisp new bill, with double figures on it, would be in their purse when they went home.

The fire of a Polish mother and the strong body of a Scandinavian father had endowed Nancy Presser with a deep-breasted voluptuous beauty that stirred men before she was sixteen.

By that time she had run away from Auburn, New York, and was waiting on tables in an Albany eatery. There she made her first major discovery in economics. A state senator, whose lawmaking evidently did not embrace considerations concerning the age of consent, left a dime tip at dinnertime. Some hours later, in his hotel room, he was more generous.

Thus enlightened, Nancy turned her back on restaurant work and headed for New York. Nancy had the natural resources to make even the big town, with its glutted flesh markets, sit up and take notice.

At first, she was a model and a play girl. This is not to be confused with the call girl or professional prostitute. A play girl deals in companionship, strictly—dinner, a theater, a night club, then a good-night handshake in the lobby, and so to bed—alone. Play girls have definite price scales: $20 to

121

accompany a gentleman to dinner (plus the price of the meal, naturally); $50 for a theater date; $75 for a full evening along the night-club belt. Call girls—those commanding the more exclusive clientele—employ the same scale, plus an additional $100 for boudoir service.

Nancy's telephone was always busy in those days of the big butter-and-egg man. One bald-headed gentleman in particular phoned every time he hit town, which was frequently. One night, after the theater, he invited her to his hotel room for a nightcap.

"At his age, it's safe," Nancy smiled to herself.

The old boy ordered up champagne. "I sat there telling him dirty jokes and drinking wine and kissing his bald spot," Nancy related to a friend afterward. "Finally, we both just fell asleep. On separate twin beds, you can bet. Next morning, he hands me a thousand-dollar bill!"

Eventually Nancy, who had not scrupled to trade her body for cash before the age of consent, decided that remaining a play girl exclusively was just throwing money out the window, now that she was old enough to give all the consent she wanted. She became the highest-priced and most sought-after call girl in New York.

Then Joe came along and wanted exclusive rights. He was a Broadway florist—Nancy could never remember his last name. Joe set her up in an apartment love nest. After a while, however, the lack of variety palled on Nancy, and she took to entertaining on the side. When Joe found out, the honeymoon was over.

Earlier, on a trip to Hot Springs, she had met Chink Sherman and others of Waxey Gordon's gang. They were the first mobsters she had ever known, and they opened an entirely new vista. As spenders, the butter-and-egg men weren't in it with these thugs, who threw money around as if there would be no tomorrow.

Nancy was only seventeen when she began running around with the hoods. She was lured by a twisted hero worship, that was soon highly colored by the false dreams of opium, to which they introduced her.

All the thugs liked Nancy—in or out of bed—including Joe the Boss Masseria and Ciro Terranova. "She's our kind of dame," they used to say. If they had to make a business stop during an evening with Nancy, they thought nothing of taking her along. Just how far she was trusted came out later, when she piloted authorities through Mulberry Bend and pointed out mob offices and hangouts—including several the detectives had never heard of.

Nancy's closest friend was a girl named Betty (who has since married a policeman). Betty raved so much about her current boy friend that one night Nancy accompanied her uptown to Tiptoe Inn to meet this paragon personally. Betty said, "Nancy, this is Charlie Lucania," and the boy friend acknowledged the introduction with the briefest nod. He was dark and sort of good-looking, but the cut of his jaw indicated flint and mystery underneath.

Charlie had not yet made his mark on the underworld, and Nancy only played with the boys who had. She was still giving him the once-over when he and Betty got into an argument. Nancy had never heard words of abuse such as Charlie heaped on his girl—vile things, to make even a call girl blush. Betty took it, trembling, eyes lowered.

"Who do you think you're talking to like that?" Nancy finally broke in. "You're no gentleman—you're a common

123

bum. And if I was Betty, I'd throw something at you and walk out! Why, you are—"

Suddenly, Nancy's heated diatribe stopped in the middle of the sentence, as if a vise had locked her throat. Charlie's face had not changed, and he hadn't uttered a word. He just stared—but in that stare were poison and murder. Nancy had never seen such cold homicidal anger in her life. Shivers raced across her shoulders. She gathered up her coat and fled.

As Nancy moved up in hoodlum society, she and Betty drifted apart. She was at a party in Joe the Boss's elaborate penthouse one night, some two or three years later, when one of her new-found companions came up with another man. "Nancy, this is Charlie Lucky; he wants to meet you," the friend introduced.

Nancy turned smiling, and then did a double take. There was a droop to the right eyelid, and scars on his face. But, in spite of the marks and the friendly smile, she saw this was the same man whose cold stare had terrorized her two years before. This was Betty's abusive boy friend, "Charlie." However, Charlie was on his way to the top now. So, Nancy was immediately cordial. Before the evening was over, they were laughing over the incident at the Tiptoe.

It was another three years before she laid eyes on him again. By that time he had become the powerhouse of the underworld. One afternoon she and a gentleman friend dropped into Kean's Tavern, across from Madison Square Garden. They were having a drink when she noticed the occupants of a nearby table. Little Davey Betillo, the torpedo, was there, and heavy-jowled Tommy the Bull Pennocchio and fat and greasy Jimmy Frederico. And in the chair at the head sat Charlie Lucky.

Nancy went over and said, "Hello, there. Long time no see."

"Sit down and have a drink," Lucky invited.

Sitting at the Boss's right, she played up to him as much as the watchful eye of her escort permitted. She slipped her telephone number into Lucky's hand, and he gave her a wink.

Several months went by. Nancy took up with Ralph Liguori. Like so many of the inexplicable molls enamored of hoods, she picked one without charm, influence, or money. When she fell all the way, it was for a runt of five feet two, thoroughly coarse and unintelligent, whose standing in the community is best conveyed by his nickname: Ralph the Pimp. His special line of endeavor was as low as even the underworld could get: he held up whorehouses. Sometimes it was individual enterprise. More often, the mob that furnished "protection" to these establishments used him in reprisal against madams who refused to pay off. He was allowed to keep a small percentage of this loot.

Before Nancy, Ralph had been kept by Gashouse Lil Cardella, a prostitute. He would book her into a house, and Lil would "case" the place, learning where the money was kept and when the fewest visitors were around. Then she would finger the place to the Pimp, and he would hold it up. It got so no madam would hire Gashouse any more. This left her in no position to support Ralph in the style to which he was accustomed. So when Nancy gave him the eye in a saloon one night, he gave it right back and leaped at the opportunity of moving in with her.

This revolting character is today still close to his pal, Lucky, in Rome. He bills himself as "Your New York Host," and in the past couple of years has opened six night clubs dedicated to entertaining lonely American servicemen who want to dance with his hostesses. It is fervently hoped that American Army authorities in Italy have their eye on this thug.

Nancy gave Ralph money, and he kept his guns in her place. On stick-ups, she went along and carried the pistol until he was ready to enter the joint selected as his victim. Sometimes she accompanied him on an extraspecial job. They'd drive to a North River pier and pick up cans of opium smuggled in by ship. On the way back, Nancy held the contraband on her lap.

"If we get nailed," she was directed, "say it's yours."

The proud call girl with the $100 clientele began to go downhill. Her phone did not ring nearly as frequently any more. Opium no longer furnished forgetfulness, and she turned to the deadlier morphine for soothing sleep. Ralph demanded more and more money, more than she had. Finally, he ordered her into a bawdyhouse.

"It's only two bucks a customer," he pointed out. "But you handle more customers than you do now, waiting for calls."

"That's not for Nancy," she fired back. So Ralph beat her up.

Late one night the phone rang, and it was Charlie Lucky.

"I'm all alone up here. How about coming over for a while?" (He was Mr. Lane of the Barbizon-Plaza then.)

Nancy went over, and they had a few drinks and talked. Nancy poured out her troubles.

126

"I need money," she said. "I'm going to have to go into a house unless I get some."

"A dame like you shouldn't be in a house," Lucky sympathized.

"Well, Liguori is making me. So what can I do about it?"

Finally Lucky said, "Look, if you need money, I'll let you have it."

He peeled a fifty-dollar bill from his bank roll. It was an outright gift.

"We never went to bed at all," Nancy insisted afterward.

Lucky called her up two or three times after that. All they did, she said, was sit and talk. Nothing else.

"Lucky couldn't . . . he had something wrong with him . . . so I didn't," Nancy pointed out.

Nancy repeated the disclosure later, out loud. It was broadcast in newspapers across the country. This was probably as severe a blow to Lucky's pride as his later conviction, this exposure to all his associates and pals that he had "something wrong"—so that a prostitute refused him as a bedmate!

When he moved over to the Waldorf Towers, the association with Nancy was continued. She felt quite the lady, strolling down Peacock Alley, to reach the Tower elevator. There was, however, one change in Lucky.

"He was no longer incapacitated all the time," Nancy said.

During the sessions devoted strictly to talk, Lucky would let his hair down. Nancy had learned, for economic reasons, to be a good listener. Like the time Lucky brought up a venture into the field of prostitution.

"The take is not good," he said. "Looks like we'll raise

the two-dollar houses to three—and boost the five- and ten-dollar joints too."

Nancy made no comment.

Gay Orlova was different from Nancy. "Gay All Over," they used to call her on Broadway, where she decorated Earl Carroll's flesh shows. Whereas Nancy had a tall voluptuous beauty that fairly screamed sex, Gay was more subtly bewitching, blue-eyed, golden-haired, and neatly put together. In her heyday, the type was known as "beautiful but dumb." Gay was, actually, about as dumb as a Ph.D.—except, maybe, in her rating of Lucky.

"He's a dear," she always insisted. "A perfect gentleman!"

Born Galen Arlova in pre-Soviet Russia, she claimed to have fled the Bolsheviks as a tiny tot, with her mother. They landed in the intrigue and mystery of Constantinople, where the yellow-curled girl learned to dance.

She was still in her teens when she hit New York in the early thirties, ambitious to set Broadway aflame. She didn't have to dance to attract Carroll's attention. With her equipment, she could have come on stage in ball and chain and still have been a sensation. The things her torso could do were just icing on the cake.

When she opened in *Murder in the Vanities* at the Majestic, she had only one problem: she had only a six-month permit to remain in the United States. That didn't trouble Gay very long. She eloped with Ed Finn a nice-looking usher from the theater's orchestra floor.

When Carroll heard the news, he sent his blonde beauty a wire:

"You might at least have picked an usher from the first balcony."

The marriage lasted some forty-eight hours. Finn got an annulment as a kissless bridegroom. Gay, however, was now eligible to remain in America.

The gorgeous Russ never had to join a lonely hearts club. Within a few weeks, a stockbroker was squiring her everywhere. She was a constant companion of a famed magazine cartoonist. When the Carroll show opened at Palm Island, which was Al Capone's playground, between Miami and Miami Beach, at the end of 1934, her stockbroker followed her to Florida and even offered matrimony.

Then one night, during the Florida run, she met a dark, beetle-browed man who didn't say much but looked plenty. From that moment on, Charlie Lucky was her man.

"I even gave up my broker friend for him," she revealed later. "He was just lovely to me."

Through that entire winter, theirs was the big romance under the whispering palms and tropical moon. No one else made passes at Gay, for word had gone around that she was the Boss's heartbeat. Here was the union of Broadway beauty and underworld beast in its basic form.

When the tourists headed north in the spring, the romance did too. Gay took an expensive suite, over near the river on exclusive East Fifty-seventh Street, within a dozen blocks of Lucky's hotel diggings. Everything was cozy through the summer of '35, until Dutch Schultz was murdered. That brought a temporary break in the beautiful relationship, for Lucky felt it expedient to leave town.

"I haven't seen him for weeks," Orlova sighed as winter approached. "I can't believe what they're saying about him.

I don't know why they say such mean things—he's just a dear!"

When Gay headed south again, she found Lucky there before her. She said she was no end surprised and pleased. She had had no idea that's where he was! They picked up where they had left off.

Later, when the Boss ran into his big trouble with Dewey over the prostitution organization, Gay was even more critical of the law.

"I don't believe any of those charges," she declared flatly. "Especially that one about compulsory something-or-other. It just doesn't sound nice—not like Lucky at all!"

("Compulsory something-or-other" must be history's prize euphemism for "prostitution.")

Gay held a press conference to voice her objections. It was held in Dave's Blue Room, Lucky's old late-night hangout. Charlie, she insisted, was just like any other fellow—even to not being so generous when she needed things most.

"He was nice," she sighed, "but he didn't give me anything too wonderful! Fact is, I'm looking for a job right now."

For a girl in search of work, La Orlova must have had some remarkably profitable side lines. She showed up for the conference in a Paris gown, a four-thousand-dollar silver fox, and dripping with jewels that never came from the five-and-ten.

Gay disliked publicity. She was no end put out when Lucky's difficulties got her name in the papers, along with several excellent photographic likenesses, which concealed her beauty by a spangle here, a tasseled G-string there. Sadly, she turned her back on her triumphs, departed the

Gay White Way, and hied herself off for further adventures in Paris.

These continued through the war years. The intriguing Russian beauty got to know her way in and out of official headquarters in those tragic years. When Hitler and Stalin signed their infamous brotherhood pact in 1939, the French nabbed Gay as a possible Russian spy. She soon won her release. In 1941, when Hitler's hordes overran France, she was picked up by the Nazis. Again, she escaped detention. The lush Orlova evidently still had all the persuasive charms that had stockbrokers dangling on the hook in her Broadway heyday.

Lucky's exile to Europe in 1946 gave Gay some moments of anticipated joy. No longer did an ocean separate her from her heartbeat. The Boss hadn't been in Italy three months before she asked permission to cross the Alps to him, to share his exile. It was refused.

As of this writing, Orlova is still in Paris, still yearning for her Lucky, for whom she sacrificed a Wall Streeter's wedding ring. The yearning, however, seems no longer mutual. The Boss is very well fixed romantically south of the border. He has not been caught struggling to reach the side of his former light o' love. Maybe the disillusioned darling is beginning to appreciate where she stands. Lately she hasn't been heard referring to Luciano as "a dear," or even "a perfect gentleman."

Such were the loves of Lucky in his palmy reign as head of the "family" and trustee of the Syndicate. In lusty, voluptuous Nancy, with whom he could talk platonically or retire to the boudoir, and in exquisite, curvaceous Gay, who was capable of arousing hidden passions, lay the extremes of his romantic bent.

There were, of course, many more—dozens of them—a remarkable feat for the scar-faced felon with an incapacity that "lighted up" from time to time. His racket-fattened bank roll helped, of course, and more than made up for the disfigurements he had acquired on the way to power. But it would be cynical to claim that this was the only reason for his success as a ladies' man. There seems to be no doubt about it—Lucky had something the girls wanted. Certain types of girl, anyway.

Some of the women he knew were considerably less than intimate, of course. Some, like Mildred Harris, differed sharply with Gay Orlova on Lucky's rating as a gentleman.

Mildred was a Dixie maid who married four times and, between husbands, shared love nests with a prominent businessman and a well-known homosexual. Her last venture into legal cohabitation was with Pete Harris. Their wedded bliss was spiced with dual careers as madam and booker in the prostitution business. Nevertheless, Mildred was most popular in her own circle.

She did have one rather unusual habit: periodic attacks of claustrophobia as far as clothes were concerned. In these stifling moments, she just couldn't stand them. The seizure took her during one soiree she and Pete threw in their penthouse a few blocks from Central Park. Suddenly, there was the Dixie damsel having a romp on the davenport with one of the male guests, and the whole roomful taking it in like a night at the opera. You could hardly blame Pete for stepping in and unraveling the human jigsaw.

"You ain't got no ethics!" he charged heatedly.

In spite of her various attachments, the only man Mildred ever really loved was Murray Marks, a Waxey Gordon hood and one of her opium-smoking crowd of close cronies. Following Waxey's troubles with the Syndicate after repeal—when the Mob was gunning for him—his hired hands began to find it difficult to get along. Marks turned to narcotics on a considerable scale, oblivious of the fact that he was infringing on a certain Mob monopoly.

One night, Mildred was in a bar, having a brandy as she waited for Murray, when she felt someone staring. She looked up, squarely into the black eyes of Charlie Lucky. Mildred was so upset she never could remember exactly what Lucky said. But it was something about, "Tell that punk it ain't healthy to move in!"

The way he said it was what unnerved Mildred. It shot out like venom, and his eyes glittered hate and rage. Then he spat in her face.

Mildred repeated the incident to her boy friend. Marks merely shrugged.

A few afternoons later, a man dismounted from a bus, high in the Bronx, and started walking along busy White Plains Avenue. The neighborhood was crowded with women shoppers and their children.

A car had been slowly trailing the bus. Now it drove up alongside the man. Before he could reach for the .38 in his shoulder holster, pistol shots vomited from the moving automobile. The pedestrian was felled in his tracks, to the horror of the passing shoppers. This was the end of Murray Marks, who tried to move in on the Mob's business.

Another landmark in Lucky's life and loves was Cokey Flo Brown, a madam. Lucky, Flo insisted, double-crossed two of her pals.

"I hated Luciano before I even knew him," she snarled. "He ordered the death of two of my best friends—guys he made a deal with, that he'd spare them if they got out of town. They kept their part of the bargain, but the dirty double-crosser sent his killers after them just the same."

Cokey Flo's story, unfortunately, ends there. She refused to elaborate, withholding even the names of the victims of the Boss's double-cross. Her disdain for Lucky included more than his ethics, though.

"He don't use such good English," she sneered.

Then there was Stone-Face Peggy, a thin spinster from New Hampshire. And Frisco Jean Irwin from California, who bragged that she smoked the opium pipe with Lucky. And a host of others who came to know the Boss only when economic conditions led him into the business recognized as the oldest in the world.

It may have increased his circle of feminine friends. As a commercial enterprise, however, it wound up most unlucky for Lucky.

7 LUCKY IN THE BROTHELS

A lawyer who never lost arouses an investigator's curiosity. . . . Girls, girls, girls drop into the net. . . . Organized prostitution, a $15,000,000-a-year business. . . . "Burn 'em and cut out their tongues if they talk". . . . The girls sing; Cokey Flo hits a high note. . . . Lucky takes the stand. . . . Siberia for the Boss.

THE RUNAWAY grand jury that swept New York's District Attorney aside in 1935, for failing to produce evidence against mobsters, delivered no easy mandate to Thomas E. Dewey, his successor:

"Get the organized crime!"

Fresh from the U.S. Attorney's office, Dewey was well aware of the Mob's power and the personnel that made it tick. But no prosecutor, anywhere, had ever sent a big-shot racketeer to prison for a real felony!

Dewey set his sights on four targets. The first was Dutch Schultz, who had beaten the income-tax rap pinned on him earlier. Next on the list was Jimmy Hines, the protection that enabled the mobsters to virtually run New York. Equally important was Lepke, who was whispered to have more than half a dozen industries by the throat. And finally, Dewey wanted Lucky Luciano, head of the infamous Italian crime society.

135

To assist his staff of "bright young men," the new rackets buster gathered a group of investigators, men and women, who were enterprising and persistent. One, Mrs. Eunice Carter, was so competent she was loaned out to other agencies.

She was in Magistrate's Court one day when a case against a prostitute was dismissed. As the defendant walked out, Mrs. Carter overheard a chance remark from a spectator.

"That lawyer never loses a case," the voice sneered knowingly. "Either he's a genius—or something's cockeyed."

Mrs. Carter had been noticing that cases against prostitutes were consistently going "out the window"—too consistently to be mere coincidence. The remark piqued her curiosity.

A check through past cases disclosed still another coincidence. This attorney who never lost seemed to have a monopoly on the defense of prostitutes. The more she checked, the more signs Mrs. Carter found that prostitution was an organized racket—that a single controlling force pulled the strings on the "oldest profession."

She brought her suspicions—they weren't much more solid than that—to Murray I. Gurfein, one of Dewey's assistants.

"What do you think?" she asked. "Doesn't it look as if there's really something there?"

"Can't tell yet," Gurfein confessed. "But there's enough to show it to the boss."

Dewey was not overenthusiastic. His sights were set on big chiefs and big operations. Harlotry in New York had never been organized on the grand scale of the Syndicate.

The take was not considered large enough to interest gang lords who raked in fancy returns from lush rackets.

Besides, pimps and procurers are social outcasts in mob-dom. As a matter of fact, through the twenties, the punks at the bottom level of crime society were thrown bawdy-house concessions as crumbs for favors performed. In return for pushing narcotics or running rum or handling a mur-der, the punk was granted three or four houses as his "terri-tory," from which he exacted what tribute he could.

Gradually, the economics of the trade changed. The punks were not talented as procurers, and in prostitution only a constant supply keeps business thriving. To main-tain supply equal to demand, four or five men of ideas appeared on the scene. Functioning like actors' booking agents, each of these men procured a number of girls and placed them in a specific chain of houses. The madams of all the establishments in any group did business only with the booker for that group. Bookings were rotated regularly inside each chain so that new faces would appear frequently in every brothel line-up.

By 1932, the top four bookers were Nick Montana, Cock-eye Lou Weiner, Pete Harris, and Dave Miller. Working independently, they controlled all of the city's vice that counted.

The law knew all this before Mrs. Carter began digging. Much of it had been uncovered only a few months before, when Montana and Cockeye Lou had been nabbed and sent to Sing Sing. But despite their absence, the bawdy-house business hadn't slowed down in the least.

Although he had no idea where it would lead, Dewey gave the go-ahead to dig further. It was long, slow work. Inquiries into prostitution always are, since those questioned are, themselves, engaged in illicit enterprise, and therefore appreciate that any revelation they make is self-incriminatory. Tapped telephones are among the few available sources of information. These were used now, and the truth began to come out. Soon Mrs. Carter's original suspicions of organization were confirmed. It was definitely established that one centralized control had replaced the four independent chains.

For five months more, the probers inched along. But at no time was there a mention of Dewey's big four. No investigative finger pointed at Schultz, Hines, Lepke, or Lucky.

In the early evening of February 1, 1936, plain-clothes men of the rackets prosecutor's staff drifted casually into the West Sixty-eighth Street Station House. Deputy Chief Inspector Dave McAuliffe detailed them off in pairs and trios. Each squad was given a sealed envelope.

"Head for the address on your envelopes," was the order. "When you're halfway there, open the envelope and carry out instructions."

In the envelopes, the plain-clothes men found detailed instructions for raids on the assigned addresses. Precisely at nine o'clock, the detective detachments swooped down on bawdyhouses from end to end of the city, with all the secrecy and suddenness of a synchronized attack by a squadron of B-17's. Forty-one brothels in Manhattan and Brooklyn were nailed.

Virtually every place was running full blast. In one joint, on Twenty-third Street, Nancy Presser, who had by this time been forced by Ralph the Pimp into a two-dollar house, was nabbed in bed with a client.

"Caught her right in the act," the detective explained to the desk sergeant downtown. "I've seen her around. She's a well-known whore."

Nancy drew herself up with dignity. "Don't be vulgar, flatfoot," she reprimanded. "The word is prostitute!"

To maintain security, the prisoners were taken to Dewey's office in the Woolworth Building. By midnight, the place was packed with more than a hundred prostitutes, madams, and their handmaidens. At sight of old friends and fellow workers, one of the girls stopped short at the door.

"Well!" she beamed. "This looks like a convention."

Meanwhile, other flying squads pounced on homes and hangouts of those the investigation had uncovered as executives of the operation. By noon the next day, a hundred women and seventeen men were under lock and key.

Behind bars were Tommy the Bull Pennocchio, Li'l Davey Betillo, Jimmy Frederico, and Abe Wahrman, chief of the ring's strong-arm section. Caught in the net, too, were three of the big-four bookers—Jack Eller, who had taken over Montana's operations; Al Weiner, son of and successor to Cockeye Lou; and Pete Harris (or Balitzar), who had fled to Philadelphia and was picked up there.

Questioning continued day after day, for there were still many holes in the case. Five days after the raids, Dewey's office announced that the headmen of the ring were the bookers. All trails in the investigation ended there, with the booking agents. Still, something seemed to be sealing the prisoners' lips. Something deadly, like fear.

It was about two weeks later that Dave Miller was being interrogated by Jacob J. Rosenblum, one of Dewey's assistants and a leading criminal attorney in private practice today. Dave recalled the time he was talking to Danny Caputo, who did some of the ring's bookkeeping. And Danny had said:

"Don't let it leak—but Charlie Lucky gives the O.K. to run!"

The economic doldrums of 1933 were reflected in the rackets. Not that Lucky had any personal problems. His take could have been cut 50 per cent, and he still wouldn't have had to worry about the rent on his plush hotel suite.

But his staff operatives—musclemen, collectors, organizers, torpedoes—made up a small army that expected payday to arrive regularly. Things got so rough that remuneration for minor hands dropped to as low as $25 a week. Instead of retrenching, Lucky cast about for some means of expansion.

"How about the whorehouses?" one lieutenant suggested.

The proposal met vociferous argument. The antis said it was only asking for trouble. But the pros contended that even a small cut of the boodle from each of more than two hundred brothels would be worth taking.

"And if we don't latch on to it," they argued, "some other mob will. They all need dough."

So Lucky gave the green light to organize prostitution.

Now, in all the millions of words spilled since—in all the squeals from inside the ring itself—there has never been one syllable of proof that Lucky, himself, extorted money from a prostitute or madam, or that he, personally, procured a girl for a bawdyhouse.

"I never took," he always insisted of his relationship with women. "I always gave." He still maintains this. "We were

140

clipping the pimps before," he goes on, unaware of the contradiction. "Why would we move in on the whores?"

Naturally, Lucky could never admit that he had the one weapon to make the whole operation work—the most feared name in crime, the name sacred to the underworld. The mere whisper that "Lucky says nix," or "Charlie gives the O.K.," or "The Boss is behind this," was a traffic signal no one dared ignore. It still is.

Early in 1933, word went out to the bookers and pimps that they'd better be in Li'l Davey Betillo's back-room office on Mulberry Street, down in Little Italy, at a certain hour.

"You guys are through," the Boss told them, with no preliminary remarks. "We're setting up the business, and Davey will handle it."

The independent operators knew better than to object—out loud, anyway.

"Each of you guys gets his take for this week," they were generously advised—a gracious gesture, considering that they'd already done the week's work!

"Maybe some of you want to stay in the new setup," a spokesman for Lucky went on. "In that case, you can buy in for ten grand."

A few had the idea they could get away with going on as if nothing had happened. One of the optimists was Dave Miller. His string of good-looking harlots were in heavy demand. He was reluctant to give up the tidy income they brought him.

Dave was a little guy with one glass eye and ears that stood straight out from his head like jug handles. He had been a constable in Pittsburgh. One day he and his wife Ruth had a row, and she walked out. Still angry, Dave

141

invited a prostitute to the house. They were in bed when Mrs. Miller, her ire cooled, came back. The windup was that both women stayed on, and Dave went into business as a brothel-keeper.

Eventually, Dave and Ruth and their three children came to New York. He peddled dresses from door to door. He soon noted that his best customers were prostitutes. It was not much of a step for him to begin booking them. With his 10 per cent "agent's fees" netting him close to $400 a week, he was not going to just walk out on it, Lucky or no Lucky.

One night, four thugs grabbed him on the street, shoved him up against a wall, and poked a knife against his ribs.

"You got twenty-four hours to get outa town," they told him.

"What's it all about?" Dave wanted to know.

"The Boss says get up ten grand—or get outa town!"

Dave did neither. A short time later, a car drove up alongside his, and a fusillade of bullets chewed up the side of his automobile. Terrified, Dave summoned his attorney. The lawyer called for police protection, without explaining Dave's business. The Mob paid not the slightest attention to the detectives stationed in his house. The phone rang while they were there.

"Cops won't do you no good," a hoarse voice threatened.

Miller was convinced. He packed up and headed for California, where he opened a gasoline station. It failed. He came back east and bought a station on Long Island. It, too, was unsuccessful. In desperation, Dave pleaded for a chance to work for the ring—on its terms.

Pete Harris, whose girls were also especially attractive, was another who tried to hold out. Wahrman, the chief strong arm, turned up at Pete's place with an assistant trigger man. They laid their guns on the table.

"What d'you want?" Pete asked.

"Two hundred a week outa your broads."

The guns were the convincers—the guns and Wahrman's assurance that Pete need have no worries about protection. "Charlie Lucky's behind this," they told him.

The original plan was less one of organizing the brothels than it was to set up extortion under the guise of "special services" like protection and medical and legal fees. This proved a losing proposition. There was not a sufficiently close check to prevent bookers and madams from holding out.

At a Chinatown restaurant meeting with Betillo and Jimmy Fredericks, another suggestion was offered: "We can take the joints away from the madams, and put 'em on salary or commission."

"It's best we run like a syndicate, like the A. & P. stores," Lucky proposed. "In Chicago there was three, four combinations had the places. Here there'd be just one. Us. . . ."

The organization was set up rapidly. His men re-formed the four independent chains into one huge combination of some two hundred brothels, covering Manhattan from the Battery to the edge of the Bronx, and all of Brooklyn. These houses catered to all tastes and pocketbooks—from the two-dollar bawdyhouse for men of small means to upper-bracket bistros for those with full bank rolls and more "refined" appetites.

The Boss himself, remember, did not soil his lily-white hands on the operation. In charge of over-all consolidation and management, he placed Li'l Davey Betillo, who was slim and innocuous in appearance and called himself a cabaret owner. Davey was, however, a vicious killer and had built a ruthless reputation in the wild Chicago gang wars of the twenties. Under Davey, Jimmy Frederico (Fredericks), a bulging, greasy slob with the build of an ape—and mentality to match—was designated field manager, to carry out directives.

The operations office was a candy store and lunch counter on Mulberry Street, around the corner from Police Headquarters. Here all collections and receipts were delivered.

A subgroup known as the Mott Street Mob was located on the fringe of Chinatown. Its chieftain was the ring's treasurer—silent Tommy Pennocchio, who had been a sage counsel in the Italian society for a quarter century.

Wahrman, the strong arm, was chief of enforcement, of course. Ralph the Pimp Liguori was taken on to hold up the houses of any madams who refused to co-operate. Heading the booking department was Nick Montana. He balked at first—but changed his mind at the point of a pistol.

The methods used on madams who were recalcitrant about agreeing to the new order were direct and convincing. Li'l Davey had to seek Lucky's advice more than once.

"Some of the madams are holding out," he informed him once, at a meeting in a Chinese restaurant on upper Broadway.

"No stalling," Lucky snapped. "Get them down and get them on the carpet. You gotta sit on them first, and then step on them!"

In a short time Betillo reported the sitting and stepping had achieved some success. There were still a few recalcitrants, however.

"I told you talking won't do no good," the Boss said. "Put the screws on."

Davey complained particularly about one madam whose brothel was so busy she was popularly known as Jennie the Factory.

"That Jennie, she's a wise guy," commented Lucky. "We'll have to take care of her."

And again the operations manager reported: "I'm having trouble with Dago Jean."

"Well, go ahead and wreck the joint," Lucky ordered.

Dago Jean's was promptly invaded. Furniture was shattered, decorations torn, upholstery ripped—even light fixtures were destroyed. Those who got in the way were thoroughly beaten.

A communications center was set up in a midtown hotel, handled by Anthony Curfeo, who fought in the boxing ring as Little Dingy Farrish. He rose from doorman of a bawdyhouse to information clerk for the ring. Into this control room came all data on the opening and closing of houses, precautionary changes of address to elude the law, and the booking of every prostitute. Word of a raid would be flashed in immediately, so that Dingy could get the legal department right to work on it.

Spike Green was a kind of truant officer. He was stationed at the phones in several East Side restaurants. There madams reported in on girls absent or late for work.

New departments were instituted, one by one. All were masks behind which the mobsters could mulct the girls and madams of more money. The section for bonding and legal counsel was to provide protection in case of raid or arrest. Bail and competent counsel were to be furnished promptly. For this service, each prostitute was charged only (!) ten dollars a week.

Generally, these functions were competently performed. However, the bonding department frequently put up only half the bail, and the prostitute or madam had to supply the balance. The ring graciously added a usurious loan shark named Ben Spiller, who advanced necessary funds— at the usual bloodsucking rates. What's more, when the full bail was returned at the completion of a case, the girl rarely saw her 50 per cent again.

Bail-supplying was under Jesse Jacobs. His bonding license had been taken away during the Seabury Investigation of 1931. Yet as late as 1936, the courts were still accepting bail bond from him!

The legal section was headed by Abe Karp, a disbarred attorney, who had an assistant to make all court appearances. Karp coached arrested prostitutes on their testimony and actually passed on a girl's ability to make perjury stand up. If it was felt she would break under cross-examination, she would be directed to jump bail and leave town until the heat was off.

Danny Brooks (Caputo) had a unique function. He made out itemized expense accounts that were given to each madam, showing her contribution to the ring, fee by fee. The statement contained the precise amounts for lawyer's fees, bonding, and all service charges.

"One I made out in August, 1934, had fifty dollars for an assistant district attorney," he revealed afterward. (No wonder a grand jury felt the need for a special prosecutor, before Dewey's appointment!)

Most of the girls lived in their own homes or hotel rooms. A number lived with members of the ring whom they were keeping. Thus the girls not only submitted to the extortions, but actually footed the bill for living expenses of the very thugs who were doing the extorting from them. Brown-haired Cokey Flo, the smartest of the madams, took in greasy Jimmy Fredericks for her bedmate. Nancy Presser kept Ralph the Pimp.

Girls always seemed plentiful. The one to two thousand prostitutes and two hundred-odd madams were recruited from every state in the Union. There were Frisco Jean Irwin from California; Mildred Curtis, the Kansas farm girl; Stone-Face Peggy from New Hampshire; Muriel Ryan of Indiana; Mildred Harris, the Dixie damsel; Jean Matthews, a dark-eyed Pennsylvania miss. Soft-voiced Helen Kelly grew up in a convent, but left it to marry Gypsy Tom Petrovich. When she arrived in New York for the nuptials, however, Tom put Helen in a brothel. She was nineteen at the time.

"Didn't you try to get out?" she was asked afterward.

"I couldn't; I was too well guarded."

"Who guarded you?"

"Gypsy Tom."

The hoods' watchfulness over their meal tickets was dictated by concern for their income, rather than jealousy of their inamorata. When Ralph Ligouri finally forced Nancy into Jenny the Factory's joint, he decided she was taking too much time with each customer, thereby limiting the number she could handle daily. Actually, Nancy had learned that for a bit of extra service, she would generally receive a tip, which she held out from both the madam and Ralph, who, between them, left her nothing. But the Pimp took to sitting in the parlor and timing Nancy with each client. If she was out more than fifteen minutes, he'd hurry upstairs and bang on her door to "hustle it up."

The girls' work day ran twelve hours, six days a week. Two meals were served daily in the house, for which the prostitute was charged exorbitantly. The madam also over-charged for "lodging," maids, towel service, and the like.

The average inmate of a two-dollar house would handle between $300 and $400 worth of business a week. Spe-cialists and speed performers ran it as high as $600 or more. Broken down, that meant the servicing of three hundred customers over a six-day week—an average of fifty per twelve-hour night, or one every fourteen minutes and twenty-four seconds! And that allowed no time out for meals, either.

The madam took 50 per cent of the girl's gross earnings. The ring extorted $10 weekly for itself, plus approximately $30 for various fees. Added to these were the booker's 10 per cent, almost $5 daily for food, about the same for "lodging," a similar amount for maid service and sundry et ceteras. By the time the breakdown was completed, a girl whose body brought in a gross of, say, $400 a week rarely had more than $50 take-home pay—and with no deduction for withholding tax, either! And when she got home, the pimp with whom she lived promptly grabbed that $50.

Under Lucky's syndicated setup, business was pushed to new highs. By 1935, it was estimated, the gross intake had skyrocketed to some $15,000,000 to $20,000,000 a year. Of this the ring very likely wound up with no less than $5,000,000. Lucky's personal end, after pay-offs, protection, and overhead, was probably in the neighborhood of $200,-000—which is a nice neighborhood to be in.

Still, for Lucky, the prostitution business was never the smooth operation his other rackets were. No one ever seemed satisfied. The boys had to keep up a constant prodding to hold everyone in line. And prostitutes, madams, and bookers, alike, howled that the extortions had them working for practically nothing.

When Dewey moved in as rackets buster, the Boss saw storm clouds ahead. He was perturbed enough to slip back from Florida around Thanksgiving, in 1935, for a meeting with his staff.

"It's getting hot," he pointed out. "This Dewey thing is going strong. . . . It's taking in all the rackets, and liable to get this too."

But he didn't order the prostitution ring halted. It was serving its purpose as a stopgap source of earnings for his hired hands during the fading business depression. Besides, Lucky was positive that he, himself, was in the clear. He was positive no signposts pointed to him, for he had not directly touched the evil racket.

He was almost right—almost! Not until Dave Miller, the booker, remembered Danny Brooks, the bookkeeper, saying, "Lucky gives the O.K.," was the Boss etched into the picture, at long last.

Miller had not been arrested in the original roundup. The afternoon following those sweeping raids, while he and his wife and three children were driving to the family doctor's office in their car, they were spotted and brought in. From the accounts in morning papers, Dave realized that both he and his wife were in the net. He looked at his three completely bewildered youngsters and made his decision.

"Let me see the prosecutor," he offered. "I'll talk to Dewey only."

The rackets buster took him into another room, and Miller came right to the point.

"Mr. Dewey," he began, "we got three kids, and there's nobody to take care of them but my wife. I know you got us cold, and I'm willing to take my rap. But you gotta turn her loose—for the kids—please!" Sobs interrupted him. Then he went on. "They're just little kids; they don't know about this. If you'll let Ruth go, I'll spill. I'll open up on the whole business," he pledged tearfully.

Up to then, the uncovered blueprint of the racket showed no executive echelon beyond the bookers. Besides, while the investigation had bared a great deal, there was not yet enough to go to trial. Facts—names, dates, places, specific extortions—had to be collected. And here was one of the bookers, glass eye unblinking, good one shedding tears, offering to lay those facts on the line.

"All right, Miller," the special prosecutor agreed. "But remember, if you don't open up all the way, the deal is off."

So Ruth took their brood home, and her husband started his song. He brought in Jimmy Fredericks and Li'l Davey and the rest of the operational bosses. And finally, in answer to the direct question from Jacob Rosenblum, he brought in Lucky.

Dewey rubbed his hands. He had figured Lucky to be the toughest of his big four to get at.

Miller's single mention would not, of course, put Luciano behind bars, by a long shot. There was, for instance, a little matter of New York State's law of corroboration.

This will no doubt come as a rude shock to the whodunit writer who, getting stuck in his plot with no outlet, simply has one mobster conveniently turn state's evidence on another. Finis Mr. Mobster. That can't happen in New York.

Section 399 of the New York State Criminal Code states:

A conviction cannot be had upon the testimony of an accomplice, unless he be corroborated by such other evidence as tends to connect the defendant with the commission of the crime.

Thus a Dave Miller could sit in the witness chair and swear all day long that "Lucky was the boss of prostitution"; he could show specifically how. But Miller, as a booker of prostitutes, was a coconspirator, with Lucky—an accomplice. Unless evidence supporting his accusations were forthcoming from an outsider, Lucky would walk out of court free!

And getting this vital corroborative evidence seemed about as likely as getting Lucky to turn State's evidence. The available nonaccomplices had the most distinct aversion to conversation with the law.

Take the madams and prostitutes. They were not coconspirators in the ring's extortions. Yet they demonstrated that awful terror of talking that is a trade-mark of the underworld.

"I know what the combination does!" cried Thelma Jordan as she was asked for the seventh time to tell what she knew. "Plenty of girls who talked had their feet and stomachs burned with cigarettes and their tongues cut up!"

Jean Martin, one of the madams who might have reported firsthand experience, knew the penalty. Once she was slugged with a lead pipe.

Mildred Harris, the uninhibited wife of booker Pete Harris, and a madam in her own right, told intimate details of the ring's machinery. When asked about the Boss, though, she blanched.

"There's nothing to be afraid of," she was assured. "No one can get at you while the Law is guarding you here."

"Oh, I'm not afraid for myself," she whispered in a scared *sotto voce*. "But my little daughter is in the South, in my home town. I'm afraid they'll get after her."

It had been confidently expected that Nancy Presser would show no such reluctance. Nancy always liked to talk—to anyone, about anything. She had demonstrated that the first night, when Dewey arrived to find all the women in his office.

"So you're Dewey, eh?" she tossed off. "You're the big shot they talk about around here." She looked the none-too-tall prosecutor up and down, slowly. "Run along, sonny, and peddle your papers," she leered playfully.

Nancy was perfectly willing to detail all her activities and those of the brutal Ralph. But about the big shots— not a word.

"What have you got to be frightened about?" she was asked. "You knew Waxey Gordon, didn't you? Well, when the Federal attorney sent him up, not one of the hundred witnesses was touched."

"Sure," she conceded. "But Waxey was all washed up by then. Lucky and these guys—they're powerhouses right now."

She walked to the window. "Look out there," she said, pointing to the el station below. "Some of the mob guys stand out there at nights and shake their fists up at us. They even know what floor we're on!"

It settled down to a long-drawn-out campaign to break down the girls through repeated interrogation and reassurance that many of the killers they feared so dreadfully were behind bars, with little or no hope of getting out.

The madams and their hired hands really were bitter over the piracy that had taken their livelihood. As the case heated up, more and bigger news stories were printed. The girls began to read that the thugs were in no position for reprisal. So, one by one, they finally overcame their terror and talked. Not all of them—but enough, so that a rough outline was taking shape.

Progress was slow and painstaking. Two months went by before Dewey was even able to go before the grand jury and get an indictment against Lucky. The day the Boss was revealed as the viceroy of vice was, appropriately enough, April Fool's Day.

"Luciano," the rackets buster announced, "is Public Enemy Number One of New York, and the man who succeeded Al Capone in the West!"

The time had come to bring in the Boss himself—but Lucky was nowhere to be found. He had skipped to Florida in his private Lockheed after the Dutch Schultz massacre, and there the trail ended.

The dragnet went out. It closed on the target in just forty-eight hours. A New York officer, in Hot Springs,

Arkansas, spotted Lucky, big as life, on the spa's famed Bathhouse Promenade, talking to Herbert (Butch) Akers, chief of detectives in the resort. The New York detective flashed the warrant. Lucky recognized him as of Italian blood. He flushed and stared, unbelieving.

"You're a helluva Dago!" he charged, with an *"et tu Brute"* look of recrimination.

"Yep," the officer grinned agreeably. "I'm a helluva Dago."

New York asked for Luciano's extradition. The resultant scramble produced some of the queerest court and law-enforcement maneuvers ever witnessed in jurisprudence.

Chancellor Sam W. Garrett set bail at a laughable $5,000—and promptly released this nationally advertised crime kingpin! (The bail bond was signed by the owners of the Southern and Belvedere Clubs in Hot Springs.) Back in New York, Dewey was stunned.

"I can't understand how any judge could release this man in such bail," he fumed. "Luciano is regarded as the most important racketeer in New York, if not in the country. And the case involves one of the largest rackets, and one of the most loathsome types of crime."

Lucky promptly issued a proclamation of his own. "Back of this action is politics," he thundered. "The most vicious kind of politics. I may not be the most moral and upright man alive, but I have not, at any time, stooped to aiding prostitution. I have never been involved in anything so messy."

Hot Springs authorities rearrested the Boss. By this time, state officials were considerably upset over what folks were saying of Arkansas and its law enforcement. State Attorney

General Carl E. Bailey ordered Lucky's transfer posthaste to the jailhouse in Little Rock. A squad of twenty Arkansas State Rangers were sent to Hot Springs after him.

"So they had to call out the National Guard for me," sneered Lucky.

The Rangers had to threaten open warfare before the sheriff would give him up. Then he was whisked the fifty miles over the mountains to the state capital.

Gangsters from various cities were reported slipping into town. The guard around the jailhouse was tripled. Machine guns were added to the defenses. When the extradition proceedings opened before Governor J. Marion Futtrell, a protective cordon of Rangers was thrown around the capitol.

Attorney General Bailey was almost at the door of the hearing room when he was accosted by strangers. They offered him $50,000 to take it easy, so that extradition would be defeated. The state's highest law officer was fighting-mad when he stood before the Governor to argue for Lucky's shipment to New York.

"It must be demonstrated that the honor of Arkansas and her officials is not for sale for blood money!" he stormed. "Every time a major criminal of this country wants asylum, he heads for Hot Springs. We must show that Arkansas cannot be made an asylum for them!"

The requisition was granted.

"I am being kidnaped," wailed Lucky.

The day Lucky arrived in New York, the grand jury handed up a brand-new indictment against the prostitution ring. It charged Luciano with ninety counts of extortion and direction of organized harlotry. If convicted on all of them, he could be sentenced to a mere 1,950 years. His bail was set at a monumental $350,000!

"I am in a fog," was all he could say.

Lucky's influence in organized crime necessitated extraordinary precautions for his trial. Forty picked policemen patrolled the corridors outside the courtroom, which was jammed with spectators at every session. More officers roved the area around the courthouse.

As the case opened, three of the four big bookers—Pete Harris, Dave Miller, and Al Weiner—suddenly pleaded guilty. The fourth, Jack Eller, followed them later.

"The vice industry, since Luciano took over, is highly organized and operates with businesslike precision," Dewey pointed out in his opening address.

"Lucky Luciano will be proved . . . to have sat way up at the top, in his apartment at the Waldorf, as the czar of organized crime in this city. Never did Lucky or any co-defendant actually see or collect from the whores. Luciano, though, was always in touch with the general details of the business.

"We will show you his function as the man whose word, whose suggestion, whose very statement, 'Do this,' was sufficient; and all the others in the case are his servants!"

To bear out these contentions, the rackets buster paraded sixty-eight witnesses to the stand. Forty were prostitutes and madams. A dozen were bookers, pimps, and male madams. The other sixteen were legitimate citizens who told of Lucky's movements and visitors in places like the Waldorf.

The top bookers put the finger on the Boss and his co-defendants. They laid the groundwork.

Some witnesses balked at the last minute. More than offsetting their loss, though, was an altogether unexpected addition to the prosecutive array.

On the very day the trial opened, a note was delivered to Dewey's office. Scribbled on a scrap of paper, it read:

DEAR SIR,
I would like to see you on a matter of great importance in the vice case.
I am and was for three years James Frederico's sweetheart.
Respectfully,
FLO

A postscript explained that Flo could be found on the fourth floor of the Women's House of Detention. A Dewey aide went over, and there was Cokey Flo Brown waiting to talk.

Her appearance in court was one of the dramatic high lights of the trial. Flo was the very last person either her boy friend, Jimmy Fredericks, or his counsel expected to show up as a witness for the state. But Flo had been languishing for days, waiting for the ring's bonding department to bail her out, and nothing had happened. Jimmy hadn't answered her letters. From the newspapers, she knew his goose was cooked. Slowly it dawned on her that her lover boy and everyone else was going to leave her there to rot. So Flo took the obvious way out.

She got on the witness stand, and for nine hours she sang. And every note buried the defense!

"I know Charlie Lucky," the tiny brothel-keeper said, and she stared right back into the Boss's cold eyes.

Jimmy, she explained, just never could learn to drive a car, so she used to chauffeur him here and there, to

157

restaurants and places. That way, she had come to meet all his friends. She had sat at table with them any number of times. They acted as if she wasn't there—just went right on talking about business "like gambling, the combination, dope." And Lucky would give the orders.

"One night," she said, "Charlie said he wanted a syndicate of houses on a big scale—the same as the A. & P. stores."

Another time, at a dinner meeting, he sternly commanded that the madams stop sending their pimps around, trying to get other mob lords to prevail upon him to lift the prostitutes' bonding fee. Charlie was thus put squarely in the middle of the whole rotten mess. And Nancy Presser and Mildred Harris added more of the same.

They were the big three: Cokey Flo, who hated them all because they hadn't bailed her out; Nancy, who hated Ralph the Pimp for dragging her down from a hundred-dollar-a-night belle-of-the-ball to a two-dollar whore; and Mildred, who hated Lucky because he spit in her face and threatened the only man she ever loved—and not long afterward the man was murdered.

The other forty brothel witnesses filled in the empty spaces. There was a sordid sameness to their stories, an unceasing reiteration of debasement and humiliation. Many of the girls were confused, and the stares of the killers and extortionists who had preyed on them were not a calming influence.

"Have you gentlemen," inquired Dewey of the jury at one point, "ever known stark, complete, and paralyzing terror?" He gestured eloquently at the witness.

By the time it was over, the picture of a degrading, filthy racket, organized by the Boss and his mob on a syndicate basis, enforced with gun, knife, and lead pipe, stood out in shocking clarity. Even the most blasé and hardboiled were stunned. Even Luciano's appearance on the stand—the climax of the drama—was weakened by what had already come from the mouths of common whores.

The Boss, conservatively dressed in custom-tailored gray and a black tie, was entirely the self-possessed business executive. He leaned comfortably back in the witness chair, completely poised, legs crossed, hands clasped easily. The direct examination was just a breeze, as he was put through his paces by one of his defense counsel, George Morton Levy (who has, for several years now, headed the Roosevelt Raceway on Long Island, which was involved in the 1953 exposure of racket labor and corruption at several New York trotting tracks). (During his trial or in subsequent appeals, Lucky's legal staff was studded with brilliant names. Besides Levy, another was Francis W. H. Adams, who today is Police Commissioner of New York City.)

"My business is gambling houses and booking horses," Lucky stated. He swore he never had seen any of the madams and prostitutes before they walked into the courtroom. If Lucky were telling the truth, then Nancy must have been really clairvoyant, because she described suite 39-C at the Waldorf minutely and accurately.

The spectators buzzed again when he denied ever in his life having met any of his codefendants, except Davey Betillo, before the trial. Just a short while previously, Molly Brown, sitting in the same chair, under the somber stare of the Boss, had pointed out various members of the Mob who had visited 39-C while she was cleaning the bathrooms on that floor.

Things got really rough when Dewey stood before Lucky

and began a cross-examination that fairly crackled. The relentless rackets buster brought in Lucky's tax returns. There were snickers when he showed that for seven years, from 1929 to 1935, the master of a dozen rackets claimed he had not made more than $22,500 in any one year. Actually, Luciano's returns for those seven years had all been filed at one time, in July of 1935, when he began to have qualms about the Dewey probe. The prosecutor hammered at him now for a detailed breakdown of the returns. The Boss refused to concede a thing.

"You just picked these figures on your income out of the sky, didn't you?" Dewey finally charged.

"I just thought it was the proper amount I should give the government," responded Lucky, smoothly.

On Saturday, June 6, the jurors retired to start wading through the endless maze of evidence, testimony, and exhibits. There were sixty-two individual charges of extortion and racketeering against each defendant. (The balance were excluded by the court.) A decision had to be made on each count against each man—a minute search calling for 806 separate verdicts.

In the milling crowds outside the courtroom, bets were made back and forth, as they are at every criminal trial by the type of ghoul who enjoys gambling on men's lives. The wagering was strong against the others. But the odds actually favored the Boss.

"If the jury has doubts about the testimony from the whores and madams," it was pointed out, "then there's no clear-cut case against Lucky."

As the church bells rang on Sunday morning, the jury trooped back in, Indian file, behind the grim-faced foreman, Edwin Aderer.

"Gentlemen of the jury," came the traditional question, "have you agreed on a verdict?"

"We have, Your Honor," the foreman replied softly.

"On the defendant Lucania, how do you find?"

The foreman read off the verdict on each count against Lucky. "Guilty as charged," he intoned. "Guilty as charged. . . ." Sixty-two times he said it. There was a barely noticeable tightening of Lucky's jaw. Otherwise, he showed no flicker of emotion as the monotone rolled on and on. "Guilty . . . guilty . . . guilty. . . ."

The chief juror turned to the others in the combination, and the vote was repeated, again and again. Each was convicted on every count charged.

Justice McCook thanked the jurors for "intelligence and discrimination," and ordered the convicted vice racketeers back eleven days hence, to hear their doom. In the interim, the customary report on each man was prepared by the Probation Officer. It provides the court with thorough background for calculation of the prison sentence and for estimating the possibility of rehabilitation. For Lucky, Chief Probation Officer Irving Halpern required eight full pages. Laid open on them, as by a surgeon's scalpel, was the inside of this crime genius who rose from the slums to sit on the highest council of the National Crime Syndicate:

He possesses average intelligence, but is a shallow and parasitic individual who is considerably wrapped up in his own feelings.

His ideals of life resolved themselves into money to spend, beautiful women to enjoy, silk underclothes, and places to go in style.

His social outlook is essentially childish, in that it is dominated by recklessness and a craving for action. His only asset as a leader consists of his apparent calmness in times of stress. This characteristic, which appears to be based on his feeling that he could escape involvement, has passed for reserve and strength.

He reads the newspapers, but chiefly looks at the cartoons and jokes. . . . His cultural pursuits are a little restricted.

He manifests a peasantlike faith in chance, and has developed an attitude of nonchalance. His behavior patterns are essentially instinctive and primitive, his manner easy, copious, and ingratiating. . . .

The document was plainly a beacon to Justice McCook, when the thugs faced him to learn their fate. The lights in the chamber were dim, and the crowd was gone now. The judge leveled his gaze first on Lucky.

"Charles Lucania," he stated, "a discriminating jury has found you guilty of heading a conspiracy to commit these crimes. Have you anything to say before judgment is pronounced?"

Lucky blinked his off-center eyelashes, as if the realization of what it was all about had just hit him.

"Your Honor," he said, "I have nothing to say outside the fact that I want to say again I am innocent."

"You are responsible . . . for every foul and cruel deed, with accompanying elements of extortion, performed by your band," the court accused. "There appears no excuse for your conduct, nor hope for your rehabilitation.

"It, therefore, is the judgment of the court that you be sentenced—"

The Justice halted a moment, his eyes squarely on the mighty gang lord who had been felled, at long last.

"—to from thirty to fifty years in the State Penitentiary!"

There was no hiding the shock. None of them had expected this. No one, as far back as the oldest courtroom observer could remember, had ever had a rap like this hung on him for a crime involving prostitution. It was a punishment truly worthy of the Boss!

Then the court turned to the others: Little Davey—"the most dangerous of the defendants except one," the judge said—twenty-five to forty years; Jimmy Fredericks—"a low and despicable character," declared the probation report—twenty-five years; Tommy the Bull Pennocchio—twenty-five years; Abe Wahrman, the strong arm—fifteen to thirty years.

Below the big shots, the sentences diminished, from seven and a half to fifteen years for Ralph Liguori ("a silly imitator of the racketeers he admires"), down to two to four years for the bookers who had turned state's evidence.

The court had one final message. The Mob's methods of dealing with songbirds were well known.

"Evidence upon the trial and reliable information since," explained Justice McCook, "have convinced the court that these defendants will be responsible for any injury which the witnesses might hereafter suffer, by reason of their testimony. Should any witness be injured or harassed, the court will request parole authorities to retain in prison those defendants against whom such witnesses testified, for the maximum terms of their sentence!"

Then to his horror, Lucky found himself relegated to Dannemora Prison, in upstate New York. To the Mob, Dannemora is Siberia!

But the Boss was not through yet. His attorneys were soon back in court, yelling fake and demanding justice. They brought affidavits from three of the witnesses, recanting their testimony, declaring all those awful things they'd said about Lucky weren't so. And of all the sixty-eight state witnesses, from which trio did the lawyers bring the recanting statements? Only from the big three, whose testimony had done most to put Luciano where he belonged. Only from Cokey Flo, Nancy, and Mildred Harris!

Dewey examined the startling claims and snorted.

"These documents reek with perjury," he charged. "They are a fraud upon the court!"

Justice McCook denied a new trial.

Three months later, an astounding affair exploded in Washington, which gave the judge's warning the ring of prophecy. In the small morning hours, a girl's voice screamed into a telephone, "Help! Police!" Officers came running and found a slim redhead, bound and carved up, on the floor of a gas-filled apartment on New Hampshire Avenue. All she had on was a sheer nightgown, and that was virtually slashed from her body.

The knife work on her anatomy was not very deep, but it was artistic. On her thigh, the incisions formed the letters "C L," about three inches square. Across her abdomen, the numerals "3-12" were etched in blood. The initials, numerical and alphabetical, of Charlie Lucky!

She said she was Margaret Louise Bell, alias Jean Costella. It developed that she was really auburn-haired Jeannette Lewis, the Cincinnati girl friend of the late Abbadabba Berman, Schultz's mathematical wizard—the girl who got a job in a brothel on Lucky's say-so. She had appeared before the grand jury in the prostitution investigation, but had not been a trial witness.

Her story sounded like something right off a movie

screen. After the vice trial, she related, a lawyer offered her $500 for an affidavit stating that her grand jury testimony had been framed against the ring's executives. She accepted the $500, and promptly skipped to Washington without making the affidavit, she went on.

On this fatal night, she had been at a club near the Washington airport when, suddenly, among the customers, the face of a member of Lucky's gang appeared. She could identify him only as Joe.

Margaret-Jean-Jeannette fled the place in terror. She had barely reached her apartment and prepared for bed, when there was a knock at the door. When she opened it a crack, a man barged in, threw her to the floor, tied her up, took a knife from a briefcase he was carrying, slashed her nightie from top to bottom, and performed the carving job. Then he dragged the roped-up redhead into the kitchen, turned on the gas, and departed. She managed to crawl to the phone, knock off the receiver, and holler for the police.

"They did it because I welched," she wailed.

That was her story. Two detectives came down from New York to investigate. A man named Joe, with a fifteen-year police record, was picked up, then let go. Jeanne could not identify him.

And then, an odor somewhat fishy was detected. It was discovered that once, in Lakeland, Florida, this same girl had come running to the police with a bullet wound and a story that her uncle had done it. The wound turned out to have been self-inflicted. Dewey checked her file and announced that he "regarded her as unreliable." Phil Davis, a patient in the Washington Veterans' Hospital, saw her photo in the papers and informed authorities that this same charmer had clipped him for $709 at a party in Baltimore ten days before.

Finally, it was established that the carving had been done, not with a knife, but with a nail file—and by Jeannette herself.

"This," announced Washington Detective Chief Bernard Thompson, closing the case, "is the greatest fabrication I have ever been confronted with."

But Lucky's going away did have major repercussions in the underworld. Police linked a number of gang killings with the resultant upheaval. No other trial witness, however, ever has been reported harmed.

Lucky and his evil crew had been hit harder than they ever were hit before. A large dent had been made in the tanklike armor of immunity that for years had shielded the racket empire. For the first time, a gang lord had been put behind thick gray walls for a real, unmistakeable felony, a major crime.

If any doubt lingered in Lucky's mind that this was for keeps, it was erased in August of that year. As a convicted felon, the State Motor Vehicle Bureau notified him that his driver's license had been revoked.

8 LUCKY GETS OUT

Dewey cleans up.... Stone walls can be a home.... Exile to Italy; a political football....

FOR A WHILE there in 1936, after Lucky was put away, it seemed that the country in general, and New York in particular, were to have the pleasure of being rid of everything that even smelled faintly of him. One by one, a number of his hoodlums, associates, and buddies followed him to the pen.

Dewey set a bomb off, too, under Charlie's political empire—in the person of Albert C. Marinelli. The slum boy who made good in Tammany was blasted out of his soft spot at the trough by a single speech. A year after putting Lucky away, Dewey got on a platform one night and took aim.

"Marinelli is a political ally of thieves, pickpockets, thugs, dope peddlers, and big-shot racketeers," he proclaimed. (He omitted whoremasters and murderers, but this may have been merely an oversight.)

Governor Lehman asked the Tammany boss for an answer. Marinelli screamed "politics," and sneered that Dewey would not dare make the nasty accusations under oath. So Dewey took an oath and repeated the allegations—plus a raft of new ones concerning political or governmental officeholders who were convicts, ex-convicts, or would-have-been convicts but for the sympathy of some court or jury.

Not even loyal party folks could stomach all this. When the next elections came round, Marinelli was heaved out, both as county clerk and Tammany leader.

Any idealistic dream that this would end the specialized brand of political control was rudely shattered. Elected Marinelli's successor was Jimmy Kelly, proprietor of a Greenwich Village night club. Jimmy was the father-in-law of Anthony Carfano, more familiar to the racket headlines as Li'l Augie Pisano. Li'l Augie's success dated back to his days as staff lieutenant for Joe the Boss Masseria.

Nevertheless, with his thirty-to-fifty-year rap, Lucky figured to be out of the way for quite a spell. Dannemora is not so far away, of course, that the Boss could not be reached—for advice, instruction, or a senior vote on important projects. What Lucky did find particularly unpleasant—besides the absence of room service, naturally—was that he was in Siberia. He discovered quickly that everything he'd been told of the grim jail's rigid discipline was understatement.

"I know now why they call it Siberia," he confided to a fellow guest. "It's un-American!"

Lucky, though, had long since learned his way around a poky and the methods of special privilege therein. Like other inmates he was put to work. Only, one newspaper reported, the erudite mob boss was put to work—in the prison library! A recent check failed to reveal any record that the Boss actually did enjoy the soft berth browsing among the old masters in the reading room. Nevertheless, he was eventually switched to the hot, steamy prison laundry, which may have been regarded as better suited to a gentleman of his standing and tastes.

Laundry or library, however, Lucky simply had to play the big shot. He had all the money he wanted, and money is just as important behind bars as elsewhere. It buys just as many favors. Fellow inmates still recall that no prisoner ever had to want for a few dollars as long as word of his need reached Luciano. They remember, too, all the fawning and kowtowing that went on over these donations.

To give him his due, Lucky did do some good occasionally. Word got to him that a local church was badly in need of funds for building. He forthwith supplied the parish with the necessary money. It has been reported, too, that during his Dannemora visit, Lucky also had his lopsided eyelid straightened out, possibly by surgery, so that today the old leering slant is barely noticeable.

Meanwhile, in the world outside, the boys had not forgotten. (He was not one to let them.) In April, 1938, his appeal came up before the New York Court of Appeals, the State's highest tribunal. It was turned down. The most eminent bench of the land, the United States Supreme Court, refused even to review the case—which was the court's way of saying there was no Constitutional ground for doubting his guilt as boss of the bawdyhouses. But the Luciano story was far from over.

Blocked in every court, Lucky waited more than six years before making his next move. On February 8, 1943, he appealed to State Supreme Court Justice McCook for a reduction in his durance vile to the time he had already served. For this bid, his earlier legal staff was bolstered by George Wolf, who was to gain nation-wide attention eight years later as lawyer for Frank Costello, in the Prime Minister's appearance at the television circus that passed for the Kefauver Committee hearings.

The basis for Lucky's plea was a shocker.

"Luciano has co-operated with high military authorities," attorney Wolf proclaimed. "He is rendering a definite service to the war effort."

It was a good try—except that the crime-hating jurist, who had already heard the most sordid details of Luciano's infamies, was not quite the man to sing his virtues to. Justice McCook said no.

Surprisingly, however, he did not slam the door all the way. The last paragraph of his opinion stated:

"If Luciano continues to co-operate and remains a model prisoner, it may be appropriate at some future time to apply for executive clemency."

Obviously, the ruling was to let Lucky know that the court was aware he was rendering some service—and that he had better keep right on rendering, if he ever wanted to get out. And if the newsmen covering the case had read down to this small type, they might have derived an inkling, way back there, of what was in the air. It would have eliminated no end of official double talk and politicking that lay ahead.

Evidently, Luciano took Judge McCook's words to heart. He waited exactly until V-E Day, and then sought the executive clemency that the jurist had said he might ask. The war was over now, so there was no longer need for the continued "co-operation" the judge had mentioned. The plea was turned over by the Governor to the State Parole Board for recommendation, which is general practice.

Finally, at the end of 1945, the board unanimously recommended his parole and exile forever from the United

States to the Italy he had left forty years before. The action, the board announced, was the result of "an investigation showing conclusively Luciano's term should be commuted." The board, too, cited his mysterious wartime service, and conceded that it had a bearing on the case, along with other considerations.

Now, there was nothing either unusual or astonishing about such a move. Ever since the parole system was founded in New York State, the same step has been used to dump hundreds of foreign-born criminals out of the country, like garbage toted out to sea in a scow. The idea has been to rid the country of undesirables (who should not have been admitted in the first place) and to save the state the cost of feeding and housing scum that the nation could do very well without, anyway.

Recommendations from the Parole Board are passed on to the governor for signature. And in the history of the parole system, rare, indeed, has been the governor who refused to sign such a recommendation. All governors have operated on the ground that the board has investigated each case thoroughly, before such recommendation, and is therefore in a better position to judge its merits. There is no more mystery to it than that.

By the time Lucky's case came up, the Governor of New York was Thomas E. Dewey, who had won national recognition for putting the Boss away in 1936. He simply activated the board's recommendation, as virtually all governors had done in similar cases. The action was a commutation, a parole based on the deportation; not a pardon, as so many mistakenly maintain. In fact, if Lucky should ever again show his leering countenance inside American borders, he will promptly be clapped in jail to serve out the balance of his original sentence.

The evidence is definite Dewey was not at all satisfied that the ex-master of the prostitutes had suddenly turned patriot. On the commutation papers, he wrote:

"It appears Luciano co-operated, though the actual value of the information procured is not clear."

The effect was to cut to about ten the thirty-to-fifty-year sentence Dewey himself had won for the Boss.

The development was duly but not sensationally noted in the public prints. Hardly an eyebrow was raised. Rather, there arose a sincere sigh of good riddance—especially from those political quarters, local, state, and national, where Lucky had built up protection and immunity. To them, he represented a threat as long as he was anywhere in this country.

A howl over Lucky's release was loosed only when a transatlantic narcotics pipeline began pouring the deadliest flow ever known across the country, by way of an east Harlem distributing outlet, and Federal Narcotics Agents pointed the trail back to the banished Boss without providing evidence thereof. Then everyone got into the act. But no one could have foreseen that "slow murder" would become an epidemic as soon as the Boss hit his native land.

Governor Dewey, who had done exactly what every other governor before him—without exception—had done, was roundly condemned. Why had he let this dope peddler get away, finger-pointers demanded? These same finger-pointers hadn't even bothered to read the news stories of Lucky's release. As a matter of fact, it will probably come as a surprise to a lot of the finger-pointers to learn that not too many years ago, sixty-four known dope peddlers were pardoned from Federal prisons, where they were doing time, and deported, in one horrible swoop. Many of them are doing business in Italy right now. And the man who loosed this ready-made narcotics-dealing army to spread its deadly poison was President Franklin D. Roosevelt!

Dewey needs no defense for his action, certainly. Nevertheless, since then, the affair Luciano has deteriorated into a messy political football, which is kicked up and down the field whenever any ambitious politician wants to grab a headline. Every hack with an ax to grind makes like a knight in shining armor over it. Candidates campaigning for office find it a handy gimmick to exploit. So do officials of investigative bodies, who are looking ahead to the time they can cash in politically—such as by running for mayor, senator, governor, or even President of the United States. Even Narcotics agents, whose batting average on Luciano facts would hardly make the big leagues, get into the act. Few, if any, bother with facts, or even with learning the background details. Even fewer, to this day, have tried to find out the real story before sounding off. Instead, it is stylish to pooh-pooh roundly the very possibility that Lucky could have contributed to the war effort in any way. This stand is all the more startling in the face of Justice McCook's revelations in his opinion and the Parole Board's investigation and findings.

In November, 1952, Michael Stern, in an article in *True* Magazine, claimed that, in discussing his release, Lucky had admitted: "It cost me $75,000 for the Republican campaign fund. At least that's where it was supposed to go." Lucky, remember, pays more attention to the cover-up and keeping his mouth shut than any gang lord before or since. He would not tell a newspaperman the time of day. You'd never get the mob boys or the veteran crime reporters to believe that he calmly confided to a magazine writer such incriminating information.

It is noted that, no matter the implication the author sought to convey, the article does not state that any money was paid to Dewey or his campaign, but rather to an ambigious "Republican Party campaign fund." That could be the fund for the campaign to elect a dogcatcher in West Squeedunk—or any other campaign.

Despite his notation on the commutation papers, though, Dewey is invariably attacked. Oddly enough, it is as often a fellow Republican who does the finger-pointing, as it is a ranking Democrat.

One of the few Democrats who tried was Walter A. Lynch, the candidate opposing Dewey in the 1950 gubernatorial election. "Unless Dewey tells why he freed Luciano, I will give the full details publicly," shouted Lynch, in a campaign speech.

His answer came, not from Dewey, but from the man who knew more about Lucky's commutation than any other individual—Dr. Frederick A. Moran, who was the chairman of the State Parole Board and a veteran of thirty years of parole work. Dr. Moran announced irately that it was ridiculous even to hint that Dewey had performed any tricks in Lucky's case. The matter, he insisted, was decided by the Parole Board with no outside initiative or pressure.

"The Board's investigation showed conclusively," the chairman insisted, "that Luciano's minimum term should be commuted so that he could be deported as an undesirable alien, in accordance with longstanding customary practice of the State. The Parole Board always has been

174

permitted to act independently and without interference of any kind or character."

Dr. Moran clearly showed his displeasure over the effort to throw the Parole Board into politics. Why, Moran declared, he, himself, was not even a Dewey appointee. He was named to the Board by Franklin D. Roosevelt, when he was Governor, and had been reappointed by Governor Lehman—both Democrats.

What, then, is the real story of Lucky's activities in wartime? Considerable of the authors' research time for this book was spent in tracking down the facts. The "inside" of one of the war's stranger developments is revealed in the following pages for the first time, to clear up a fairy tale that has become most malodorous. What the research developed was startling—especially in light of the fact that so many men of standing knew so little of what they were talking about. And tried to impress the public with the fact that they knew a lot more.

9 LUCKY AND OPERATION UNDERWORLD

Sabotage, submarines, and spies menace a life line. . . . SOS from a desperate Navy. . . . Lucky sends the word out. . . . "Charlie's behind this": password to information. . . . Counterespionage à la mob. . . . Mobsters and politicians at a going-away party. . . . Dock worker hoods show the law who's boss. . . .

IN THE early months of World War II, the Allies' life line hung by a slender thread. No one outside official walls knows, to this day, just how close it came to being snapped off altogether, under the torpedoes of German U-Boats.

The Navy was desperate.

Hitler's submarine pack actually ringed our very front doorsill—the Eastern seaboard. They struck savagely, day after day, at the convoys that made up the shaky life line. In the first ten months of the war alone, some five hundred of our ships were sunk in the Atlantic!

The mad-dog underwater horde lurked around the vast exposed New York shore line, which spreads over perhaps five hundred miles of Long Island (much of it sparsely inhabited), New Jersey, and nearby New England. And they roved in our very harbors. They were actually sighted in New York waters!

The ring of death remained so constant and in such

numbers that it was perilously obvious the killer pack did not have to return to bases for supplies. The dreadful thought, then, was that they were getting food, fuel, distilled water, and whatever else they needed from American shores! It was no more than simple—though fearful—logic that such supplies could very likely be coming from the fishing fleets that put out from Boston and New York and the Philadelphia-Baltimore waters; from traitors who, for money or to aid a native land at the expense of their adopted home, were selling out.

There are many fishing-boat stations on this long exposed coast. The Navy had to find out if there was a real basis for the fears. Some way must be devised to put undercover operatives aboard the smacks and on the trucks that hauled the fish from landing dock to market and at the fuel dumps where the boats were serviced.

Adding to the menace, there rose the specter of sabotage on the water front, against the docks and the ships and the life-and-death cargoes they carried.

In February of 1942, the French luxury liner *Normandie* was burned virtually to the water as she stood at her pier in the Hudson River. She was being converted for United States Navy use as the auxiliary ship *Lafayette*. So strong were the signs of enemy agents at work that an all-out investigation was ordered, under Lieutenant Commander Charles Radcliffe Haffenden, a brilliant intelligence officer.

Then, in June, a dozen enemy spies were landed by submarine near the village of Amagansett, on Long Island. They were caught, through the ever watchful FBI. But, having tried once, what if the foe dared again, slipping in elsewhere on the long miles of lonely sand—and this time eluded detection?

New York was the main port for troopships, for matériel, for the formation of convoys. The large number of sinkings indicated definitely that information was leaking. Word of ships' being loaded, data on convoys gathering were getting to the enemy. A blackout was imposed on the harbor. Agents of the various military services were posted atop skyscrapers along the water front, sweeping the area with binoculars for suspicious activity, any movement that might be a signal to the lurking foe.

Nor were these, pressing as they were, the only worries piled on the Navy, which is the security watchdog of water front and shipping in times of crises. Espionage was an ever present, very real threat.

Most of the out-and-out pro-Nazis were spotted in the front-door cities on the Atlantic. But there were great numbers of pro-Mussolini-ites and Fascist Italians. And they were unchecked in those days when the brand-new war effort was still clogged with duties and tasks by the thousand. A considerable element always works in and around the water front; Germans do not. Among this set are many with criminal background—men who will commit murder for a price. To the Nazis, here was a recruiting ground for a mercenary force to do their dirty work. Here could likely be found men who would plant bombs or sell information. Nor was it entirely inconceivable that the enemy might try worming and weaseling its way into labor and labor unions to stir up agitation, and thus break the steady flow of war goods just then starting to roll.

In wartime, not even one slip-up is allowed. The Navy had to know definitely what was going on. Agents or operatives had to be placed in critical, sensitive spots—in factories devoted to war production, on piers and trucks, and in night clubs, hotels, restaurants, where military personnel gathered. Few are not talkative when drinking. Remarks men made among themselves could be picked up by ears tuned in for that purpose. A man in uniform, seeking pleasure, could be placed in an embarrassing position without too much difficulty—and given the alternative of exposure or supplying information to save himself.

Investigators—city, state, and Federal—have long recognized waiters, elevator boys, bellboys, and chambermaids as prime sources of information, simply because they see and hear people off guard. Bars and grills, lounges, restaurants, hotels are sensitive spots in wartime. In them, large numbers of military men congregate. And in such places, they are off guard. The Navy was anxious to place its own agents in such spots, to check for espionage.

But these places are almost exclusively unionized. The waiters, the building employees, the hotel service workers all have their labor organizations. And it was imperative that the identity of the Navy's agents remain covered. A building superintendent, for instance, could not be tipped off that a new man was actually an intelligence operative, who might have to do a job of second-story work in the office of a suspected business firm that tenanted the building. The only sure method was to equip the agents with bona fide union cards and union books, so that when they showed up for a job, it would be with the real appearance of normal employees, sent by the union. Blank legitimate union credentials were a necessity.

In downtown New York, just back of the Woolworth Building, the watchdog to combat all these threats was housed. This was 90 Church Street, headquarters of the Third Naval District, comprising that considerable chunk of Atlantic seaboard that includes New York harbor. S. S. Concrete, it was humorously called by the Navy men assigned there. Here, too, was Naval Intelligence Headquarters, which had the particular job of putting the cork in espionage and sabotage, of building up counterintelligence, of laboring and sweating over ways and means in those days when the war was young.

Daily, Captain Roscoe C. MacFall and his staff of officers and civilian intelligence agents huddled over the tremendous task and what to do about it. The Navy had picked unusually well for this pulse beat of the war effort. On the intelligence staff were prewar F.B.I. men, detectives, District and Federal Attorneys and their investigators, Treasury Department operatives, lawyers—all now in uniform.

Many of them were accustomed to the use of informers in law-enforcement work. Among Federal and local police agencies and prosecuting offices, it has long been routine to get an "in," to develop stool pigeons who talk from the inside. That's time-honored technique. It was only natural, then, that in the daily brow-knitting sessions in the Third District Intelligence Office, with so many peacetime law officers present, the idea eventually would come up for meeting the many-sided menace they faced. And from there, the use of underworld characters, with fingers in many pies, was considered. It was simply the application of civilian law enforcement to military necessity.

But could it work for so sensitive a project? Take a mobster mixed up in murder and racketeering and any number of other projects designed to wreck American economy. Could he be convinced? Was he capable of making the switch to working with the law, even if it was a branch of the law that had no particular immediate concern with his standing as gang lord, killer, or dope dealer? What of the Mob's long-established credo of a bullet for the squealer? And above all, could such a thug be trusted?

Among the intelligence officers were Lieutenant James O'Malley and Commander Anthony Marsloe. Jim O'Malley had been an assistant District Attorney under Prosecutor Frank Hogan in New York. And Tony Marsloe—a specialist in Sicilian dialect and head of the Third District linguistic squad—had been an investigator on D. A. Hogan's staff.

Hogan's office is the largest prosecuting office in the world. It maintains an outstanding rackets bureau, which includes a grand jury squad of sixty detectives alone. They probably know more about the underworld than any similar group. Jim O'Malley and Tony Marsloe pointed out that Hogan's office was not only particularly acquainted with the water front, but was virtually a repository of the Who's Who in the underworld, generally. The social register of the Mob was kept there.

The Navy had theories—and only theories—with no idea of precisely what it wanted or how to get what it wanted, even if it did know. Why not, then, go to Hogan and see if he had any ideas about transforming this nebulous possibility into working fact?

In no time at all, Lieutenant O'Malley and Captain MacFall were in the District Attorney's office. They sat down with Hogan and Murray I. Gurfein, a former assistant U.S. Attorney, and just then in charge of the District Attorney's rackets bureau. This was the same

Gurfein, incidentally, who had been on Dewey's staff during the brothel probe and exposure that sent Lucky to prison. He had been studying the Mob a long time.

On a day in early March of 1942, the Navy men outlined for the two prosecutors the dangers to the nation in the New York area—its water front and harbors, its hundreds of gathering places and offices and buildings. They revealed how they had considered all ways, chewed over every possible method. And they laid the problem in Hogan's lap.

"What can we do about it?" pleaded Captain MacFall. "Frankly, we're in a tough spot. And we have to work fast."

"Anything we have you can have," Hogan pledged at once. "The information we have, the underworld characters . . . anything at all."

"Well," Captain MacFall came right to the point, "we have considered using informers, even from the underworld. But is it practical? Can they be trusted and would they help? We're worried about Mussolini sympathizers and Fascists. We're also concerned about those who used to be rumrunners, and might know how to make contacts at sea—for a price."

"I think you'll find that a lot of these Italian racketeers are loyal Americans," was Hogan's unexpected reply. "Besides, I understand a lot of them don't like Mussolini."

Obviously, the District Attorney was thinking of those Sicilians and members of Old World Mafia who had been run out of Italy by Mussolini in the twenties. Il Duce chased them as a threat to his own iron-handed racketeering rule, and they fled by the dozens—to America.

From that first discussion, the possibility of tapping the

underworld became something definite to work on. Hogan and Gurfein promised to line up a program.

"Let us have several days to go through our files and pick out likely candidates to work on," they explained.

To get the ball rolling, Captain MacFall set up the nucleus of an organization for the project before he left that day.

"I have a man in charge of the investigations section who will be the Navy's representative in this operation," he said. "He is Lieutenant Commander Haffenden. Since Lieutenant O'Malley knows your office, he'll be the liaison man between the Navy and you."

To complete the setup, Hogan designated Gurfein as the D. A.'s representative for the campaign.

Captain MacFall did not just pick Haffenden's name out of a hat. The Lieutenant Commander had been in the service in 1917 and was back in for another wartime hitch. He was known through the Navy as a resourceful man. Willis George, a secret Treasury Department agent, in his book *Surreptitious Entry,* declared flatly that Haffenden "was largely responsible for the success of the Naval Intelligence unit of the 3rd District."

"He was ready to take long chances," wrote George, who was a wartime civilian operative for Naval Intelligence. "Had he been less ready to gamble his Naval career for the things he knew ought to be done, our surveillance work would have been far less successful."

Two weeks after the first session, there was another get-together in the District Attorney's office. O'Malley introduced Haffenden around. They talked briefly to Hogan, then sat down with Gurfein to begin shaping definite plans from the nebulous theories.

A lot of underworld names were tossed back and forth. Haffenden was all for the frontal approach: Find one of the top hoods and put it right on the line with him.

"I wouldn't do it that way," countered Gurfein. "It would be better to lay some groundwork first."

The prosecutor's idea was to start unraveling the mob source by making initial approaches to the lawyers who represented the thugs. They were members of the bar; they could be relied on.

"It's best to move up to this cautiously," he advised. "Find out first whether these characters will co-operate— and if those we want can be trusted."

Since the early emphasis was on the water front and the fishing boats that might be supplying enemy submarines, the job obviously required someone well acquainted in those fields.

"It just so happens," Gurfein brought out, "that right now there's a beautiful opportunity."

The biggest man in the entire fishing industry in the East, if not the entire country, was Joseph Lanza, also known as Socks Lanza, Joe Socks, and Joe Zocks. These are the varied labels of a ruthless extortionist who controlled the rackets aimed at a rich industry, which offers all kinds of targets to the mobster.

In downtown Manhattan, the Fulton Fish Market, a municipally owned institution, is the second largest fish mart in the nation. Salt- and fresh-water denizens, brought to shore from Maine to the Carolinas, are shipped in to Fulton Market. It is, too, the distribution point to retailers as far away as Mississippi and Indiana. The business it handles each year runs well over a quarter-billion dollars.

And vicious, overjowled Socks Lanza was the actual (if

off-the-record) boss of the whole works. Through his iron-fisted domination of half-a-dozen illicit labor and management rackets, like the thousand-member Sea-Food Workers Union, the Fulton Market Watchmen's Protective Association, and a dealers' group, this quarter-billion-dollar industry was permitted to run—or could be brought to a grinding stop. He was "in" on a canning company, and he was boss of the vast retail market, near the parent Fulton establishment.

Legitimate dealers had to go along—because they knew what could happen to them and their businesses if they didn't. Through the twenties and thirties, Socks was good for a "take" well up in six figures from these and allied extortions.

In the mid-thirties, he clutched so much authority in his racketeering palm that he was called a monopoly by the Federal Government. He even established and maintained price control and marketing, it charged, through an army of muscle men. They beat up buyers, smashed trucks, destroyed fish stocks, heaved stink bombs and acid. Such were the pleasing prospects faced by the fish retailer or wholesaler who wanted to run a legitimate business.

And just at the time the Navy, in desperation, was deciding to turn to the Mob for wartime help, Lanza was up to his ears in further trouble. He was under a new indictment for more and similar racketeering—and stood an excellent chance of winding up as a guest of the state for quite a spell.

With the approaching prosecution by the District Attorney's office—and with Socks's water-front and fishing-boat connections—it is plain to see why Gurfein felt here was golden opportunity, indeed.

"Let's first contact Lanza's attorney," he suggested. "That's the safer approach, instead of going directly to the bums themselves."

He phoned attorney Joseph K. Guerin and asked him to stop in at the D. A.'s office. The following morning, the lawyer was apprised of the Navy's problem.

"I feel sure Lanza would be willing to help," he acknowledged quickly.

"First, as representative of the District Attorney's office," Gurfein warned, "I must point out there will be no promises, no deals, no considerations in Lanza's trial for doing this. Whatever he does will be out of patriotic duty.

"The most important thing—we have to work fast," he added.

What Guerin may have thought of the warning was something else again. Nevertheless, he saw Lanza. "I want you to meet Gurfein," he proposed. "He'll explain what's wanted."

Lanza was willing—except for one point. If any of the boys saw him—a hood under indictment—putting his head together with the boss of the D. A.'s rackets bureau, it might give them ideas that would be unhealthy for him. He laid out minute arrangements for the meeting.

At midnight that night, a taxicab pulled to a stop at the corner of 103rd Street and Broadway. The door swung open. Two men, standing on the corner, hopped quickly in and joined the lone figure inside. The cab drove on, turned west to the Hudson River front. At Riverside Park, a tiny strip of lawn and benches in sight of Grant's Tomb, it came to a stop. In daylight hours, children cavort over almost every inch of green; here and there, a sailor and a girl dally on a bench. At this hour, it was deserted.

The three men walked away from the cab. The faint beam of a nearby street light showed Gurfein, Guerin, and Lanza. This was the way Socks had set up the meeting—so none of the boys would spot him in the "suspicious" company of a D. A.'s man.

Once more, Gurfein told the entire story—how the Navy, in fact, the entire nation and its war effort, faced a desperate situation.

"I might be able to help," the hoodlum conceded. "I'll do what I can."

A few days later, the same trio was in a suite on the mezzanine of the Hotel Astor. It was here Commander Haffenden maintained offices for conferences with people he preferred not to expose to the more public Third District offices downtown, where Navy men abounded. The officer explained in detail what was so badly needed.

"O.K. . . . I'll do what I can," Socks repeated.

Lanza gave Haffenden two phone numbers where he might be contacted. What neither of them knew was that, with Lanza awaiting trial for racketeering, his phones had been tapped. The District Attorney's investigators were somewhat confused later to hear Naval Intelligence and the rackets boss discussing mysterious matters in such code-like words as "Harlem spot" and "Brooklyn Bridge deal."

The Navy gave Lanza certain assignments that required quick action, and he went right to work. Intelligence agents were placed on fishing boats. Socks knew many of the truckers who hauled fish from the docks stretching along Long Island's water-front miles to the markets in downtown Manhattan, or from the markets to as far west as Ohio. He saw to it that Navy operatives got on the trucks under concealed identities. A chain reaction developed.

The head of a trucking company would introduce agents to the captains of fishing boats and to operators of piers where they tied up to buy oil and supplies.

In two weeks, a network of intelligence and counter-intelligence was working. Ship-to-shore and ship-to-ship telephones were installed on fishing boats. Codes were assigned. That way, any suspicious antics, ashore or afloat, could be reported immediately.

In those days, when ships carrying war matériel were being sunk with deadly regularity, such a network had tremendous advantages. A fishing smack at sea would come upon wreckage—crates, debris, bodies. With the phone hookup, the Navy could be notified immediately. If the discovery was made soon enough, planes and destroyers could be dispatched to the spot, and might locate the U-boat itself. The wreckage also told the mute story of what ship had been sunk. In that way, it would not be weeks or months before authorities learned of the fate of a missing freighter, and what vital cargo had to be replaced —or what personnel had been lost.

Over a period of weeks, the operation expanded. But as more and more demands were made, it became apparent to Lanza that his power was limited. His influence on the water front ended with that part of it dealing in the fish industry. The Navy's wants took in far more territory. The docks on the Hudson and East Rivers and in Brooklyn, where war convoys were loaded with men and matériel for war, were sensitive and exposed. Sabotage was the perpetual fear.

"Ins" were vitally needed on the docks; ins that would never be connected with the Navy by suspicious minds. Ins were needed, too, in various labor unions, to obtain credentials for placing agents in touchy spots.

Much of this was beyond Lanza's scope. On the big docks —those where the fishing industry meant nothing—he carried no authority. What's more, a lot of the men he sought out were shying away from him. He was under indictment, awaiting trial. When he intimated that he was working for the Government, he noticed an immediate obvious distaste toward himself. To those characters, there was no differentiation between Navy and District Attorney. It was all the law.

The particular period didn't help Socks's activities either. The entire water front was under investigation from several directions. The Brooklyn District Attorney's office was in turmoil over the gangster-racketeering infection on the docks. Everyone knew that not only the D. A., but even a special prosecutor, had been looking over the water front. One particularly vicious murder, laid directly to the mob grip on dock labor, was causing nasty repercussions. Things were so hot that the No. 1 figure in the racketeering on the Brooklyn water front, Albert Anastasia, had disappeared. The boss of the Murder, Inc., killer department was not to be heard from again for more than two years, after the heat had subsided. Albert A. had faded into the best spot for a man to lose himself in those years. He joined the Army.

So, among his contacts, it was not startling that Lanza suddenly found himself suspect. He might, they felt, be putting the finger on them—to help himself.

In mid-April of 1942—about a month after he began his intelligence work—Lanza stopped in to see his attorney.

"Look," he told lawyer Guerin, "a lot of guys won't talk

to me. They think I'm a stool . . . that I'm trying to help myself. All I know is the fish business. The Navy is asking more and more things which got nothing to do with fishing. There's only one guy can do what they want . . . can send word out, and get things done." He hesitated momentarily. "Y'gotta have the O.K. from Charlie," he concluded.

"Don't tell me about it," the attorney replied. "You're working for Haffenden. Tell him and let him figure out what he wants to do."

Lanza went to Haffenden and mournfully explained that he had gone about as far as his say-so in the rackets could be felt.

"There's only one guy for this job," he insisted. "And that's Charlie Lucky. What he says goes."

It was not the easiest job in the world for the Navy. Here was a thug buried deep in the most inaccessible prison in New York—Clinton Penitentiary at Dannemora, far upstate. Hardened criminals were inmates—men who had known Lucky on the outside. If he were suddenly to receive visitors, strangers who had a look of respectability about them, a finger would very likely be pointed at him at once. Lucky's name, as a symbol for vice and organized crime, had been trumpeted around the world. He had been given a thirty-to-fifty-year term because he was what he was. Law enforcement would hardly be pleased over any proposition about letting any number of visitors come up to see him, regardless of their purpose. And who knew if Lucky would even be willing to go along with the Navy? He was a noncitizen; he had no cause to be anxious to stick his neck out for the United States—not after this country had handed him the longest stretch ever doled out for such a crime as he had committed.

Haffenden headed once more for the District Attorney's office, for help and advice. "Lanza insists only Luciano can open the door for us," he declared.

This was too touchy even for Gurfein to decide alone. He took it up with Hogan. "Well, we've got to help the Navy," the prosecutor concurred.

The first step would be to contact one of the attorneys who had represented Luciano during his vice trial. The one they chose was Moses Polakoff, himself a World War I Naval veteran and a former assistant United States Attorney. He would recognize both the need and the pressing time factor.

"Can you come over here? It's very important," Gurfein told the lawyer over the phone that afternoon. "I want to talk to you about Luciano."

The cryptic message only nettled Polakoff. All the courts, right up to the highest, had turned down Lucky's appeal. The Boss had been locked up for keeps.

"The case is closed," Polakoff demurred. "As far as I'm concerned, I'm not interested any longer."

"But this is urgent," Gurfein pressed. "I want you to come down. It's very important."

Polakoff hesitated a moment more. "All right, then," he finally conceded. "If you insist, I'll come down."

In the District Attorney's office, he was let in on the entire picture: how Lanza had been working for Navy Intelligence on this job so highly vital to the war effort; how he had run into a wall whenever he stepped out into something not concerned with his own domain—and how he had maintained that the "O.K. from Charlie Lucky" was the only key that could unlock places now closed to the Navy.

191

"Now, there are two questions," Gurfein finished. "Would Luciano be willing to help? And can he be trusted?"

"I'll do anything I can," Polakoff pledged. "But frankly, I don't know Luciano that well. I only represented him in his trial." He sat back in thought for some moments. Then: "I think I know someone who might be helpful," he finally went on. "This fellow knows Luciano a long time; he's an intimate friend. He can give you the right steer. At least, he could find out if Luciano would be willing to go into this. I'll get hold of this party and arrange for you to meet him."

Without mentioning names, he made a breakfast date for the following morning at a fashionable Fifty-eighth Street restaurant. A dark-haired stocky man was with him when Gurfein arrived.

"Mr. Gurfein," Polakoff presented his companion, "meet Meyer Lansky."

It was a shock to the prosecutor. Meyer Lansky has been high in the rackets for many years. (He still is.) As far back as the late twenties, he was the infamous Buggsy Siegel's buddy, and they ran the notorious Bug & Meyer Mob between them. Some said the Bug & Meyer Mob made murder its chief business. It provided a strong-arm crew in labor-industry strife, and worked with Lepke in industrial extortion.

After a night-club man was slain in New York in the course of one extortion, Bug and Meyer extended their activities to Philadelphia and did exceptionally well economically. In the early thirties, Lansky was one of that group, which included Frank Costello, Joey Adonis, Lepke, Owney Madden, Lucky, Joe the Boss, and Dutch Schultz, that just about ran New York City under the benign protection of Jimmy Hines, the politician. Lansky, Lucky, Hines, and Adonis were a familiar foursome on the wintertime links at Hot Springs, Arkansas, in those days. And when Prohibition was repealed, the old pals, Meyer and Bug, were among those who put much of the wholesale liquor business under their collective thumb.

As the years went on, Lansky lost none of his prestige, but turned more to the billion-dollar gambling enterprises. In 1933, he was a partner—with Adonis and Costello—in the Piping Rock Club at Saratoga, New York. He was in the Beverly Club in New Orleans with Costello, later selling his end, it was said, for $100,000. He and Adonis were in the Colonial Inn in Florida, with members of the Detroit Purple Gang and, very likely, the Cleveland mob as well. His brother, Jack, was Costello's associate in the Louisiana Mint Company, a vending-machine enterprise.

Even more recently, Lansky has followed the fashion of moving into entirely legitimate enterprise, in the belief, no doubt, that a halo of legality can suddenly sprout. It is hardly convincing, however, since his associates in a television company in 1949 were Costello and Adonis.

Since 1952, Lansky has had his troubles. He was placed front and center in the gambling syndicate that operated the hot spots in Saratoga. And he caught the eye of Immigration authorities. They have been trying to deport him to Russia.

Gurfein remembers that breakfast back in 1942 as the most uncomfortable he ever sat down to. He shuddered at the possibility that some knowing eyes would spot the head of the D. A.'s rackets bureau real cozy like with a notorious racketeer in a popular spot. As quickly as he could, he outlined the details, concluding with the reason for summoning this notorious hoodlum. Did he feel Lucky would go along with the plot?

"I'm positive of it," Lansky brought out without hesitation. "He'll help out. Besides, he's got nothing holding him to the old country . . . nobody left in Sicily. All his family is here . . . his parents and brothers and sister."

Thus reassured, it became now a matter of finding out for certain. And the only way to do that was to see Lucky himself. It was decided that Polakoff and Lansky—the attorney and the close friend—should carry the Navy's plea to the penitentiary.

"But Dannemora is a waste of time," Polakoff suggested. "It's at the other end of the state. To go there and back takes two or three days. If this plan is put into operation, time will be very vital. Besides, the way it's situated, any strangers would be noticed in Dannemora. The thing to do is to get Luciano transferred where it is more accessible. To Sing Sing, perhaps."

There was no denying the wisdom of the attorney's proposal—provided the transfer could be arranged. Haffenden addressed a letter to Commissioner of Corrections John A. Lyons, a former Police Inspector in New York. He had been appointed to his state office by Governor Herbert H. Lehman.

"In connection with a highly confidential mission," it said, in effect, "the Navy would greatly appreciate your co-operation in arranging the transfer of Charles Luciano from Clinton Prison at Dannemora to Sing Sing. It is planned to have him interviewed in private and confidence by various persons working for Navy Intelligence.

"This letter," it concluded, "is to be destroyed as soon as it has been read."

So top-secret a missive could hardly be entrusted to the public mails. It was given to Lieutenant Commander Lawrence Cowen and Ensign Arthur V. Lamberson, to be delivered by hand. They went to Albany, saw Commissioner Lyons. The Commissioner read the letter without comment. The two officers then burned it in each other's presence.

In the ordinary course of events, before making any change in a prisoner's status, the Commissioner of Corrections looks to the District Attorney who prosecuted that prisoner. Commissioner Lyons would undoubtedly have contacted Prosecutor Hogan about so highly irregular a request. To expedite the action, Gurfein made a trip to Albany to carry the District Attorney's backing for the Navy's plea personally to the Commissioner.

Lyons agreed to a transfer—but not to Sing Sing. It would, he pointed out, be impossible to do there what the Navy wanted—carry on confidential interviews with Lucky. Besides being a penitentiary, Sing Sing also is the reception center for all convicts. After their convictions, they are sent there, to be shipped out to their "permanent" addresses. Too many eyes would spot strange visitors coming to see the thug who, as the Boss, was the center of attention of other inmates. Facilities for interviews were not airtight for the security the Navy demanded. Instead, the Commissioner selected Great Meadow Prison at Comstock, sixty miles north of Albany, as the more likely institution for this purpose.

Through the years, those who—for one reason or another —have been loudest at pooh-poohing the entire idea of the

Navy and Lucky working together in any way, have been most wrong about Great Meadow. They say the transfer was made to give Lucky a soft touch. A "prison farm," it has been called; a "country club," as compared with "Siberia" at Dannemora. Actually, Great Meadow is a "maximum security" penitentiary. As a penal institution, it is in precisely the same category as Sing Sing, Dannemora, and Auburn, New York's three other maximum security institutions.

Commissioner Lyons activated the orders for Lucky's transfer. Following out the plan for concealment, he arranged for the switch of half a dozen more Dannemora inmates at the same time, so that Luciano's shift would not be pin-pointed.

The warden at Great Meadow, Vernon A. Morhous (he still holds the post there), was notified of the delightful bundle of gangdom upper crust he was about to receive. Luciano, Commissioner Lyons explained, was to help Navy Intelligence. In that capacity, he would be permitted visitors other than relatives and known friends.

The Navy was advised that, although the State was anxious to help all it could, certain of the regulations would still have to be complied with. After all—and particularly in the case of a convict of Lucky's standing—there were set rules governing registration and fingerprinting of visitors and advance notification of impending visits. All of these could hardly be washed off the boards.

After considerable discussion, a routine was laid down to which the Commissioner agreed. Attorney Polakoff would be present at every visit. As a member of the bar, he had the standing that would meet the requirements of the State. He was to telephone Commissioner Lyons a day or two in advance of each trip, advising him how many would accompany him, and their approximate time of arrival.

Polakoff was the only one required to sign the prison register, stating the number in his party. Thus, it would show: "Mr. Polakoff and two," or "Polakoff and four," etc. Fingerprint requirements were waived. In view of the personalities likely to be called into service on this project, this was just as well. The type involved would as soon join the police force as have their prints taken.

Warden Morhous was to send a memo to Commissioner Lyons after each visit, detailing how many visitors had come, how long they stayed—and their names, if he learned them. All, it was understood, was to be entirely confidential.

Lucky, of course, knew nothing at all about the plotting and planning on the outside. He was startled when he was loaded onto a van at Dannemora and switched to Great Meadow—and he didn't know why. Three days after he arrived at Comstock, he was taken from his cell and ushered into a room, outside of which two guards were stationed. He had been there a minute or two when, off to the side, the door to an adjoining room opened—and Lucky plumped into a chair, his eyes popping. Entering were Moses Polakoff, his attorney, and, even more of a stunner, Meyer Lansky, as close a friend as the Boss had in his palmy days.

"What the hell are you guys doing here?" was all he was able to gasp.

On that first visit, the ideal security arrangement to meet the requirements of secrecy became apparent. The visitors arrived and were ushered into the warden's office at once. There, Polakoff presented himself and his party to the warden alone. Thus, no trusty or grapevine messenger could connect them with any particular inmate. Then, Lucky would be marched out of his cell and into a room adjoining the warden's office, outside of which guards kept any prying eyes and ears away. After he was inside and the door secured, Polakoff and whoever accompanied him entered through the inner door from the warden's office—again frustrating potential snoopers.

When Lucky's surprise passed on that first visit, Lansky and Polakoff proceeded to fill him in on recent developments.

"Joe Lanza has been doing the best he can," they said. "But he's having trouble making the right connections. He says if you were behind it, the job would be done."

"We're here to see if you'll help the Navy in this," Lansky went on. "We think you ought to do it."

Lucky thought it over. "O.K., I'll help," he promised. "Only . . ." Again he hesitated. "Look," he finally blurted, "practically the same day I got sent away, there was a warrant put out for my deportation. No one knows how this war is gonna turn out. Suppose I get sent back to Italy someday. If it's known I helped the U.S. Navy in the war, I'm a goner over there. They'll lynch me. So . . . whatever I do gotta be quiet. Nothing leaks!"

"Absolutely, Charlie," he was reassured. "Everybody in this wants it quiet about themselves. And the Navy can't afford any leaks either. There'll be no tip-off."

"Then it's a deal," the Boss approved. "Send Joe Socks up here, and I'll tell him who to see and what to do, and how to get it done."

Thus was launched "Operation Underworld"—perhaps the strangest campaign for intelligence and counterintel-

ligence military history has ever sported. Certainly, no
other ever had its central point, its direction, in a penitentiary cell—with an alien already marked for exile to a
then-enemy nation (and a master criminal, to boot) as the
very key to the workings.

Two weeks after that first visit, Lucky was taken from
his cell to the "consultation room" once more. This time,
in addition to Polakoff and Lansky, Lanza also walked
through the connecting door. The greetings were most
cordial.

"The thing is," Lanza reported, "a lotta things the Navy
asks me, I can't do, because I just don't know the people.
Then, there's places there's no co-operation. A lot of the
gumbari don't want to get mixed up in anything. If you
give the green light it'll move."

"O.K. Tell 'em I'm behind this thing," Lucky directed.
"And I'll get the word around, too."

"Certain guys I can't do nothing with ... like Johnny
Dunn and the Camardos."

Johnny (Cockeye) Dunn was a tough, ruthless killer—
and boss of the West Side docks fronting the Hudson in
Manhattan. He was, that is, until the law put the finger on
him for a dock labor murder after the war. Then he sat in
the electric chair at Sing Sing. The Camardo Brothers were
(and are) powers along the Brooklyn piers, and they ran
certain of the water-front labor groups as their own private
domains to such extent that they were known simply as
"Camardo locals." Emil Camardo was a vice-president of
the racket-ridden International Longshoremen's Association, which was kicked out of the American Federation of
Labor in 1954 for its crime-packed operations.

"For them," Lucky ordered Lanza, "go to Joey A. and

Frank Costello. Tell 'em I'm for this. Joey A.'ll straighten out the Camardos. I'll also send word out."

Somehow, too, the word did get out from behind prison walls. Sometimes, Lansky carried it, to quarters where Socks's say-so on the "O.K. from Charlie" was doubted. Sometimes Lucky got it out through channels only he can tell about, even today.

"There's a lotta Army piers in Jersey," Lanza went on. "I ain't got connections there, neither."

"I'll see that word gets out to the right people," Lucky nodded again. The "right people" in this case were Willie Moretti and Mike Lascari. Willie was the gambling impresario of the Mob's Bergen County (New Jersey) stronghold and a successful laundry operator who got business by being "polite," as he put it. He did, that is, until the boys fired a lot of bullets into him in an eatery one morning. Lascari and Lucky were kids in the streets together, before Mike moved across the river. He got to know Jersey boss Longy Zwillman and dipped into certain aspects of the restaurant-saloon business. Once the "O.K. from Charlie" reached them, both Willie and Mike went to work for the Navy.

For the next two years—and sporadically thereafter for two years more—there were visits to Great Meadow every few weeks. As late as 1945, even after Haffenden was transferred to duty in the Pacific, the work was still going on. Polakoff would call Commissioner Lyons on each occasion with the word that he would be up on such-and-such a day, accompanied by so-and-so many persons.

He never had to identify his companions, but Warden Morhous was "cute" in this respect. He would make conversation in his office, delaying the visit with Lucky, until

Attorney Polakoff would feel called upon to introduce those with him—if, that is, he knew their names, himself. Sometimes, he could identify them only by their first names—Joe or Frank or Willie. Sometimes, he never did learn the identity of those with whom he made the long trip to Comstock. Lansky would make a date for the trek, and would meet him at the appointed time and place with two or three characters. Lansky would not introduce them to Polakoff, and Polakoff would not ask to be presented. So, he never did find out with whom he traveled.

After the third or fourth visit, the pattern for the work was progressing smoothly. By this time, lawyer Polakoff felt it was no longer necessary for him to go along. As a member of the bar, a man of standing in the community, he was deriving no pleasure from periodic elbow-rubbing with the worst brand of hoodlums, while visiting another notorious thug. He sought to beg off.

Commissioner Lyons, however, balked at even the thought of known racketeers and bums having carte blanche to call on the boss gang lord unchecked by legal, legitimate hand. There had to be some semblance of control and regulation, he insisted—and authorities were already leaning over backward in waiving visitors' fingerprinting and registration rules at the penitentiary. Besides, the Commissioner's old policeman's soul revolted at the mere thought of known mobsters casually calling him up to announce they were on the way to visit the Boss. So, the attorney continued leading the parties.

"But I want it understood that the man in whom the responsibility rests is Lansky," Polakoff stipulated. "He must be the intermediary with Luciano. As a lawyer, it's obvious I certainly should not deal with the underworld myself."

Thus, the attorney and Lansky were the nucleus of each visiting party. Polakoff had not designated Lansky by chance, either. First, he was a mob lord on whom the lawyer knew he could rely. Secondly, it was entirely obvious that if word had to reach certain quarters that "Charlie wants this done," such word carried by Lansky would wield the same authority as if Lucky delivered it personally. That was Lansky's standing in the syndicate.

Everything was done in the strictest secrecy, with the elaborate cloak-and-dagger trimmings that invariably are the icing on the cake of intelligence work. No one was identified by name. Each hoodlum was given a code number as soon as he got into the act, and that was used, without exception, in any naval work. Not even the Third District office or headquarters in Washington knew these identifications. They were kept in a small black book, which only Haffenden held. Cryptic phrases and code words were used in telephone conversations.

Lucky and his visitors—those he sent for, to meet particular Navy requests—took no chances on the walls having ears, even the walls of the consultation room next to the warden's office. They knew there were trusties around, and guards. And that no particular difficulty would be encountered by authorities installing a microphone in the room. After all, in doing the work the Navy required, they were exposing the Mob's chain of command—and this they insisted on doing only among themselves. So, invariably they carried on their discussions in Italian, and in an idiom only they practiced. Lawyer Polakoff does not understand the tongue.

"What did you do on those occasions?" he was asked recently.

"Me? Oh, I sat in a corner and read a newspaper," he recollected.

A hoodlum or a racketeer was "tapped" by another thug for the work only once. After that, he dealt entirely and exclusively with Haffenden, or intelligence agents Haffenden designated. The Navy officer became a magic and mysterious figure to the underworld. "Working for the Commander" was a password on docks and fishing boats, in restaurants and night clubs and even labor unions. Only a very few knew that "the Commander" was a Navy officer, and not a nickname given to a gang lord, like "the Boss" or "the Prime Minister" or "the Judge."

"Haffenden wanted a job done," Lansky explained the workings not long ago, "and we'd get the man, the right guy for the job. From then on, that guy worked for Haffenden only. I didn't know what he was doing . . . or nobody else, except the Commander."

There will be no attempt here to evaluate the work done by Lucky and his hoods. Only Navy Intelligence knows how valuable it really was—and N.I. isn't talking. But . . .

It is positively astounding that for the duration of the war, not a single proved case of sabotage was found on the hundreds of miles of New York water front. Some of the bums even bordered on rabid patriotism as they joined the Operation. Johnny (Cockeye) Dunn, boss of the West Side docks who co-operated thoroughly once the "O.K. from Charlie" came down, even volunteered extra service. One day, greatly upset, he came to see Lansky.

"Geez," he reported in shocked excitement, "the way

things are on the docks, it'd be easy to plant a bomb in one of them boats going to Europe."

Security arrangements in the loading of ships carrying war matériel and men were horrible, he went on. There was only slipshod watch. He was really worked up over it. Lansky took him to Polakoff, who passed him along to Haffenden. From then on, things were changed, under the hold the Mob had on the docks. Joey Adonis went to the Camardos, and they co-operated. Frank Costello entered the picture; more co-operation.

Subversive material began to show up in uptown New York. The source was localized in the Harlem area, and one particular printing establishment was suspect. Navy Intelligence wanted to learn more of the plot and the personnel before landing on the plant. If an agent could be placed on the inside . . .

Through the chain of command, characters influential in the Harlem numbers rackets were pressed into service. On the "word from Charlie," hoodlums like Willie McCabe and Whitey Carney went to work on the problem. Union cards and union books were obtained. And a Navy Intelligence agent was actually placed inside the subversive printing shop as a workman, complete with bona fide labor credentials.

Civilian N.I. agents recall one conversation with McCabe while working with him, which should set at rest any doubts as to the source spring of the co-operation. "I'm doing this for the Boss," he confessed. Actually, the agents were not sure whom he meant—but they had a pretty good idea.

There was a certain night club where, it was suspected, talk among servicemen was being picked up and relayed to espionage centers. Through the hat-check union, more Navy agents were placed in advantageous spots.

In one area, Falangists—Spanish Fascists—were especially active. The signs pointed to spy work. Here, again, the numbers mobs—"working for the Boss"—went into action, and counterespionage activities were installed. The action was most convincing.

Certain business firms in skyscraper office buildings came under the eye of intelligence. It was vital to get into their offices, to look over their files close up. Again, union books were mysteriously furnished in the building employees' union; in the elevator operators'; in the office workers'. Building superintendents never knew that a number of their nighttime cleaning help or maintenance men were actually Navy agents. Or that a good part of the hours they were supposed to be cleaning and maintaining were spent in searching the offices of tenants.

Armed with the "O.K. from Lucky," Lanza made one trip from Maine to South Carolina—considerably outside the territory of the Third District—trading blank union credentials, among other things.

"Let me have four, five of your books," he would propose to an acquaintance who had connections in a union in which he was interested, similar to those he boasted among his organizations. "I'll give you four, five in my outfit," he proffered.

Thus, for credentials in those unions in which he had the big say, he would obtain membership papers necessary to put agents in potential espionage or sabotage sore spots. Armed with proper union cards, no one would ever suspect them as anything but legitimate members of the trade they adopted.

Nor were the boys averse to taking direct action, when required. Late in 1942, Harry Bridges showed up in New York and began to move in on water-front activities, seeking to organize dock labor under his left-wing banner. A no-strike pledge had been signed by all unions in a patriotic gesture, but it was felt that the presence of the notorious pro-Communist labor man from the Pacific Coast would cause interunion strife and general unrest, particularly among the tough Camardo locals on the important Brooklyn piers.

No break in the steady flow of shipping could be risked. Nor could the Navy be detected in a position of taking a stand in labor disputes. There was no time for the conference table, anyway. So, the word went out to the Mob agents: See that the unrest is settled. The project was called "Brooklyn Bridge" for obvious reasons. Joey Adonis had already seen to it that the Camardos were "co-operating." Lucky had sent him the word on that. It was not long before Lanza telephoned Commander Haffenden with a most satisfying message.

"That Brooklyn Bridge matter is all straightened out," he reported. "That fellow got on a plane back to the West last night."

Interested only in results, Haffenden did not have to be advised—and as a Navy man did not really care to know—of details as to how Bridges had been made to see the light so suddenly and decisively. If you believe what you hear from old-timers along the Brooklyn docks even today, he was given a thorough going over, as only the Brooklyn boys are experts in providing, was told that Communist organizers weren't welcome on the Flatbush piers, and then he was hauled to LaGuardia Field and loaded on a plane west. Which may or may not be the reason why he has been somewhat hesitant about invading the East personally ever since.

Late in the summer of 1942, with the tactical battle against espionage and sabotage running well, interest in Third District Intelligence was shifted. The Allied Joint Chiefs of Staff had decided on a landing in North Africa to aid Montgomery's beleaguered forces. Information was needed on what came to be known militarily as the Mediterranean Basin.

After the landings and liberation of North Africa, Roosevelt and Churchill met at Casablanca and laid plans to follow up by striking at the soft underbelly of Hitler's Fortress Europa. The first punch was to be thrown at Sicily, with the Italian mainland to follow.

Now the information was absolutely essential. The Third District was directed to find out all about Sicily. A group known informally as "Target Section" was set up. Later, it became "F" (for Foreign Intelligence) Section, dealing less in tactical work on this side of the Atlantic than in strategic counterintelligence overseas. And to command it, the Navy designated the daring Commander Haffenden, who had been running Operation Underworld for half a year.

Although shifting to long-range tactics, Commander Haffenden appreciated at once the potential value of the same sources that had been so useful along the local water front. Many of his mob contacts were Sicilian born or of Italian extraction. They or their families knew the Island firsthand. Some still had friends and relatives in Sicily and felt no love for Italy's Fascist government, which had run them out.

Haffenden's first move was simply to get these same underworld aides to start "thinking strategically," rather than tactically. And to open this trend, word went out to Lucky, up in Great Meadow, once more. The Navy wanted everything it could get on the terrain and topography of Sicily—any little bit of information anyone knew or remembered on harbors and channels, rivers and bridges, water supplies and physical characteristics of villages.

Most needed of all were the identities of natives still on the other side who could be relied on to be friendly, once landings were made. That was the chief concern: Who could be counted on for counterespionage for the invading Allied forces?

Once more, directives were mysteriously issued from behind the grim walls. The response was almost immediate. Here a person stepped forward to report on the village he had left perhaps fifteen years before. There, someone who had been a fisherman back in the old country gave details on a harbor or a little-known channel that might come in handy for landings or commando work.

A huge war map was prepared in Target Section. A cellophane "overlay" was placed on it. Each titbit of information was crayoned onto the overlay in exact position on the map. In Navy Intelligence's Washington headquarters, the same thing was done, only on a larger scale, since the bits of information were coming in there from many sources besides the Third District. Periodically, something especially hot would be reported. On those occasions, Haffenden took it personally and posthaste to Washington, instead of relying on the usual communication lines.

The names of Sicilian underworld figures and old-country Mustache Petes of Mafia who could be counted on were dropped into the files by the Mob operatives. And finally, as the Navy's demands persisted, the names of legitimate, law-abiding citizens of Sicily who could be called on were supplied.

Lucky got a message out to Joey Adonis. Joey A. formerly owned a restaurant in Brooklyn that attracted a class clientele. Some of the biggest names in business and politics in New York tasted of the viands at Joe's Italian kitchen. The owner, for all his hoodlum background, got to know many of them real well. He made the contacts firmer by contributing to political campaign funds—to either or any party, as is the mob's practice to ensure being on "the right side."

Joey A. was thus able to bring in any number of people to help the Navy compile its counterintelligence information —people who might otherwise be recalcitrant about a war against their motherland, or to expose relatives and friends, still in the old country, to reprisal and possible death. A word from Joey A. carried a lot of weight. It still does.

At Lucky's suggestion, Adonis enlisted a new name in the fight. "See Vince; tell him I'm behind this," Luciano directed through the grapevine.

Vince was—and is—important in the gangland upper crust. He is Vincent Mangano, and he is a ranking member of the Italian Crime Society. His power is such, it was testified during the Murder, Inc., trials of the early forties, that when he had a complaint—real or imagined—of a small-time bookmaker moving in on his territory, Albert Anastasia felt more or less obliged to turn loose his killer crew on the matter. The result was one of the nastier Murder, Inc., jobs of garrotting and ice-picking, after which the bookie's body was roped up, deposited on an empty lot, saturated with gasoline, and set afire. In some quarters, Vince Mangano was regarded as Albert A.'s partner in certain Brooklyn mob operations.

This was, though, aside from an import-export firm in which he was interested, and which gave him standing in the community that he did not deserve. Now, when the word that Lucky wanted help for the Navy got around, Vince came forward just like the rest. With his connections in legitimate quarters, he supplied particularly important reinforcements for the expanding network of Sicilian contacts.

Even former civic officials of Sicilian towns, who had migrated to America, showed up and furnished information and names of contacts who could be relied on for counter-espionage assistance. It has been often reported since the war that Don Calogero Vizzini, who was, until his death in July, 1954, chief of the Sicilian Mafia, aided American forces considerably during the island campaign. In fact, when he became the first postwar mayor of Villalba, it was said the nomination was a reward for that assistance.

No top-level official in the Navy will, to this day, be quoted officially and specifically on this phase of Operation Underworld. There can be no doubt, however, that the worth of the counterintelligence furnished through these contacts was extremely valuable. Here and there, an individual will let on, off the record, that from the data collected in this country, American forces found the nucleus of a ready-made set that aided the push across the island. One intelligence officer even admits that of the Sicilian contacts given by the mob—and by the legitimate citizens the underworld moved to come forward—40 per cent turned out to be most useful.

These are the simple facts of Lucky's wartime activities, set down for the first time. Who can say if what he did should or should not have warranted awarding him a medal, as one columnist suggested afterward? Only Navy Intelligence and the Parole Board had the authority to evaluate his services; the Board alone could decide whether he should be paroled—or be left to rot in Dannemora.

Only portions of the story have been told in the dozen years or so since the Navy, desperate over the twin menace of sabotage and espionage, launched Operation Underworld. A bit of it was exposed to view in 1943 when Luciano appealed to Justice McCook for reduction of his sentence. The judge actually was acquainted with the general nature of the project to a greater degree than he let on. When Attorney George Wolf, claiming that Lucky rated consideration, brought up the subject of war service, the jurist suggested he'd like to hear more. He took the case behind the closed doors of his chambers, and had Gurfein and Commander Haffenden speak their pieces. It was as a result of what they told the judge, that he—a World War I veteran, himself—left the door open for the Boss to make a future bid for freedom.

In 1945, with the war in Europe over, the State Parole Board took up the case and launched its full dress investigation that ran for many months. The probers found they had to dig over, under, and around some of the strangest snags thrown in their way—especially by the Navy. They interviewed Polakoff and Commissioner Lyons, Lansky, Lanza, and Lucky himself, and began to uncover definite details of Operation Underworld. But as the details began to leak, it was noted that the Navy grew more and more reticent.

The reasoning behind this odd silence involved mental gyrations bordering on the class conscious. It seems Navy brass was not especially pleased to have it known that the service had been dealing with the scum of national crime. This Fauntleroy outlook is a mystery. After all, anything goes in war. If mobsters or murderers or anyone else can help, surely no one takes any particular exception to even the worst being used.

Individually, this attitude was by no means universal among Navy men, particularly among those intelligence officers who had been in civilian law enforcement. They felt no compunction about using any source of information —so long as it got the job done. The feeling of this minority was perhaps best explained in a statement by Colonel Angelo Cincotta, who was borrowed from the Marines to head the Italian Section of Navy Intelligence in Washington.

"We don't care where we get the information," he observed. "It's a one-way conversation, anyway. They talk to us; we don't talk to them."

But the prevailing feeling, especially in command echelons, was otherwise. Critical word drifted through the ranks. The Navy had been "indiscreet" in its methods, it was said. With the war over, the scrambled-egg set in the Pentagon shuddered at the thought of having it become known that the Navy had relations with the mob. It kept its official mouth shut—and took a position best described as "official ignorance."

What this meant was soon sadly discovered by the Parole probers and Lucky's attorneys—even Polakoff, who had helped in the Operation. The result was a ride on a merry-go-round.

Polakoff went after affidavits from Haffenden and Gurfein. By this time, Gurfein had departed the District Attorney's office in favor of an army uniform and a post with the Office of Strategic Services in Paris. He did prepare an affidavit, explaining Lucky's part in the Navy's intelligence network, as he knew it. Especially security conscious himself, now that he was in the highly cloak-and-dagger OSS, Gurfein sent the document to his former boss, District Attorney Hogan, for relay to the Navy for clearance.

"If you think it shouldn't be sent to the Parole Board," Hogan pointed out to the Navy, "please advise us."

Back came the reply: Clearance refused. The affidavit never did get to the board.

The investigators sought out Haffenden. He did not have authority to disclose the name of any informant—Lucky's included—he pointed out.

"You'll have to get clearance from the Third District Intelligence officer," he told them. Clearance was denied.

Haffenden did undertake to write a personal letter to the Parole authorities. But he was still Navy and security minded. He would reveal only that Lucky had been of "value." (Five years later, the Kefauver Senate Crime Committee Counsel, Rudolph Halley, sought to convey the idea that Haffenden had written that Lucky was of "great value." Waving what purported to be a copy of Haffenden's letter, he questioned the Navy officer vigorously during a Committee hearing. Haffenden, ill and suffering from war injuries, eventually conceded that if Halley said he had written the words "great value," then he supposed that's what he had written; that he no longer recalled definitely. The letter, however, does not reveal those words.)

Coincidental or not with the Parole Board's investigation, the Third Naval District office began to weed out and eliminate a large part of its wartime files just at that time— and among those disposed of were the records of Operation Underworld! Even Haffenden's black book of code numbers assigned to each informant disappeared. He had left it in the intelligence office when he shipped out for Pacific duty. Yeoman Kathleen Mitchell, the WAVE who had been stationed in his office, remembered that. But the secret black volume had vanished!

When the Parole probers went looking, the District office maintained its policy of "official ignorance." The files have been searched in vain, the investigators were informed.

"There is nothing in the way of an official record," was the Navy's bland message.

It was a slick way of putting it. Note that the Navy was very careful not to deny that there ever had been an official record; just that there was "nothing" in the files at present. And it was very, very careful not to reveal that the files had been eliminated! This is "official ignorance."

But the probers were persistent. And after months and months, the board had a fairly clear-cut presentment. Clear enough, at any rate, so that Lucky's part in the Navy's wartime operations could form a part of the basis for consideration of his parole.

Obviously, then, sufficient facts were available for later investigations to have learned what went on. Weird, indeed, therefore, have been the ways of officialdom any time the commutation and deportation has come up in the years since then. And weirdest of all were the antics of the Kefauver Crime Investigating Committee of the United States Senate.

Now, official bodies—formally appointed investigative groups, Congressional committees, and the like—have vastly more authority for getting at facts than the ordinary, unofficial researcher. Their strength is great, indeed. The biggest stick they wield is the power of subpoena and the authority to hang contempt citations—with resultant jail sentences—on recalcitrant witnesses.

Yet, armed with such potent weapons, the Kefauver Committee, by even the kindest calculation, missed the boat on that portion of its probe dealing with Luciano's parole, even more than it did on other aspects of organized crime in its costly (to the taxpayers), year-long cross-country junket. It seemed, almost, as if the entire committee, plus counsel, had officially formed—in advance—the opinion that some flim-flammery attended the case, and that nothing should be elicited which did not conform to this preconceived notion.

When the committee brought its TV circus to New York, it made much of one story of Lucky in wartime, dressed up in cloak-and-dagger trimmings and utterly fantastic in detail. Or, as Luciano, himself, described it later, "Baloney!"

Federal Narcotics Agent George White revealed this one. Agent White, seeking to establish himself as an "expert" on the subject of Luciano, began by claiming that he had interviewed Lucky on occasion. Actually, White once went to Dannemora with another agent while Lucky was an inmate, and requested prison officials to let him see the Boss. Lucky was brought into the room used by government officials to interview prisoners. The agent introduced himself. He got no further.

Lucky spun on his heel. "Take me outa here; I don't want to talk to this guy," he demanded of the guard, exercising a prisoner's privilege. The guard took him out.

Thus, White's "interview" was strictly a brief one-way affair. It lasted about 20 seconds. White managed to announce his name; Lucky didn't talk to the agent with so much as a grunt!

Along in 1943, said Agent White, he was approached by a character named August del Grazio with a most remarkable suggestion.

"Del Grazio claimed that he was acting on behalf of two attorneys, George Wolf and Moses Polakoff, and a man named Frank Costello, who was spearheading the movement to get Luciano out of prison," the agent revealed.

White described Del Grazio as a notorious criminal. Actually, he was little more than a punk—the lowest form of mob life—throughout his illegal career. A far-reaching revolution, indeed, must have hit the underworld to have placed a punk in the high society of two prominent attorneys and the Prime Minister, to plead for the Boss's freedom, especially when Luciano had any number of political pals who would have carried more weight. Especially odd is the fact that no law-enforcement files—not even the dossiers of the Narcotics Bureau—show that Del Grazio ever had any connection with Lucky, or that Lucky was even one of his known associates.

The deal brought by this "notorious" punk, according to White, was that, since Lucky knew many important persons in Sicily, he should be slipped onto the island somehow, to set up an intelligence service so United States forces would find the island a softer target. And all Lucky wanted in return was his parole.

White explained that it was widely known at the time that American forces were soon to invade Sicily. Now, in wartime, nothing is more top-secret than plans for an invasion. Once the secret is compromised, it means more American soldiers are going to be killed hitting the beach. It is surprising that Agent White would not have immediately put the arm on this underworld punk and run him into the nearest intelligence office, to ascertain how and where he picked up top-secret information.

However, White simply told Del Grazio that it would be impossible to have Luciano paroled, and that no such deal could be made. Just how the agent, with no official status in the New York State Government, knew that Lucky could not be paroled, he did not disclose.

Now, there is no intent here to dispute White on his story that Del Grazio came to him. But if the punk sought out the agent in Lucky's behalf in 1943, surely neither Polakoff nor Frank Costello would have been behind it. By the start of 1943, Lucky already had been a part of Operation Underworld for a full nine months—and both the attorney and Frank C. knew all about it. Why, by then, Lucky had been supplying names and sources for espionage in Sicily, itself, since the fall of '42! And these facts, remember, are documented.

Thus, if he or his pals had any idea for turning him loose in Sicily, why would they have gone to White? Is it not far more logical to assume they would have tried to do it through the Navy—for whom he already had been working almost a year—rather than through so completely dissociated a source as the Narcotics Agent? White had no connection with any contemplated Sicilian invasion, and even less with the state authorities who, alone, could grant a parole.

Moreover, as early as February 8, 1943, some word of Lucky's wartime activities was already a matter of record. That was the date on which Judge McCook handed down his opinion, and in it he publicly referred to them.

Completing his 1951 Kefauver Committee testimony, Agent White related that he had made an investigation concerning Lucky in wartime, and that his investigation included the Army, Navy, Marine Corps, and OSS.

"All categorically denied that Luciano had furnished any information or given any services of value whatsoever," the agent averred.

He did not say—and the committee counsel did not ask him—by what authority he, an agent for the Narcotics Bureau, undertook to investigate the Army, Navy, and Marines concerning wartime intelligence, which hardly has anything to do with narcotics law enforcement. Nor was he asked just how thorough could such an investigation have been which did not seek information from such Navy men as Captain MacFall and Commander Haffenden—the officers who knew the entire story—from District Attorney Hogan, from lawyer Polakoff, from Lansky and Lanza and the rest of the hoods who were in it!

Besides White, the Kefauver Committee also summoned Haffenden. As we have previously noted, he was a sick man, weak from wartime injuries and a long hospital stay. During his entire period on the witness stand, the intent of counsel seemed to be to disparage him and his testimony.

Four days afterward, the Senators sent a wire to Governor Dewey.

"If you desire to appear, please communicate with the committee," it invited.

As usual, Senator Kefauver announced his action to

newsmen. His announcement, however, mentioned only "the question of gambling at Saratoga." There was absolutely no reference to the Luciano affair, either in the wire to Dewey or the announcement to the press.

At the time the wire was sent, Dewey had been in bed a week with virus pneumonia, and the newspapers had duly reported this. It is assumed the Senators read newspapers. The Governor wired back that he would be "delighted to give you my views on organized crime," if the committee could come to Albany to hear them.

That night, Kefauver told a reporter, "I've already heard Dewey's story." The following day, the Senator waited until he was on his television hookup to declare, "Governor Dewey has not seen fit to come and give us the information." It was confusing, to say the least: the Senator had "already heard Dewey's story" in his first statement; yet was still after "the information" the following day.

Now, with the Senators so heated up about getting the information on Lucky's release, it is remarkable how many witnesses they failed to hear who did have knowledge of the case. Five months earlier gubernatorial candidate Lynch had alleged he knew the "full details." Dr. Moran, the Parole Board chairman, certainly knew the case better than anyone. The committee had heard from White that August del Grazio and Frank Costello were interested.

The committee, which claimed a thorough and sincere interest in getting the facts, did not call Dr. Moran (or any other member of the Parole Board) to find out why the action was taken. The committee did not call Lynch to tell the "details" he said he knew. It did not call Haffenden's commanding officer, Captain MacFall, who is still available to this day, though retired. Certainly, the Senators and their counsel must have realized that no one with the comparatively lowly rank of lieutenant commander, such as Haffenden held, could have negotiated so touchy a deal as Operation Underworld for the United States Navy without higher authority.

In fact, the number of interested and knowledgeable parties the committee did not call in this investigation easily outnumbers those who were brought in. And a number of those summoned—who could have supplied details—were not even asked a single question about Operation Underworld or Lucky's part in it. For instance, attorney Polakoff, in a closed session, informed the august Senators that Lansky and Lascari were among those who visited Lucky in connection with the operation. Lascari was called as a witness—but neither counsel Rudolph Halley nor any of the Senators asked him so much as one question about Lucky's or his own work during the war! Nor was a single query about it addressed to Costello in his three full days on the stand!

But the Senators did summon a man who was publicly known to be in bed, seriously ill. And when he asked them to come to him, they resorted to snide remarks. Oddly enough, less than three weeks before, an official Kefauver Committee hearing *was* held in Albany, at the Wellington Hotel. Subpoenas were issued for witnesses; various civic officials gave testimony. If Dewey's statement was so compellingly vital, it could just as easily have been obtained while the Senators' representatives were only a few blocks away. Or, if there had been developments in the intervening three weeks, it seems a member or an investigator could have been dispatched to interview Dewey, even without TV cameras.

Surely the committee's appropriation, which was not far from half a million dollars of the taxpayers' money, could have stood the expense of a train trip to Albany, and perhaps one night in a hotel room!

Lucky's release is brought up generally for some individual headline-making purpose. Yet, there is never more than a cursory, somewhat sidelong glance at a shameful series of incidents attending his going-away party, which are still crying loudly for exposure and fumigation.

Among the proud boasts of these United States are: (a) a free press and (b) the fact that law and order never give way before mob rule without putting up the best fight they can (except, maybe, in the South, where law officers have, on occasion, abetted and even encouraged lynching).

At the time of Lucky's going away, though, the free press was stifled by the underworld, and mob law openly and defiantly took command of both Federal and city authority. And both governments meekly submitted!

Lucky, armed with his commutation of sentence, had been brought down from prison for deportation. Before starting out, however, he had carefully attended to one important matter: he paid his state income taxes.

During his trial, Dewey had brought out that Lucky's tax returns from 1929 to 1935, filed simultaneously in the summer of 1935, admitted incomes of: $15,000 for 1929, $16,500 for 1930, $20,000 for each of the next four years, and $22,500 for 1935. If Luciano's clothing bills alone hadn't run that high, any given year, it would have surprised the friends who so admired his sartorial splendor. On the witness stand, Lucky admitted that he had never paid any state income tax.

"And that is because the Federal Government prosecutes big gangsters for income tax, and the State does not," demanded Dewey. "Isn't that so?"

Lucky said he wouldn't know about those things.

Perhaps it was not quite so simple as Dewey put it. It is true, nevertheless, that the State is far more patient with recalcitrants. While Lucky was in jail, the only notice New York took of his tax debt was to send a messenger over to the jailhouse with a bill for $4,000 due. This was promptly dropped into the file-and-forget drawer. But with a chance to get out of prison, Lucky wasn't going to let a little matter of $4,000 stand in the way or delay him. He paid up.

Then, surrounded by immigration guards, he was hauled to Ellis Island for a brief wait before boarding the ship for Italy. The island immigration station in New York Harbor is reached by government ferry from a slip on the lower Manhattan water front. Robert Dwyer, a New York *Daily News* reporter, was at the pier, trying to get across, that day Lucky was on the island.

Suddenly, two men came up to the slip, one of them carrying two valises. The newspaperman recognized one as an individual whose photograph was frequently in the public print. If this wasn't Frank Costello, then the Prime Minister must have an undisclosed identical twin.

"What cooks, Frank?" asked the reporter.

The gambling czar spun around. His brows screwed into a frown.

"Look, fella, I don't make you," he insisted. "You didn't see me, eh?"

The mere sight of Frank C., heading for the ferry that would take him to his old chum, had piqued Dwyer's news

222

sense. Now his curiosity was thoroughly aroused by the mystery Costello sought to attach to the incident.

"What's going on. Where are you heading?" the reporter inquired.

Costello nodded toward the other man, who was Lucky's faithful attorney. "Me and Polakoff here are just going over to see Lucky," he said. He did not add that the suitcases contained a varied wardrobe, so that the Boss could embark on the forthcoming sea voyage in the tailored splendor to which he had been accustomed (before Dannemora, that is).

Dwyer sought to make further inquiries. An official guard had been taking in the brief interchange. Now, however, he turned to two Coast Guard shore patrolmen on duty at the pier and pointed at the newspaperman.

"Throw this fellow out," he ordered.

The two Coast Guardsmen, wearing the uniforms of the United States, forcibly heaved the newspaperman off the slip—but allowed the gang lord and the gang lord's lawyer to enter the government pier, get aboard a government ferry, and sail over to the government's island to see the mobster who thought he was bigger than American laws!

This was the first of the nauseating incidents which revealed, in neon brightness, that mobsters enjoyed special privilege on government and city property, while law-abiding citizens had no rights at all. To this day, so far as was ever revealed, no official action has ever been taken to reprimand the Coast Guardsmen who manhandled the reporter or the guard who gave them the command, while holding out the glad hand to one of the top gang lords in the nation's underworld!

And that was only the beginning. The next afternoon, immigration officials and enforcement officers escorted Lucky to Brooklyn's Bush Terminal, perhaps the largest, and easily the busiest, covered dock-and-storehouse area in the world. Here, at Pier 7, the liberty ship *Laura Keene,* as worn and frowsy as the prostitutes under Lucky's vice administration, awaited him. Both pier and ship were heavily guarded.

The newspapers were, naturally, interested in the exile of the slum boy who had risen to a directorship in national crime, and in any plans for the future that he cared to discuss. Consequently, a shipboard press conference had been arranged by the U.S. Bureau of Immigration. Every newspaper, wire service, and news photograph organization in the metropolitan area sent representatives. Some thirty to forty news- and cameramen were duly accredited by Federal Immigration authorities to board the ship and receive any pearls that might fall from the Boss's lips. Each had the proper entrance pass. A security officer from the Immigration Bureau shepherded the group. The forces of law and order arrayed along the pier had been instructed to let them pass.

At the dock, however, they discovered that the water front apparently is part of neither New York City nor the United States of America. At least, the Law had nothing to say there. Only Albert Anastasia, big boss of the hoodlum longshoremen, had—and Anastasia is not even in the United States legally.

At the pier entrance, the newsmen ran into a solid picket line of about half a hundred stevedores. Each carried an ugly baling hook, a long, curved, sharp-pointed, heavy metal tool used by dock workers to heave huge cases and

barrels about. Lined up as an honor guard for the depart-
ing boss of the bawdyhouses, the longshoremen let no one
pass but Luciano's friends.

When the Boss himself arrived, well concealed from prying eyes and camera lenses by the escort of Federal men,
the dock men opened their ranks and let him through.
The representatives of the press tried to follow. The dock-
ers closed lines and brought the newsmen up short.

One chunky, evil-looking thug, acting as commanding
officer, stepped forward.

"Nobody goes on the pier," he announced, "because
somebody might get hoited. We gotta watch out for law-
suits. Somebody'll trip over somepin', and the foist thing
you know, there's trouble."

Now it should be pointed out that the dock workers do
not own the piers. The city does. The dock workers do not
lease the piers. Shipping companies do. The dock workers
are simply unskilled labor hired to take freight off and
put freight on ships—and that is all. Period.

Neither they nor their racket union, the International
Longshoremen's Association, have any responsibility for
loss or injury on the piers. On the contrary, dock labor has
been responsible for countless murders, has pilfered or co-
operated in the stealing of millions of dollars in freight,
and has thrown up phony picket lines as a means of extortion beyond its regular piracies. The sudden solicitude that
some visitor might get "hoited" drew sly grins from the
chunky spokesman's followers.

The water-front thugs made good their threat. Although
sponsored by the Federal government, and with city police
by the dozen within eye- and earshot, the newsmen did not
get on the pier. Those reporters who persisted were threat-

ened with bodily harm if they defied mob law to carry out their assignment!

Admission to the pier was granted only to certain select guests and a line of attendants bringing baskets bulging with the choicest food and vintage champagne for Lucky's *bon voyage* frolic. The guests—evidently thought to lead charmed lives that wouldn't get "hoited"—were armed with cards stating they were "stevedores."

As the picket line closed behind the provision bearers, a burly longshoreman was seen to approach Lucky on board the ship and clap him on the shoulder.

"Keep punching, Boss," he boomed in a voice that carried across the dock. "You'll be back in action before you know it."

The immigration official assigned to guide the newsmen decided to board the ship on the chance that there might have been a misunderstanding. After a brief delay, the dock laborers let him through. In a short time, he was back with the announcement that Luciano had canceled the press conference—which the Federal Government had set up! The Boss had been neither subtle nor indirect.

"I ain't gonna see any God-damn reporters," he had stated with finality.

The immigration man became apologetic. "I want you fellows to know it wasn't the Bureau of Immigration that kept you off the boat," he whined.

Here was a how-de-do, indeed. The combined authority of the United States Government and the City of New York was being defied openly by gangster rule. Why a squad of police was not summoned at once to run these thugs, baling hooks and all, right into New York Bay, no one has ever found out. Nor has there ever been, so far as has been disclosed, any effort on the part of either city or nation to learn who was behind it, and what officer or officers were responsible for so shameful a blot on law and order. Certainly so revolting a state of affairs demands investigation, even at this late date, far more than the recurring, politically inspired shouting for the reasons behind Lucky's release.

Later it was learned what prompted the underworld to take such precautions at Lucky's going-away party. After all, it was no hush-hush matter that he was being booted out on the *Laura Keene*. It seems, however, that some of the guests preferred it this way. At the farewell party were a number who felt it would be beneficial neither to their careers nor to their positions for the multitude to be advised, in public prints, that they were on hand to wish the exiled prince of gangland Godspeed.

These, naturally, were not the notorious hoodlums present—such as Frank Costello, the Prime Minister; Meyer Lansky, Buggsy Siegel's old murder-mob partner; one or more of the violent Anastasias; and Mike Lascari, who grew up with Lucky and has made a name as partner of New Jersey's notorious Longy Zwillman in a vending-machine company. They were expected to be there and would hardly have made a point of keeping the newsmen away.

Those on hand to bid the exiled Boss *bon voyage* who *were* wary of news coverage numbered certain personalities in New York politics—a former judge of General Sessions Court, a Tammany district leader, and the like. The politicians demanded anonymity.

If the picture of esteemed judiciary cavorting with dope peddlers, extortionists, killers, and brothel magnates leaves a repellent taste, remember that it goes on all the time. And the reason it continues, very likely, is that the voters rarely boot these mobster associates out of office.

So, surrounded by the cronies, mob and political, of his palmy days, Lucky enjoyed a champagne and lobster party that was more a fete of honor than a deportation.

The boys hadn't forgotten, either, that he was going to a foreign shore after nine and a half years behind bars. From his prison earnings he had exactly $196 in his pocket. Consequently, several of the *bon voyage* guests left business envelopes with him before they departed. Frank Costello, it was said, arrived with a brief case that looked considerably flatter when he returned down the gangplank. Lucky was no doubt delighted, when he counted up, that his $196 was bolstered, according to varied reports, by something between $50,000 and $150,000.

Eventually, the *Laura Keene* tooted her whistle, and the guests, shouting words of cheer and farewell over their shoulders, walked from the pier to where the frustrated newsmen were still at bay. Gangplanks were pulled up, and the frowsy liberty ship slipped away from Pier 7, bound for Naples.

It was a long, dull trip for Lucky. He was prepared to dislike everything about Italy by the time Capri and Vesuvius's high column of smoke appeared on the horizon. His feelings did not improve when he was taken into custody as soon as he set foot on Italian soil.

Since his status was that of an Italian citizen who had violated no Italian law (as yet), he was released after brief detention and questioning. He was entitled to live as a free man. But Lucky simply doesn't like his native land. In fact, he lets you know he has an almost pathological aver-

228

sion to the country, the people, their mentality, and their way of life.

Almost as soon as he had his suitcase unpacked in the Quirinale Hotel in Rome, he began to lay plans for a change. The first step was to seek an Italian passport. He acquired one legally in a matter of days.

Thus armed, he could now proceed to any country on the face of the earth—providing it would grant him a visa. And just eight months after the United States had shipped him across the Atlantic, supposedly for good, Luciano was back in this hemisphere!

10 LUCKY IN CUBA— OBJECT: HOMICIDE?

The exile comes back, with the law watching. . . . Crime, Inc., convenes among the rum and the rumba. . . . . Buggsy and Virginia Hill; ah, romance. . . . Buggys holds out, and the Syndicate pays off—for good. . . . How to get thrown out of Cuba.

LATE IN February of 1947, the weekly newspaper, *Tiempo de Cuba,* of Havana, exploded a bombshell on its front page.

Lucky Luciano was not in Italy; he was not even in Europe. *Tiempo* had discovered the Boss right here in Havana—in the Western Hemisphere! What's more, he had already been in Cuba for nearly four months, living lavishly in a fashionable home in suburban Miramar, overlooking the rolling sea.

Just how he did it has not been entirely unraveled to this day in all its conniving detail and cunning corruption. That it was not all open and aboveboard was obvious from the devious ways Lucky traveled. He had not one, but two passports, both in the name of Salvatore Lucania. He obtained a Cuban visa on one, and approval for landings in Colombia, Bolivia, Venezuela, and perhaps Brazil and Mexico, on the other.

Instead of using a direct route from Italy to the Pearl

of the Antilles, the Boss flew first to Brazil and then to Venezuela. It was fairly well established, too, that he touched down in Mexico. He landed at Camagüey, Cuba, accompanied by fourteen characters, men and women—all with one common denominator: each had a record with the F.B.I.

Of course, all this could not possibly have been done without help. As usual, Lucky had the best. In obtaining a visa from the Cuban Consulate in Rome, he was aided by a certain highly placed islander with powerful political connections. There were reports that this influential individual was a public officeholder and a partner of Luciano in some venture or other.

Others lent aid and material comfort. Politicians, bankers, wealthy sugar-plantation magnates have been vaguely mentioned. From the day Lucky hit Havana, the most influential of his connections was listed as a Cuban senator. His identity has never been publicly proclaimed. Among Luciano's Cuban friends, one of the closest was Senator Edouardo Suarez Rivas. (Later, Rivas' brother, Representative José Suarez Rivas, got into the picture.)

In the ensuing weeks, the reasons behind Lucky's astonishing presence in Cuba became an international quiz show, with more contestants than in the Atlantic City beauty parade. All the guesses had to do, naturally, with lawless enterprise of one sort or another, in spite of his continued insistence that the trip had no ulterior motive.

"What are you doing here?" someone asked him point-blank.

"Enjoying myself," he tossed off cryptically. "I came because it's near my home, nearer my relatives. I like it here; I like the climate."

He did not elaborate on why he found the West Indian weather utterly delightful, yet heartily disliked everything about Italy, including the climate. They are, in fact, quite similar. Obviously, he was telling the truth about being near his family, for his sister came down from New York to spend the New Year holiday with him.

His Havana address was also most convenient for all his friends to drop in and pay their respects. At one point during that winter, it seemed the Syndicate was holding a convention on the island. Joe Adonis was on hand; so were Frank Costello, the Fischetti boys, Willie Moretti (the general manager in charge of New Jersey gambling), and practically the entire board of directors of the crime cartel. In fact, there were repercussions for years afterward.

As recently as 1953, when deportation proceedings were brought against Adonis, the trip to Cuba formed the groundwork for the charges. Since Joey A. was foreign-born, Immigration authorities claimed, he violated his right to stay in this country by leaving the mainland of the United States and returning again without obtaining a re-entry permit. Mr. A.'s answer to that one was that he was not foreign born, unless you call Passaic, New Jersey, foreign. The court believed the Immigration department. At this writing, Adonis is still appealing.

Several of the gang lords have been questioned about the get-together amid the rum and the rumba. Costello insisted he just happened to drop over to Cuba on his way from Florida to New York (?), and whom did he bump into but Lucky! Willie Moretti, an old chum of the Boss, when interrogated, rose to Lucky's defense.

"He is the most persecuted man in the world," avowed the gambler, who, every mobster pledged, was like a godfather to them. They thought so highly of Willie, in fact, that nine months after this incident, some of the boys caught him in a North Jersey eatery and filled him full of bullet holes.

The most astonishing aspect of Lucky's elusive travels was, of course, how he managed to get to Cuba and then to run around Havana for four months before someone spotted him. He was there through the heart of the tourist season, when New Yorkers are almost as numerous on Cuban streets as the troubadour panhandlers. He was at the track every day and at one of the play spots, usually the Casino Nacional, virtually every night.

And day or night, at track or trap, Lucky was in the company of celebrities. The press agent of the Casino introduced him to a United States society belle, just then convalescing from divorcing the heir to a New York realty fortune. The dope peddler and the gay divorcée appeared together everywhere, and she presented him to others of her set.

He had frequent guests at his impressive seaside home and treated them to the *salsa di pomidoro* that was the specialty of his culinary skill. He made regular appearances on the golf links. All in all, he could hardly have been more prominent if he had dug the big sunken diamond out of the lobby floor of the Capitol Building or disputed the right of way on the Malacan with one of Havana's accelerator-happy cab drivers.

Yet, for four months, there was not a single mention of his presence until the sharp-eyed *Tiempo de Cuba* reporters uncovered him. The editor, Roland Masferrer, revealed that, after exposing Lucky, both he and his staff were threatened with violence by the boys who had gathered 'round the Boss.

Incidentally, a certain New York columnist—with a reputation of never sacrificing trick phrase and sensationalism for accuracy—took bows all over the place (and still does) for the "scoop" of discovering Lucky in Havana. The dates of publication of the stories, though, prove that he definitely was "borrowing" from *Tiempo de Cuba*.

This same columnist also saw in Lucky's Cuban presence a far-flung narcotics organization already submerging the United States. It would have taken considerably longer than Lucky was in Havana to have set up such an operation. What's more, if a major enterprise had been in the making in Cuba, Luciano certainly was not needed on the spot to make it run, any more than he had to be in east Harlem when the 107th Street Mob started distribution of the many-million-dollar smuggled shipments through the United States. As a matter of fact, there had been dope-running from Cuba for a number of years before Luciano appeared on the scene, especially by plane from Havana to Tampa, Florida, which had been a stronghold of Unione.

There was a story, too, that Lucky planned to take over all gambling on the island. He did make some motions in that direction, although not by moving in for his customary grab. He merely associated himself with two already established sucker traps, primarily intent on luring the tourist money. Once Lucky became interested in these joints, connections were established with the full-pocketed Americans who play away their winters in Daytona, Palm Beach, and Miami Beach. Chartered planes began to make regular week-end runs from Florida, bringing in loads of tourists (with loads of cash) most of that 1946–47 season.

That Lucky may have had eventual designs on the island's gambling enterprises is probable. Certainly, he had ideas that he might stay on indefinitely, instead of returning to the Italy he found so revolting. Officially, he had entered Cuba as a tourist, with a visa good for six months. His plans to fix continued residence there became obvious very quickly.

"Everything appears to indicate his influential friends, who are accustomed to selling Cuban citizenships, had arranged for a Cuban girl to marry him," insisted Roland Masferrer, *Tiempo de Cuba*'s alert editor, in a copyrighted story. "After that, citizenship would come his way easily —for a price."

But narcotics or gambling or the climate—none of these seems to have been the prime motive that impelled Lucky to Cuba. The decision, it appears, was made by his old gang-lord playmates of the Syndicate. And it had its inception four thousand miles or more from the murmuring palms along the Malacan—far away in southern California.

When gangland put together the Syndicate in the early thirties, the organization reached to every corner of the United States—except California. Oddly enough, through the wild Prohibition era and afterward, the sun-kissed shores, although just as ridden as any other place with individual lawless enterprise, knew nothing of organized crime. The Mob had not yet spotted the gold in the Golden West.

Along about 1935 or the beginning of '36, however, the board of directors, their greed tickled over the affluence and success of Syndicate operations, decided to expand. And their eyes lit on the one remaining virgin territory— Southern California.

After some months of spadework, they selected as general manager for the new Los Angeles branch Lucky's old pal, Buggsy Siegel. "Benny is a natural," insisted Lepke. Already reposing in Dannemora, Lucky had no objection to the appointment. He knew Buggsy as a capable, cold organizer whose only fault, perhaps, lay in his single-track approach to settling all business problems with a gun.

So, with the blessing of Lucky and all the rest of the mob lords, Buggsy packed his gripsack and headed west. The subdued rumble accompanying his departure very likely was Horace Greeley spinning in his grave.

A thoroughly arrogant, uninhibited hoodlum, the Bug had an ego that was incredible. The Mob had pinned the "Buggsy" label on him as a complimentary token for his indifference under fire. Yet, he would kill a man who called him Buggsy out loud. Even old friends, like Lucky and Lepke, addressed him as "Ben" or "Benny."

Buggsy was handsome and smooth-talking and fancied $200 suits and $25 silk shirts. He was a natural for Hollywood.

He set up his wife and two daughters in a cozy thirty-five-room $200,000 cottage, complete with his own private bath in maroon marble.

Even while he was up to his elbows in extortions, he was hobnobbing with top-name movie stars. In fact, some of the very stars with whom he was playing footsie were simultaneously paying him tribute on one of the rackets he set in motion! He possessed a *bon vivant* charm that made him a darling of the film elite. A blonde beauty, still recognized as a star of film and television, was linked romantically with him.

That, of course, was before Virginia Hill came into his life. The Alabama marble-polisher's daughter bowed into the public eye on the Midway at the Chicago World's Fair. She had made a large splash as (a) a honey of hoodlums and (b) a collector of cash in such fancy figures that she tossed $10,000-a-night parties as unconcernedly as buying the morning paper.

There have been times the Dixie damsel was suspected of being the Mob's "bagman" or money messenger. Virginia considers this the back-fence babble of envious rumor mongers. "The only money I ever carried was my own," she stoutly avers.

She married four times in less than sixteen years. A girl with a yen for variety, her mates ran the divergent gamut from Mexican rumba dancer to Austrian skier and fire-extinguisher salesman.

But Virginia won far more fame for her beautiful friendships with some of the hottest hoodlums ever to decorate a police line-up. From time to time, she has been mentioned as a favorite—to one degree or another—of Lucky, the Fischettis, Joey Adonis, Meyer Lansky, Frank Costello, and Frank C.'s New Orleans negotiator, Dandy Phil Kastel.

"Virginia doesn't look too hard to know," was the cogent observation of Longy Zwillman, the director in charge of New Jersey operations, after seeing her on a television screen.

When she hit California, la Hill met Buggsy, and a spark ignited. The Bug established her in a fancy Beverly Hills nest and even gave her a wedding ring—not, it is assumed, the same circlet he had bestowed upon his patient lawfully wedded wife.

By 1937, Buggsy had established a firm beachhead of organized crime in California. He put together an operational staff and laid political pipelines in the approved underworld manner. Of special note were the torpedoes and assorted experts sent in from Syndicate branches in Cleveland, Chicago, and New York to man his office. One was Mickey Cohen, a loud and somewhat ludicrous figure who was far more adept at assorted larcenies than he was as a featherweight fighter.

Mickey knew a lot of the right people. One acquaintance, for instance, was Arthur Samish, a gross, three-hundred-pound character who has been, for a number of years, a lobbyist attaching himself to the California legislature with remarkable influence. His outlook on political and lawmaking authority is unique, indeed.

"To hell with the Governor of the State," he shrugged once, in explanation. "I am the governor of the legislature!"

In a manner of speaking, it was basically the same political philosophy as the credo of the Mob.

"We don't run for office," Buggsy frequently said. "We just own the politicians."

One of the few local hands Siegel chose for his staff was Jack I. Dragna, a survivor of the 1931 purge of Mafia and a gambling power in Southern California. Although the Kefauver Senate Committee adopted an odd attitude toward this character—failing even to mention him in the section of its report on California—his proper position was accurately tabbed by James Ragan, who was murdered in Chicago for the race wire service he operated.

238

"Dragna is the Capone of Los Angeles," Ragan gasped, when he lay dying of mob gunshot wounds.

Of all the services Buggsy performed for the Syndicate, none was so valuable or so successful as that in the war for control of the race wire business, known to the boys as "The Service."

The race wire is vital to bookmakers. The Service operated a broadcast over its own nation-wide network, on wires leased from commercial telegraph companies, of all racing information, including advance data on jockeys, horses, and sudden shifts in betting odds at all tracks. Its most vital function is the clandestine transmission of results, immediately after the horses cross the finish line. Under legal procedure, the result of a race is delayed until after it is declared official. Sometimes—in the cases of claims of foul or photo finishes—this takes many minutes. A bookmaker without wire service is at the mercy of sharpers. Informed promptly by wire service of the order of finish, a sharper can "past post" the bookie—make a bet on a race already over, but which on legal wires, has not yet even been announced as having started. As a monopoly, the service thus controls bookmakers and exacts enormous tribute from them.

Continental, flung from coast to coast, was the largest of the services when the Mob turned its hungry grab toward this rich source of income. A rival network was set up by the Capone combination in the far-western areas of Nevada, Arizona, and California. Buggsy, as west-coast manager, applied tremendous pressure toward putting it in the number-one position. He succeeded comparatively quickly in the legal gambling environs of Nevada. Soon his personal take was $25,000 a month from Las Vegas alone.

In California, though, Continental held out longer than most of the Mob had expected. Buggsy and his boys had to go all out to wean the bookmakers away. The war was finally settled, however, when James Ragan, who had evaded gang guns for six years, was cut down in Chicago in August, 1946.

In Nevada and Arizona, Buggsy turned the industry over to the Syndicate swiftly. But in California, he suddenly and astoundingly defied the cartel, although he was just as aware as any hoodlum in the underworld that defiance of the Syndicate carried a mandatory death sentence.

"I put the service together here," he proclaimed. "And I am gonna run it. It's all mine!"

The Mob was patient. Buggsy had always been both valuable and popular. For months, the other directors sought to cool off their hothead chum. This was the first time—and the only time to this day—that a member of the board of directors threw a monkey wrench of defiance into the smooth mechanics of the National Crime Syndicate, in its entire two decades of lawlessness.

An additional consideration, if not a deterrent, against reprisal lay in the fact that Buggsy's lieutenants, such as Dragna, stood loyally by him. The capable California Crime Study Commission learned afterward that two Chicago characters descended from an airplane in Los Angeles about that time and held a conference with Dragna. He apparently was convinced that he had more to lose than to gain. All of a sudden, he was a neutral.

A few days later, Buggsy was ensconced on the ornate living-room sofa in the nest he had feathered for Virginia Hill in Beverly Hills. An unfriendly person poked a gun in and blew his head wide open.

Virginia was not there. Four days earlier, she and Buggsy had had a quarrel because she had taken aboard a quantity of distilled grain and whacked another lady soundly on the chin in the gaudy Flamingo Hotel, a $6,000,000 joint Buggsy built in Las Vegas. The irate Dixie damsel threw her nightie and toothbrush into a satchel and flew to Paris. She was, of course, sorely grieved over the sudden passing of her light o' love.

All of which is by way of getting back to Lucky and his astonishing appearance in Cuba—halfway around the world from where he was supposed to be. The likely connection between Buggsy's defiance and demise in California and Lucky's transatlantic hop a few months before the shooting, is brought out in the book previously referred to, *Murder, Inc.* It explains a story whispered in gangland everywhere:

Buggsy's continued defiance was affecting the Mob's pocketbook. Naturally, this upset the directorate. But, because it was Buggsy, these ganglords who made operational decisions, as a rule, with unhesitant certainty . . . felt the need for the highest voice of authority. . . .

With Lepke gone (to the electric chair) by then, Lucky's was the most respected counsel extant. . . .

To go to Luciano was out of the question. . . . So, on the plea of the Board of Governors of the Syndicate, he somehow managed to elude the spotlight and cross the Atlantic. . . .

The most monstrous collection of gang rulers ever in one batch met on solemn business in Cuba. They assembled . . . from all over this country. It was the Supreme Court of crime —bent on ironing out a touchy problem.

No action had been taken on Buggsy's defiance up to then. Not too long after that Cuban conclave of the "justices" of gangland's kangaroo court, Buggsy was "hit."

With the kangaroo proceedings wrapped up, Lucky settled down to working his strings to remain in Cuba. He was beginning to produce encouraging results when he was uncovered.

Even then, Cuba was neither particularly irate over his presence nor co-operative about getting rid of him. For forty-eight hours, he was not even picked up by authorities.

"Oh, he has maintained contact with certain interests in the United States, and he has been receiving money from business interests which allow him to live lavishly," Chief Benito Herrera, of the Cuban Secret Police, conceded. "But so far as we have ascertained, there is no evidence that he is mixed up in any illicit business in Cuba."

Interior Minister Alfredo Pequeno made a check-up to see whether Lucky had met the requirement that every alien or visitor must obtain an official employment permit if he plans to work on the island. The cabinet minister found nothing affecting Lucky.

"He is a dangerous character and a perjurer, to be sure," *Señor* Pequeno conceded. "But his papers are in perfect order."

In the United States, meantime, news of the Boss's presence at our doorstep had the effect of a sudden enemy attack. The Narcotics Bureau began issuing frantic bulletins.

"His presence makes it exceedingly dangerous for legitimate drugs to be shipped to Cuba," asserted Narcotics Commissioner Harry Anslinger.

Washington announced that Immigration officials at every port of entry had been alerted against an attempt to sneak Lucky back into the country. Was one to suppose that these officials had *not* been alert previously to the possible return of a deported criminal alien?

The day after Lucky's presence was exposed, U.S. Ambassador to Cuba R. Henry Norweb was ordered back to Washington, to give firsthand information on the situation.

Cuban authorities, however, apparently remained not at all interested in checking the menacing mob lord. The United States was forced to play a trump to get action. After forty-eight hours, the Government advised Cuba flatly that as long as Luciano remained there, this country would ship the island no more narcotics, for medicinal or any other purpose. The embargo was slapped on at once.

"Luciano should not be permitted to live where he can exercise his dangerous influence over the American underworld!" asserted Colonel Garland Williams, New York District Federal Narcotics Supervisor.

Lucky couldn't get over all the tumult and shouting. "I got good moral character," he proclaimed. "I'm too old for any funny business."

The embargo produced prompt results. Cuban medical men were at once alarmed over the cut in the steady flow of pain-killing drugs. They demanded government action. Interior Minister Pequeno bowed to their pleas.

That morning, Lucky, decked out in white linen suit, was having breakfast with two of his bodyguards in the fashionable El Jardin Restaurant, out in suburban El Vedado. They were just finishing their coffee when Assistant Chief Hernandez led a squad of secret police in and put the arm on the Boss.

Surprisingly, Luciano offered nary a complaint. He stood up, yanked his jacket into place, and nodded a pleasant "See ya later" at his companions. He even posed agreeably for photographers, with his captors. His actions were, for all the world, those of a man who had completed his business anyway, so this minor indignity was not interrupting a thing.

But Lucky was not altogether happy. The right side of his face was swollen from an ulcerated cut inside his mouth. Deep lines along his jaw and across his forehead were testimony that it pained severely. Nor was the pain eased when he was thrown into Tiscornia Immigration Camp, Cuba's Ellis Island, across the bay from Havana.

"He can leave tomorrow if he wants to," sighed Interior Minister Pequeno wishfully. "We'll be glad to put him on the first plane out."

"If the Cuban government doesn't want me here, I'll go," Lucky tossed off easily.

It was not, however, that quick or that simple. Suddenly, Representative José Suarez Rivas, brother of Senator Edouardo Suarez Rivas, came to the fore. If the United States insisted on highhandedly ramming its edict down Cuba's throat under pain of a narcotics embargo, said the Representative, then how about giving Uncle Sam a taste of the same? He pointed out that the head of the wartime sugar black market, allegedly Spanish-born, had been deported by Cuba, but the United States had not shipped him back to his native land.

"I shall ask President San Martin to stop all sugar shipments to the United States, until the United States deports this man to Spain," Rivas declared.

Lucky's attitude remained comparatively placid, but the row waxed warmer. Two petitions for habeas corpus were filed by Attorney Alfonso Gonzalez. They were drawn up "on behalf of the people of Cuba," and made some unusual claims.

244

"His arrest is due to political persecution," they declared, and:

"The United States is opposed to him, because he is an anti-Nazi."

As day after day went by, Lucky grew morose, depressed. Tiscornia, like any immigration and deportation center, is not the most pleasant place to be incarcerated. What irked him most, though, were the charges leveled by narcotics officials in Washington and New York.

"I'm taking bum raps," he cried. "Now they got me handling junk. It's just one headache on top of a headache. If I can't be left alone, what am I gonna do?"

"Did you get a lawyer?" an acquaintance asked.

"What do I want a mouthpiece for?" he challenged. "Five thousand cops can investigate me. I'm clean. I'm takin' it easy!"

He even granted an audience willingly, to a newspaperman, so that he might expound further on his "persecution."

"Have you made any contacts in the United States?" the newsman inquired.

"What connections you mean?" he demanded.

The reporter was forthright. "Like rackets, for instance."

"Are you kiddin'?" the Boss exploded. "I been 'away' [meaning Dannemora] all these years. What racket could I be in?"

His air of injured innocence was belied in the next breath: "If I could open up a nice legit business, I'd do it," he vowed. Thus, for all his declamation of "good moral character," Lucky still admitted that, up to that moment, he had not stooped to "nice legitimate business."

In the end, of course, Lucky had to go. He was loaded

aboard the Turkish ship, *Bakir,* and summarily sped from Cuba. Any idea he might have had of lighting elsewhere in the Western Hemisphere was rudely dispelled. Venezuela and Colombia, which had granted him visas when he left Italy, announced loudly that they would not accept him now on a gold platter.

Still acting like a man with his affairs completed and in order, Lucky was philosophical about it. "If I'm gonna have trouble other places, like here in Cuba, I'm going back to Italy," he announced. It was hardly an ultimatum; there was no other place he could go.

From the looks of the luggage he toted aboard the *Bakir,* the Boss would have no worry for some time to come about his wardrobe—if, that is, all the shiny suitcases were loaded with clothing. Actually, there have been frequent reports that one or more may not have contained articles of apparel. His friends, it seems, had been so gracious in their contributions that he simply could not carry all the money in his pockets. In fact, if you believe all you hear, he took as much as a million dollars in cold hard cash back to Italy.

There was no promise of a joyous welcome awaiting him on the Continent. Italy had been most upset over the indications that an embarrassing astigmatism had afflicted Latin law enforcement. Even before Lucky started back from the West Indies, the Rome Government announced that he would be clapped into the *questura* just as soon as he ambled down the gangplank.

"The charges are clandestine departure without proper credentials," announced Police Chief Luigi Ferrari of Genoa, where the *Bakir* was due to dock.

The trip back on the puffing little vessel took the better part of a month. As advertised, Police Chief Ferrari nabbed the home-coming native son at the pier and tossed him into the jailhouse. As usual, he was out in a day or two.

Authorities promised that from there on in, Lucky's flitting about would be a matter of their especial attention.

"He will be under permanent police surveillance," it was officially announced.

If Lucky's accomplishments in the ensuing years are any indication of the efficacy of "permanent police surveillance," Roman style, it might be a good idea to include a load of seeing-eye dogs with the next Marshall Plan shipment to Italy!

ADMIRAL LUCKY: PIRACY, OLD CLOTHES, AND HIGH FINANCE

*Steady money from the States....
"Permanent surveillance": Italian
law's waiting game?... Candy factory, pastry shop, and slot machines.
...Lucky's Sixth Fleet, or pirates
out of Tangiers....Luciano, the
old-clothes man: he who gets slapped.*

AFTER THE ILLEGAL exit charges were dismissed, Lucky left
the mainland for his native Sicily—by police invitation
and under police guard to see that he didn't lose his way.
Among his personal effects were reported to be several
gold bars, a diamond-studded belt, and an assortment of
one hundred handmade neckties—the boys' little offerings
when they dropped in at Havana.

Arriving in Palermo, the Boss again was clapped into
jail, just like any ordinary bum, while officialdom considered the proper way to handle a public enemy. As usual,
Lucky was given the benefit of all doubts. He was freed
with a warning: stay out of (*a*) trouble and (*b*) the public
eye.

For two months or so, he lay low. As soon as he felt reasonably safe, though, he sneaked out of Sicily—right back
to Rome! There he rented a swank, ornate apartment and
settled down with his new (and blonde) girl friend.

They were living in high style, when the Marchesa Sandra Rossi, who spends much of her time at fashionable Montelera, got back to town. It turned out she owned the apartment. It had been requisitioned by Allied Occupation authorities during the war, then rented to someone, who in turn leased it to Luciano without a word to the landlady.

"I," the Marchesa announced, "am horrified!"

She told Lucky and his lady to get out or she would have the law on them. The Boss was embarrassed. Not even on the East Side had he ever suffered the humiliation of an eviction.

The inconvenience was brief, however. He was already planning to settle in Naples, anyway.

For quite a while, he lived in the Hotel Turistico there. Then he acquired an ultramodern, American-style penthouse on the exclusive heights of the famed Vomero, far above the city. To this, he later added a villa on Capri and another on the Tyrrhenian Sea.

Luciano's style of living today obviously demands ample and sustained resources. He has them, of course. They are, however, unaccounted for by any apparent occupation, legitimate or otherwise.

"He lives like a king, but has no legal income," police officials sighed with an air of futility when he moved into the penthouse. "He says he gets his money from friends."

"Luciano has more United States dollars than anyone else in Italy—maybe more than the Government," Walter Winchell reported some time ago. The Government has not denied it.

Lucky, on the other hand, insists that, all signs to the contrary, he "needs dough badly."

His net worth is anyone's guess—and the best guesses

range up to three million, in cash. Observers close enough to the scene to be authoritative estimate that his take from Italian operations alone runs up to $250,000 a year.

That not "all" of the income is from legitimate sources is the understatement of the decade. He does have, or has had, assorted enterprises on the peninsula—from real estate to candymaking—that may be labeled legitimate, or a reasonable facsimile thereof. But his shady operations in Italy very likely far outnumber the legal. As a matter of fact, the chances are that the legitimate ventures would just about stand off his horse bets.

Lucky, it seems, has hardly been as expert a handicapper on the Italian turf as in the palmy days at Jamaica and Hialeah and Hot Springs. There is evidence that the horses have been running cold for him over quite a period now. One recent losing streak is said to have skipped blithely over the $50,000 mark before luck came back to Lucky.

What with bad horses and good living, the estimates of $250,000 a year from local enterprises seem far too conservative to keep Lucky in the lush style he has always fancied—and still does. Obviously, then, fresh supplies of folding money must be shoveled in constantly, and in king-size bundles.

The sources of Lucky's income are, beyond any question, chiefly American. Practically all his multiple manipulations have an American angle and, more important, yield good American dollars—a priceless commodity on the Continent today.

Conversion of dollars into Italian spending money, without running afoul of currency control or catching the tax collector's eye, is a major problem of those interested in beating the law in Italy, just as it is anywhere else on the Continent today. The best tax sleuths of both Italy and America have had a close watch on Lucky and have come up with very little, indeed. In covering assets and camouflaging income, the Boss is practically a genius. Not for nothing did he absorb the lesson learned and practiced so well by the American mob lord—that the income-tax collector is to be feared above all menaces, except the electric chair.

One rumor concerns a particularly helpful financial gimmick Lucky is said to have cooked up. He met ex-King Farouk, Egypt's obese abdicator, while both were lolling around Capri. They reached an agreement, this story goes, for Luciano to keep his records clean by using Fatty Farouk's foreign banking accounts for monetary transactions. Naturally, there was a slight charge for the service.

Lucky frankly confesses that old friends from across the sea continue to bring him gifts of green bills. In the same breath, though, he denies that he holds any property or transacts business in America.

"Nuthin'—I got not a piece of nuthin'—in the States," he vows vehemently.

However, he did slip once, not long ago. In an interview with a reporter for *Milano Sera (Milan Evening)*, he was waving the usual banner of innocence.

"The only charge that can possibly be made against me," he was quoted as asserting, "is that I received $60,000 from my American administrators. It was mine, and I had a right to use it."

Well, if he has administrators, then there must be an estate or business for them to administrate!

Who brings this tribute, gift, cut, salary, dividend, or

what have you? And how? Since his exile, an uninterrupted parade of visitors has been toting him presents. Some say he entertains an emissary from America as often as once a week. Friends, relatives, business associates, or just plain couriers for the Syndicate arrive periodically from New York and Chicago, Las Vegas and Miami, and the west coast. The Kefauver Committee claimed it had turned up reports that several of the Boss's old buddies pretended to be Holy Year pilgrims to Rome in order to confer with him. On each visit, a billfold or envelope stuffed with greenbacks changes hands in the seclusion of a men's room, in a private car in a lonely spot, or, if the visitor is not too conspicuous, in Lucky's apartment.

Since the guests from overseas invariably forget to report to authorities how many dollars they bring in, there is no way to make an accurate check on their bank rolls when they depart. Hence, no possible direct trail to Lucky.

Several of the gift-bearing visits are on record. Mike Lascari once took $2,500 to the unforgotten exile.

"I just thought he might need it," Mike explained candidly.

Lucky's two brothers, Joseph and Bert (they have also been Leo and Tony at times), have visited their deported relative in Sicily and departed with emptier pockets. Mike Spinella, dropped in on the Boss, too (Mike has since become a fellow deportee). Gaetano Martino, representative of the racket-ridden Brooklyn docks, was an early visitor, and has been back more than once, but insists he didn't take a cent to Lucky.

Then there was Meyer Lansky, Buggsy Siegel's old murder mob partner. His was the sincerest of all the gestures of friendship. It was so unrehearsed and unexpected that it was, in fact, practically unconscious.

Through a mix-up in the travel bureau, Lansky related afterward, he suddenly and unexpectedly found himself sailing in a $2,600 suite on the smart liner *Italia*. He hadn't planned to visit Italy at all.

"I couldn't get out and walk, could I?" he demanded.

Imagine, then, his surprise when the Italian boat docked in Italy! And imagine his further, but ecstatic, joy when the telephone rang, and who was on the wire but his old buddy and business pal, Lucky!

"I says to him, 'How the hell did y'know where I am?' " Lansky related. "And he says, 'Well, I get it from the papers.' "

Which just goes to show how alert the Naples newspapers are. They knew where the old mob mogul was going, even before he knew himself.

And what did the old gang playmates, thrown together by sheer accident, talk about? Oh, nothing much, the visiting hood remembered. Just an exchange of gripes about being "crucified" by press and public. And Lansky gave Lucky a bit of cash—just for old times' sake, you understand. This was Lansky's story, and he stuck to it.

Even Virginia Hill turned up in Naples on unexplained business in June, 1953. The visit provoked much wonder as to whether the Dixie damsel brought Lucky loot from pals in Las Vegas. This is very unlikely. Although reputed to have been the Mob bagman at times, la Hill never was too fond of the Boss. And since her lover, Buggsy Siegel, was erased by the Syndicate, she has had a solid hatred for all of them.

The favorite of the felons could, of course, have come to borrow from Lucky. Or maybe she just dropped in to re-fresh the Boss's memory. The underworld grapevine has long whispered that her enlightening memoirs are in a safe place and will be turned over to authorities in case any of the boys get ideas that she should be silenced because of her considerable knowledge of their affairs.

Things may be getting tougher in Italy, however. The police, who have had Luciano for breakfast, lunch, and dinner for more than seven years, have lately been gloat-ing and rubbing their hands in anticipation of the coun-try's new and tighter income-tax laws.

"With stiffer sentences for false returns and regulations more severe, Luciano will have some explaining to do," observed one investigator. "We'll get him sure, next year."

There is no doubt that up to now Lucky is carrying the same charm, as far as police go, that he bore in the palmy protections days in New York. Time after time, he has been tabbed by assorted authorities as the secret overlord of the drug traffic (not to mention other illegitimacies). Yet he still remains at large.

"Luciano is behaving himself," was the astonishing state-ment of one police official early in 1952. It almost sounded like the Boss himself talking.

"Luciano is an ordinary citizen, and I can't have him shadowed all the time," declared Naples *Questore* Fausto Salvatore. The police chief was being asked about the re-ports that Lucky flits in and out of Italy, even though his passport has been lifted.

Lucky's comment on all this is: "If I'm guilty of all I been accused of, why don't the Italian police arrest me and put me in jail?"

There are at least three possible explanations:

1. Italian authorities—with the approval of their opposite number in America—are playing a waiting game, on the theory that, given enough rope, he will hang himself.

2. Lucky is up to his old tricks of buying protection at fancy prices. The authors have been informed on good authority that Naples Police Chief Salvatore is aware that one of his high-ranking subordinates—in the very department responsible for keeping an eye on drug operatives—has been "on the take" from Luciano. "For administrative reasons," the story goes, the Questore can do nothing about it.

3. Lucky's apparent immunity is due to politics in America! A number of persons entrenched in high places in the States must still shudder at the very thought of what Luciano could tell. They fear that should authorities bear down on him, Lucky may decide to sing chorus and verse about those of his onetime political friends who are still on hand and in the public trough.

Virtually all of the finger-pointing at the crime mogul has emanated from the U.S. Narcotics Bureau. In fairness to Italian authorities, it must be pointed out that with Lucky under Italian jurisdiction, the Bureau in Washington can make any charges against him it pleases, without having to back them up with proof. In Italy, on the other hand, authorities face the almost impossible task of getting evidence to prosecute specific charges. The two situations are vastly different.

Quite a few competent observers, as a matter of fact, remain unconvinced by the Narcotics Bureau's allegations. One seasoned Rome newspaperman flatly maintains that the Washington Bureau, fumbling in the dark, "pops off" about Luciano for lack of any other headline-making name to serve as a peg on which to hang its hat.

When Lucky was brought back from Cuba in 1947, Italian authorities pledged that he would, from that moment on, be under "permanent surveillance." This watch has been about as effective as a yawn in a typhoon. One of the authors of this book had several meetings with him in Naples. Any juicy deal could have been arranged, any amount of dollars handed over, had the writer been another racketeer. Yet no one was more surprised than the local police when they finally heard about it—because the author went and told them!

It is no wonder, then, that Luciano has managed to launch or become involved in businesses galore, legal and illegal, personally or through dummies and fronts, since his deportation.

Perhaps the clearest picture of how far he has spread himself can be seen in a listing of his business investments as they came up—good, bad, and revolting:

In 1949, police searched a candy factory at Palermo, alleged to be owned by Lucky. Rome papers speculated on the possibility that they were looking for candy containing narcotics.

A young American businessman came to Italy with the idea of setting up a chain of launderettes throughout southern Italy. Two hard gentlemen dropped in at his hotel quarters in Naples and informed him that any plans for launderettes south of Naples would require "the O.K.," and that such approval would be forthcoming only if the Boss were cut in.

In 1951, Luciano filled out, on official request, an affidavit in which he said the one real commercial venture he had attempted in Italy was a pastry shop at Palermo. "It was forced to close after two and a half years," he reported.

In April, 1952, Lucky was said to own and race a string of six horses.

Early that same year, back in New York, a heavy packing case, marked for Genoa, slipped its chain as it was being hoisted aboard ship at Pier 84, on the Hudson River. The box crashed to the dock and split open. A sharp-eyed customs man froze in astonishment at the contents: slot machines! The next day, right in the middle of the ensuing investigation, a truck drove up to the pier loaded with identical cases—and identical contents! All told, there were thirty-nine one-armed bandits, consigned to "C. & M. Enterprises, Genoa." The truck driver, Jack Anthony Marraffa, said the machines were purchased from a novelty company in Chicago. Chicago police reported they had never heard of the firm. Lucky was not the consignee, but few, indeed, doubted that, had the slots reached Italy, the Boss would have had quite a bit to say about them—and even more about the "take" from them.

In October, 1952, Canadian officials were considerably worried over a tremendous upsurge in the clandestine transportation of aliens from Canada to the United States. Consider this news dispatch of October 18, 1952:

St. Albans, Vermont (UP)—Canadian border officials said today they have "strong evidence" that deported vice overlord Charles (Lucky) Luciano is running one of several rings smuggling perhaps 33,000 European aliens a year into the United States.

Chester Woish, chief Border Patrol inspector at Rouse's Point, N.Y., charges that Luciano is linked with the Society

[that] ... recruits hoodlums in Sicily for gangster organizations in principal U.S. cities.

Border Patrol agents recently seized a husky Italian youth as he tried to cross a Vermont farm that straddles the U.S. Canadian border. Questioned by Immigration officials, the youth tearfully said:

"To talk is to cut my throat!"

And then there is the enterprise which, for want of an official label, might be titled "Admiral Lucky and his Sixth Fleet" or "Who said Captain Kidd is dead?"

Anyone who has the idea that the Barbary Coast and the Spanish Main are just legends should visit Tangier. Not far from the straits of Gibraltar, at the western gateway to the Mediterranean, this melting pot combines all that is mysterious and bizarre in North Africa with the cloak-and-dagger intrigue—political, commercial, and criminal—that blossoms up in any free port.

Tangier is renowned the world over for unmatched business facilities, an easygoing international administration, and an absolute minimum of restrictions. In recent years, the port has become the funnel through which American goods are unloaded onto the black markets of Spain, France, Italy, and countries across the Mediterranean. And it is unanimously cursed by customs authorities of these countries as the worst smugglers' den on earth.

Tangier tradespeople buy goods from America and store them in the bonded warehouses (*entrepôt fictif*) of the free port. Then, one day, the stock is taken out, loaded aboard freighter, fishing vessel, or even private yacht and sent off into the Mediterranean.

Up to that point, everything is perfectly legal and aboveboard. Thereafter, things get very tricky. The American goods shipped out of the free port are seldom unloaded at their declared destinations. The freighter that puts out for Malta or Athens or Istanbul generally winds up in a rendezvous with "fishing boats" just outside the territorial limits of Italy, Spain, or France. In the dead of night, cargo and cash change hands. Then the small craft, now loaded with contraband, dash through customs patrol lines to land their freight in secret cove or lonely, unguarded beach.

It is a lush business. In Mediterranean countries, import duties on American cigarettes, nylons, and other products are extremely high. A smuggler can undersell official prices and still make out handsomely. In Italy, for example, American cigarettes cost up to 300 lire in stores; street hawkers offer almost any brand at 200 lire a pack.

The wholesalers in this illicit importing make astronomical profits. A single trip from Tangier nets a good-sized vessel $15,000 to $20,000. Annual earnings of $500,000 to $750,000 are not uncommon for the important operator.

Behind the usual array of fronts, a flotilla of smuggling boats, including freighters, yachts, motor launches, speedboats, and even small submarines was rounded up for the operation. The modern touch was added in the form of a few light airplanes, to guide the smuggling ships, scout for customs vessels, spot unguarded coasts—and pin point suitable targets for hijacking. Considerable of the transportation equipment—air and sea—came from American war surplus stocks.

This powerful task force has been known throughout Europe for years as "Lucky's Sixth Fleet."

Not, however, until the dramatic voyage of the *Combinatie* was the Syndicate's interest high lighted.

The 249-ton *Combinatie,* Captain Johannes Van Delft commanding, was a freighter of Dutch registry, owned by the Mavotrans Shipping Company of The Hague. In the fall of 1952, she was chartered by one *Signor* Pedemonte for Mediterranean cargo service.

Typical trafficker in the import-export business is *Signor* Pedemonte. He holds two passports—one Italian, one Argentine. Tradesman Pedemonte does very nicely for himself, but he has remained a "loner"—holding aloof from organized smuggling. As proven by the case of the Mustache Petes of Mafia in America, independence is an antiquated business method. Now that Crime, International, and Lucky are in the Mediterranean, it is a grievous error.

A magistrate of the International Court in Tangier described the situation this way.

"In order to obtain a virtual monopoly of the contraband traffic, the big racketeers have taken steps to eliminate the small fry of smugglers."

On October 3, 1952, the *Combinatie* put out of Tangier harbor, bound for Malta (it said on her papers) with a mixed cargo of fountain pens, American nylon stockings, and three thousand cases of cigarettes. Press reports of the incredible voyage that followed were wide of the facts in several respects. We believe the following is the first authentic and reasonably complete account, based on information gathered from unimpeachable sources at The Hague, Tangier, Naples, and the International Police in Paris.

At about 1:00 A.M. on October 4, the *Combinatie* was churning through the western Mediterranean, sixteen miles off the Spanish coast, with Captain Van Delft on the bridge. Suddenly, a small vessel, running lights dimmed, loomed out of nowhere and bore down on the freighter. And it kept on bearing down until, a few moments later, the mystery ship rammed the *Combinatie.*

Six masked men, tommy guns in hand, swarmed aboard and took command. Captain Van Delft, his son Cornelius, and his eight-man crew were herded below decks at gun point. For ten days, they huddled there, locked in a dirty hold, while the buccaneers ran the ship. The brigands' first port of call was a tiny town on the Spanish island of Majorca, where three hundred cases of cigarettes were unloaded. Then, some four hundred miles northeast, they put in at an isolated spot on the coast of Corsica, not far from Ajaccio. There they discharged the remaining 2,700 cases and once more stood out to sea.

On the eleventh day, the prisoners became aware that the *Combinatie* had stopped moving. From their smelly dungeons, they heard a boat come alongside. Footsteps clattered across the deck over their heads. The boat pulled away. Then—silence.

Only the slap of the wavelets on the ship's sides broke the stillness. Captain Van Delft and his men realized their captors were gone, taken off by the mystery boat. They went to work on a skylight, and managed to pry it open and scramble out on deck.

The *Combinatie* was practically cleaned out. Not only the cargo, but everything else not bolted down had been pirated. About the only item left on the bridge was a chart, showing their position off the African coast. The buccaneers had abandoned the ship—after sailing her twelve hundred miles around the Mediterranean—in almost the identical spot at which they had boarded her twelve days before!

International authorities at Tangier were hard put to believe the captain's wild story. Not since pieces of eight were legal tender had anything like this happened. Nevertheless, the tale was corroborated by the entire crew—plus $3,000 damage to the ship itself, and the absence of $100,-000 in cargo.

The International Police in Paris were alerted. INTERPOL is a combination of law-enforcement agents from many countries. They know the dives and dark corners in many capitals. Their net was spread, and before long, little by little, the answers were coming in.

The pirate ship that had rammed the *Combinatie* was identified as the motor launch *Esme,* formerly of the British Navy. She is now owned by one Rue Wright, native of Colorado City, Colorado, U.S.A., but currently a resident of Tangier. However, it developed that the *Esme* had recently been chartered by two Americans in Tangier—Sidney J. Paley and his junior partner, Elliot B. Forrest.

The thirty-four-year-old Paley is a former G.I. from Jersey City. Around the Mediterranean, they call him Nylon Sid, because importing and exporting American stockings is his business. A dark, rather insignificant character, he was something of an exhibitionist in the free port. He sported splashy clothes and a Cadillac convertible. His partner, Forrest, is a tall, tanned roisterer of thirty-one, who, according to the newspapers, "looked and acted the part of a pirate." Back in 1948, he was stopped by the Coast Guard when he and five other men tried to sail a war surplus submarine chaser from New York to Tangier.

Both men had vanished from their haunts when INTERPOL came calling. In a matter of days, though, Nylon Sid was picked up in Madrid.

Under an old treaty with the Sultan of Morocco, American citizens in Tangier are exempt from local and international jurisdiction. As a result, Nylon Sid went on trial before a United States Consular Court for piracy on the high seas. It was the first such case in the court's history, and the legal procedure had to be dug out of the distant past.

There was no evidence that Paley had personally taken part in the piracy. Forrest is generally credited with leading the foray. Paley was, however, in on the conspiracy.

A bearded Australian seadog named Ernest (Tony) Townsend gave startling testimony. He had run smuggling errands for Nylon Sid & Company before, and he linked Sid directly with the Luciano organization. He discovered this not long before the *Combinatie* incident, he vowed, when he had met Paley in Rome, and listened to the Jersey City smuggler discuss the piracy plot with others.

An even closer link with Lucky was forged by the testimony of one of the original British crew members of the *Esme*.

"The whole business is so well organized," he swore, "that we'd rather not talk unless we are guaranteed safety. The line stretches from Chicago to Lucky Luciano in Naples—and it is really dangerous!"

That the scheme had been hatched by an organization with world-wide power was confirmed by Captain Van Delft. He remembered that when the buccaneers stormed aboard that night, their leader (presumably Forrest) warned him to "keep your trap shut."

"If you don't," the raider menaced, "We'll get you—even if you run to Hong Kong or Buenos Aires!"

Nylon Sid was convicted and sentenced to three years in a Federal Penitentiary back in the States. He was granted a new trial—and again convicted. But he came off better this time. Instead of being imprisoned, he walked out into the free air, on probation.

As for Forrest, not until 1954 was he tracked down. On January 21, he was ferreted out of an obscure village in the Vancluse region of the French Alps, where he had been living quietly for months, masquerading as an invalid. At this writing, his case is still unsettled. At a preliminary hearing, he was fearful that if he talked there would be reprisals against his parents, who live in New York.

The affair of the pirates of 1952 is still unfinished. The rest of the *Esme*'s crew of buccaneers, including the skipper—a Dutchman named Eddie Engelsman—are awaiting trial. Pedemonte, the Italian-Argentine man of mystery, is suing the owners of the *Combinatie* in Holland, charging a dastardly double-cross, a put-up job. Captain Van Delft knew all along his ship was going to be hijacked, the *signore* cries bitterly. On the other hand, Pedemonte himself is charged with the double-cross. The hijack job was really his doing, it is alleged, so that he could collect double damages—from the ship's owners and from the insurance company!

Nor does it end even there. After the pirates had put the 2,700 cases of cigarettes ashore on the Corsican coast, the small Danish ship, *Jess B. E. 106,* picked up the loot, by prearrangement. Authorities caught the ship in the act of sneaking it onto the French mainland, near Toulon, at a private beach formerly owned by the Italian statesman, Count Carlo Sforza.

264

Just as in his New York racket days, no finger points directly to Lucky. The Boss denies all. In fact, while Nylon Sid was on trial, Luciano called a press conference in Naples to cry out his innocence.

"Look, fellas," he confided, "I need dough bad—but I ain't in no racket. Why don't they leave me alone?" Then, hamming it up, he waxed indignant. "I ain't no cigarette smuggler," he sputtered. "I'm disgusted with that kinda talk!"

A very well-informed source in Naples, however, stated to one of the authors of this book that port authorities there definitely suspect Lucky of having organized the *Combinatie* raid, with the help of Sicilian friends. Paley and Forrest were simply stooges.

It is apparent, then, that Lucky still has the touch. Though up to his eyeballs in this affair, on the basis of evidence no one can put the pirate's cutlass in his hand or place him on the bridge of the smuggling ship. Or even seat him at the conference table at which the piracy was plotted. As usual, he is out of reach.

Crime, International, it is evident, handles anything— from dope to women to cigarettes, from nylon to rags. That's right—rags!

The boys around the Waldorf—even those along Mulberry Bend—will find it hard to picture this, but Lucky's latest trade is—in the old-clothes business! Naturally, with Lucky's fingers in it, the profits must be fancier than those of the well-known ragman piloting a bony nag.

In Italy, especially in the southern areas of stark poverty, there is a crying need for clothes of any kind. A few years ago, the Boss decided to do something about filling it.

He organized a transatlantic commerce in secondhand garments. Shirts, underwear, haberdashery, suits, dresses—anything wearable—are shipped in regularly from New York, in huge bales. These are hauled to the nearby market place of Resina, and auctioned off to the highest bidders.

The bales are sold unopened, contents unseen, on a straight-sale, no-return basis. They bring about $800 apiece under the hammer. The wholesalers are gambling against rags. Sometimes the buyer will find an only slightly used tailored suit or a fashionable evening gown discarded by a fastidious Park Avenue belle after two or three wearings. Then the wholesaler has won. Just as often, he discovers nothing but a bundle of tatters, unusable even by the sadly ill-clothed Neapolitan and Calabrian.

Thousands of customers come to rummage for some article to fit their frames and their pocketbooks. A working girl in quest of an inexpensive trousseau; a small-town pimp, eager to add class to his wardrobe with a hand-me-down from the New World; the hard-pressed housewife, who must seek bargains to cover her all-too-numerous brood—these are the ultimate consumers who make Lucky's old-clothes mart a fancy business.

From the drab and uninteresting old-clothes trade came an amusing incident neither prostitution nor piracy nor any of the more exciting evils could match. For the second time in his charmed life, Lucky experienced the humiliation of physical assault. It differed in two respects from his famous ride to Staten Island twenty-one years before. The only punishment he took this time was a few fast punches.

Word of Lucky's hand-me-down auction had spread. It began to attract others besides customers—smugglers, thieves, fences, and the rest. Among the hoodlum *hoi polloi* was a sleek character named Vittorio Nappi. He billed himself as "Il Re dei Guappi" (pronounced "gwah-pee"), which translates to "King of the Thugs."

The handsome profits accruing to the "foreigner" from his old clothes made King Guappi's mouth water. And, since Lucky was working what Nappi considered his own territory, he felt that some of the profit should rub off on him.

He paid a call on the Boss, duly set forth his qualifications, and hinted broadly that perhaps it would be a good idea for Lucky to cut him in. The local punk should have realized that Luciano learned his trade in the very rough and highly competitive American racket school. He wasn't likely to give way to the muscle at this late date—especially from one of the local hoods, for whom he has the greatest contempt.

However, Lucky had learned that an out-and-out "no" sometimes stirs up resentment and trouble.

"I'll think it over, chum," he promised casually, assuming the *guappo* would get the idea and retire.

But Nappi didn't get it. In a couple of weeks he button-holed the exile in his favorite restaurant. Once again, Lucky was diplomatic.

"I gotta talk to some guys who are in with me. As soon as I get ahold of them, I'll contact you."

The would-be muscler still didn't catch the signal. Back he came the third time. Lucky had run out of patience and tact.

"Look, bum," he snapped, taking off the kid glove. "I've checked up on you, and you're N.G. Now get the hell outa here, or I'll get you heaved out!"

Nappi's dignity was bruised. A Napoleon should not

suffer such insult in his own territory. He forgot all about whom he was dealing with. He vowed to get even.

On Thursday, November 13, 1950, after enjoying his Neapolitan lunch in his habitual corner at Da Giacomino's, Lucky slipped through the restaurant's back door, into his green Oldsmobile and headed for the Agnano Hippodrome. The fall racing season was on.

The afternoon went fine. After the last race, Lucky was on his way to the parking lot, when Nappi suddenly popped out of the shrubs and grabbed the Boss's mob-sacred person. Lucky's bodyguards were momentarily nowhere in sight.

Nappi whipped out his right hand and smacked the swarthy face with a resounding one-two blow that sent Lucky reeling. It was all over in a flash, and King Guappi, having let off steam, was gone before anyone could get into the act.

The only damage was to Lucky's pride. He felt a stinging humiliation as he drove back to town.

The newspapers never learned the identity of the brash attacker, but the underworld knew—and gasped. From one end of the peninsula to the other, the startled grapevine buzzed the sensational news: "Il Re dei Guappi slapped Lucky! Il Re has the nerve of the lion!"

The tidings reached dull-witted Pasquale Simonetti, who had once been a close friend and business partner of Nappi. His pals nicknamed him Pascalone, meaning Big Pasquale, and the reason was obvious. An ex-pug, Pascalone's 230 pounds loomed tremendous in a country that leans to the undersized man.

Eventually it dawned on Big Pasquale that his quick-witted co-worker was splitting the take in a most inequitable manner. Nappi was making a patsy out of Pasquale. The friendship dissolved, with very hard feelings on Pascalone's side.

The big oaf saw golden opportunity in Nappi's attack on Lucky—opportunity for revenge and for self-improvement, to boot. He had long heard of the smartly dressed bodyguards surrounding American gangsters. The United States hoods always had money and pretty girls. The Nappi incident proved the Boss needed someone to watch over him. Why shouldn't that someone be Big Pasquale?

Fired with ambition and vengeance, he went after his onetime pal. He caught up with Nappi on Piazza Garibaldi, in front of Naples' Central Station.

Nappi was just dismounting from his flashy automobile when the onrushing giant thundered down, brandishing a monkey wrench. Il Re ran—but not far. The heavy tool crashed down on his head and all but drove him into the sidewalk, blood spitting from his shattered skull. Pasquale, his slow mind unusually active, took advantage of the immediate furore. He dashed into the station and jumped aboard a train just pulling out.

The police were warned that Pascalone was too dangerous (and too big) to be taken singlehanded. But when they finally caught up with him, two years later, they found his viciousness had been highly overrated. Cornered at a roadblock spanning the entrance to the *Autostrada,* the superhighway between Naples and Pompeii, Pasquale showed no more fight than a kitten.

Big, dull Pasquale was disillusioned. For two long years, while he dodged the law, he had waited for the call from Lucky. But the big Boss from America sent neither flowers nor funds—not even a "thanks" to the devoted dunce who had paid off for Nappi's insult. And when Pascalone was caught, Lucky disavowed him completely.

Almost miraclously, Nappi survived. His skull was fractured in several places, but the surgeons did a nice stitching job. Perhaps the *guappo* king's mind won't be quite so nimble as before. But it is no doubt agile enough to appreciate the fact that slapping the Boss does not pay.

12 LUCKY AND THE SLOW MURDER

*The dope pipeline, Rome to New York.
... Trieste, main station on the "White
Road".... Moles work underground in
vice, too.... Four hundred pounds of
H to America annually.... Doctors,
professors, and a* Commendatore *of the
King: fronts for the heroin mob....
The biggest haul of them all—and
Lucky still untouched.*

IN ANY DISCUSSION of Lucky's rackets, all others run second
to narcotics.

There is no doubt that Italy is one source of the pipeline
flooding America with dope. And agents of the U.S. Narcotics Bureau unhesitatingly nominate Luciano as the kingpin of the killing traffic, without a contest. To back up their
claim, the agents produce quite an array of coincidental
data, information, and surmises—albeit little concrete evidence:

1. Luciano has been a known drug trafficker since 1916.

2. Luciano is the acknowledged head of Unione—and
narcotics has long been the Italian crime society's business.

3. Luciano reached Italy in 1946, and, coincidentally—
say agents—the flow of dope into America began to in-
crease the following year. Drug arrests in New York jumped
from 712 in 1946 (with 23 under 21 years of age), to 2,482

in 1950 (with 521 under 21). (This, however, can be in large measure accounted for by the fact that in the same period, the Narcotics Squad of the New York Police Department was boosted from some two dozen officers to over 100.)

4. Narcotics Bureau Supervisor Garland Williams charged that three months after Luciano's return from Cuba, in 1947, the first large shipment of heroin—worth $250,000—was smuggled into the U.S.

5. A number of people in Italy, Federal Narcotics men claim, are listed in the Who's Who of Dope at INTERPOL Headquarters in Paris.

In the face of increasing accusation, the Boss keeps up a bold front of protestation and denial. The more the Federal Narcotics Bureau in Washington points a finger, the louder Lucky screams "persecution." At one time, he even hired a press agent to make him "respectable"—a former American Army man who had been tub-thumper for the Commanding General of United States Forces in Italy!

Early in 1952, a mass dragnet covering every major American city—appropriately labeled "Operation Big Sweep"—culminated in the indictment in San Francisco of twenty-three alleged members of a nation-wide ring.

"These fellows were dealing with just one source," asserted Assistant Narcotics Bureau Chief George Cunningham. "And that was the illegal Italian traffic controlled by Luciano!"

A spokesman for the Italian police declared that if this were so, then Lucky must be a magician: "If he is running a world-wide narcotics ring, he is doing it by some of the cleverest remote-control operations we have ever encountered!" the official insisted.

Nobody denies that. "The cleverest remote-control" operator is Lucky all over. Not since he hit the top of gangland has the Boss soiled his own hands handling the actual dope, pistol, or prostitute—any more than the president of a meat-packing corporation personally cuts the top round, the tripe, or even the filet mignon. However, when Italian authorities pleaded for evidence from Cunningham, so that they could nab Lucky, none was forthcoming.

Although apparently reluctant to label Lucky as the man in control, Italian authorities do concede that he may well be connected with the traffic. Yet, in spite of intense investigation, they have found no evidence with which to haul him into court in connection with any dope seizure—and they have been trying for half a dozen years now.

In the summer of 1949, a team of U.S. Narcotics Agents arrived in Italy to work with local authorities against the traffic in slow murder. At the head of this mission was much-publicized Charles Siragusa.

Shortly afterward, Siragusa and Captain Guillermo Oliva of the Guardia di Finanza (Italy's equivalent of the Secret Service) nabbed a young fellow boarding a New York-bound plane at Ciampino airport, outside Rome. In a secret compartment of his suitcase the agents found sixteen pounds of cocaine. When he was stripped, another three pounds were extracted from a rubber container which he carried "inside his body." The hoard was worth half a million!

The young man's passport identified him as Charles Vincent Trupia, and he said he was on his way home to his job as an automobile mechanic in New York. He gave an address on Broome Street, in New York City—practically next door to Police Headquarters! But when the address was checked that same day, it was found to be the home of Vincent Trupia, Sr., and Vincent Trupia, Jr.—and both of them were at home. They insisted no member of their family was bouncing around Europe, and they couldn't figure why anyone would be using their name or address. The identity of the man—who obviously either held a phony passport or was using a phony name—has never been cleared up.

He said his supplier was a fellow named Francesco Pirigo of Milan, a native Sicilian. He also related, reluctantly, that he was under specific orders from the New York dope syndicate. The Italian courts put him away for a year and a half. In less than a week, Lucky was involved and was brought in. The Rome police held him nearly two weeks, while they dug into any possible link between him and Trupia. There was none, so he was released. Italian newspapers speculated frankly that his arrest may have been nothing but a "smoke screen."

(The day Lucky was set free marked the ultimate order barring him from Rome and exiling him to his birthplace of Lercara Friddi. The exile lasted one day.)

Sometimes, Rome officials work Lucky into a case in a peculiarly backhand fashion, as in the report the Italian Government submitted a couple of years ago to the International Criminal Police Commission, for forwarding to the United Nations.

One paragraph concerned "one of the largest" heroin seizures in 1951. Police arrested an American, whom the report identified only as "C. . . Frank," and later took into custody the prisoner's uncle, named "C. . . Francesco." Then the report added this gem:

"Their accomplices included L. . . Lucky, and others."

From the inconspicuous and casual manner in which this was tossed in, one would suppose that the Italian government had never heard of Lucky Luciano, or else considered the whole affair trivial. And this mind you, in a report to the United Nations, which has been studying the world-wide narcotics menace for years!

Fantastic, also, is the coy omission of all other full names from the report. "C. . . .Frank" actually is Frank Callace, a thirty-year-old self-styled New York "businessman," closely connected with the 107th Street mob of east Harlem. In fact, he lives on East 107th Street. And "C. . . Francesco" is Francesco Callace,* young Frank's uncle, whose twenty-five-year career in American crime ended when he disappeared while the FBI was after him for a spot of blackmail in Milford, Connecticut, in 1948.

The case of the initials began toward the end of March in 1951, when Frank Callace was sent to Italy by the Syndicate to pick up a large parcel of dope. Following his travel orders to the letter, he disembarked in Sicily, consulted with his Uncle Francesco, a local power in the crime society, and then proceeded to Milan, to get the "snow" from one Joe Pici. Other contacts were established en route.

What none of them knew, though, was that Callace had been a marked man even before he left New York. There was a tail on him through the entire trip. For, this was one of the capers about which Gene Giannini, the stool pigeon, had informed the Narcotics Bureau. In fact, it was this job he referred to afterward, when he wrote Agent Irwin Greenfeld from the Rome jail and brought up the earlier

---

* Francesco Callace turned up in New York and was murdered on November 14, 1954.

arrests of dope smugglers "on information I gave you." His information was that this outfit had purchased heroin in various parts of Europe, including Germany, and sold it in several United States cities for $500,000.

As a result, when Frank Callace reached Rome airport on his way back from Milan, the trackers closed in. He had more than six pounds of heroin in a false-bottomed suitcase. Frank came up with the usual insipid explanation—a total stranger gave him a sealed package in Milan for delivery to another stranger, etc., etc. The authorities nodded —and went out and grabbed Uncle Francesco at the airport in Palermo, where he was waiting for his nephew.

The Guardia di Finanza set out after the supplier, Pici. "Peachy" looks the part of the gangster—and has acted it to the hilt.

Narcotics Agents frequently and insistently describe Pici as a New York gangster. They stoutly maintain that he is a prime example of old American gangland associations Lucky has renewed in Italy to build up a dope mob. Actually, Joe Pici's entire life of crime, until his deportation in 1946, was spent in Pittsburgh. If he ever was in New York, it was probably to take in the shows or buy a new spring wardrobe, for it certainly is not a matter of police record. And he was far more notorious solely as a stick-up man and a pimp, than for any connection with organized crime or rackets which might have thrown him into contact with Syndicate directors of Luciano's social standing in the underworld. In fact, he was never mentioned in connection with dope in this country. Lucky, himself, paints a considerably different picture of his relationship with Pici.

"This guy comes to me with a proposition three years ago," the Boss told authorities in 1952. "I don't like it, and

I tell him to get the hell away from me. I ain't seen him since."

This ex-Pittsburgh pimp has, nevertheless, put together a deadly drug setup in Northern Italy. In one operation in 1948, Pici dispatched thirty-three pounds of 99 per cent pure heroin to the Kansas City chapter of Unione. He bought this junk for $22,500 and sold it for $150,000. In the Syndicate's hidden American laboratories, it was cut and recut with milk sugar until there were several hundred thousand individual shots, available to addicts at one to two dollars apiece. There are reports that Pici also has even personally delivered batches of "junk" to the Kansas City branch, his deportation to the contrary, notwithstanding!

Peachy's northern Italian territory is a center of heroin traffic. Milan is the heart of Italy's manufacture of medicinal drugs, with Turin second only in importance. Genoa is the principal export port for American shipments. And Trieste is the entry and smuggling point for raw material from Turkey, Greece, and Yugoslavia. Within a few months after Pici's arrival, there was set up in this area one of the most tightly knit, smoothly functioning rings ever organized, and uncorking a source of almost unlimited supplies of H.

The hunt for Pici led over the rough mountain and lake country above Milan, to a tiny inn on the southeastern shore of Lake Como. But as the *carabinieri* closed in, the elusive dope operator got away, one jump in front of them.

The inn was not altogether empty, however. Among Pici's belongings was a checkbook in which ninety-two stubs bore the names and addresses of his business contacts. It has since brought no end of embarrassment to a number

277

of behind-the-scenes operators who sported convenient respectable fronts.

In Italy, just as elsewhere, law-enforcement officers sometimes have a way of looking hard—in the wrong direction. Sometime during the ensuing months, in which Peachy was the object of a country-wide manhunt, he took unto himself a buxom blonde bride—and followed his marriage with a noisy and very unsecret celebration!

Three months after Pici's public wedding, the *carabinieri* received an anonymous tip that he had been seen at a secluded villa, not far from the inn where he had gone out the window months before. An army of police set out in a fleet of cars. Roadblocks were set up, and an armed cordon thrown about the cottage, with orders to shoot on sight.

The raiders rang the bell and walked in. Brushing past a luscious blonde, they strolled into the kitchen—and there sat their man, having breakfast. He was neither very surprised nor perturbed.

The officer in charge advised the long-sought dope dealer he was going to Rome for questioning. "If I gotta travel," Peachy sneered, "I go in comfort. I want to buy first-class tickets on the train for myself and whatever *carabiniere* goes with me."

The expense could hardly have worried the gangster. He was carrying 2,800,000 lire—approximately $4,000.

Placed on trial, at long last, he drew an eighteen-month sentence—and then did not serve a day of it! Nor did Frank Callace do any time behind bars. A gimmick about an amnesty was found by officialdom, just to fit their cases. At this writing Pici is back in Milan—doing business as usual.

Meantime, however, Narcotics Agents once more alleged a hook-up between Lucky and a dope case. As a result of their claim, Italian Police picked up the Boss again. And again, after thoroughly running down all leads, they found nothing to connect him with it. Since the U.S. Agents had said so, they did include him as an "accomplice" in their report for the United Nations.

Perhaps the closest Lucky has come to being definitely nailed occurred early in 1952, when the alert INTERPOL nabbed Serafino Mancuso at the ancient Mafia citadel of Alcamo, in the Sicilian hills. Serafino is one of three Mancuso brothers—the other two are Salvatore and Giuseppe—who have one thing in common: law enforcement on both sides of the Atlantic has frequently had its eye on all of them.

Back in the thirties, the Mancusos were front and center in a particularly revolting bit of business. A French seaman was kidnaped in New York and was treated to all the vicious tortures that have come down from Mafia and Camorra, plus a few sadistic stunts the torturers thought up on the spur of the moment. There were whispers that the sailor had double-crossed one or more of the brothers, after agreeing to smuggle a batch of heroin into the United States for them.

Salvatore was given forty years for kidnaping and drug dealings, and his wife, who helped in the affair, got a three and a half year stretch. After the war, however, Salvatore was deported to Italy, where his brothers joined him, and all of them took up where they had left off.

When Serafino was nabbed there in Alcamo in '52, he was in the act of claiming a trunk, inside of which, cleverly tucked in the ribbed walls, were twenty-five pounds of heroin!

The trunk, it developed, belonged to one Francesco Coppola, who was then a wealthy gentleman farmer with a hundred-acre estate hard by Anzio's blood-soaked battlefields. The country gentleman turned out to be a former New Orleans and Detroit character (friend of Frank Costello), who left the United States after the war, just as deportation proceedings were to be instituted against him. Some agents have said he is a brother of Trigger Mike Coppola, who has been named by Narcotics authorities as lieutenant in the setup of the 107th Street mob of east Harlem dope distributors. There is, however, no such relationship between the two.

The discovery of the trunk set off a chain reaction that stretched from Sicily to Milan and brought several others into the bag.

Coppola's estate was raided, and another batch of heroin discovered. The country gentleman was gone, however, and at this writing, is still at large, probably holed up in Sicily's inaccessible mountains. Giuseppe Mancuso, charged with complicity, is also in hiding. Brother Salvatore is too—but not in Italy. Brought back to the United States, to serve as a government witness in another case, he promptly escaped from American agents—proving that not only Italian officers are fallible.

Curiously, several of those involved in the case had been, at one time, residents of New Orleans and associates, to one degree or another, of Dandy Phil Kastel and Frank Costello. One was Sylvester Carollo, formerly of Memphis, Tennessee. He has been labeled by police as "one of the most important" nabbed since the all-out drive against dope began. Before his eventual exile, Carollo bore a charmed life where it concerned deportation. Once, a Louisiana Congressman had his banishment delayed by introducing into the House of Representatives a so-called "private bill" sparing the racketeer. This is an insidious practice, largely secret or unpublicized, known as "by request" legislation. Through these little-known bills, duly elected representatives too often have tried to keep killers, dope peddlers, and gangsters from exile. They are generally passed on a you-vote-for-mine, I'll-vote-for-yours understanding in the House.

Where Luciano got into the heroin-in-the-trunk caper was that just before Serafino's arrest he was seen frequently with Lucky. The morning after the trunk was found, Lucky hurriedly flew to Palermo, checked in at the ornate Delle Palme Hotel, made a mysterious telephone call, and returned to Naples the following day.

It would be impossible, of course, to name all the operatives in Lucky's far-reaching organization—for the Boss does not put the payroll lists on public display. However, research and occasional prosecution have uncovered several of those around him. Generally, in accordance with Lucky's personal views toward provincial Italian blood, they are deportees.

Here, at any rate, is a listing of some of those who, by their very proximity to the Boss in Italy in recent years, have made themselves at least available to him—if he wanted them—as playmates, hired hands, and/or associates up and down the Boot:

Nicolo Gentile— A long-known dope trafficker, and member of the inner council of Unione during his U.S. days. His arrest in 1937, in the United States, marked the most valuable break of the era, for his two address books contained the names and addresses of practically every important trafficker of the thirties, from coast to coast. In 1940, Gentile jumped $15,000 bail in the States and fled to Italy. He is generally credited with being in over-all charge of channeling heroin to the U.S.

Gaetano Chiofalo (Charley Young)— Former Brooklyn hoodlum, although the New York Police Department has no record on him. He is said to run the northeast Italy district, with headquarters in Trieste. Whenever things get too hot in Italy, Charley skips across the border to his cozy mountain cottage in Switzerland's canton of Tessin. He was deported by President Roosevelt.

Giuseppe (Giacomo) Giometti— Known as Jean the Frenchman, forty-eight years old, arrested in Milan in 1951 round-up—said to be a "big wheel" in Rome office of the dope organization.

Mike Spinella— Deported in June, 1953, after charges of operating a disorderly house in his motel in the New Jersey mob stronghold of Hackensack. He claims this is all wrong, that he's a legitimate owner of "hotels" in Florida and New Jersey. Fifty-eight years old, he insists Lucky "is a helluva nice guy," although there is no record they ever were associated in any way.

Joseph de Simone— A top Kansas City dope trafficker, convicted in 1943 of narcotics charges and deported to Italy in September, 1953.

Carmine Tufarelli— One of seventeen tried with Pici in Milan. Had served time in Sing Sing and had a police record for 20 years.

Joseph LoCurto— A most elusive exile, who was twice deported to Italy, and twice sneaked back into U.S. Freed from life sentence he was serving in connection with holdup killing of a policeman, he was first exiled with Lucky in 1946. In 1953, he was found back in the States for the second time—selling the same house to two women and taking a down payment from each.

Michael Cerani— General activities unknown except that they centered largely in New Jersey and New York, but described by authorities as "a key Luciano mobster."

With all the available information on his henchmen, aides, and associates, with the knowledge of the activities of his organization, and the continuing arrests and seizures, it is truly remarkable that no trail has ever been uncovered leading to Lucky, himself—a trail of evidence that would stand up in a court of law. This has been the major mystery in the entire long and bitter war against the traffic in terror drugs.

But just as elusive, just as confounding to investigators as the dead-end roads that never get to Lucky, was the problem of where, if he does control the deadly racket, he got the dope to pour into the pipeline to America, since manufacture of opium in Italy is done only by strict regulation. And here, at last, the first glimmer of light gets through.

One day, in late summer of 1950, a new face showed up among the hard-boiled habitués of the dives and the joints in the free city of Trieste. The newcomer had the Mulberry Bend earmark and spoke New York-ese with a dash of Sicilian accent. He let it be known that he was acquainted with all the right people. Frank Costello and Lucky Luciano were his pals.

This was not particularly strange in Trieste. Like any international free port, the city at the head of the Adriatic attracts the cream of the criminal element from all over the world. And its geographical location makes it a main station on the "White Road" from the poppy fields of the Near and Middle East to the heroin addict in the United States.

On one side, the free territory adjoins Yugoslavia, a major opium producer herself, as well as a main-line route for raw opium from Greece and Turkey. On the other side, it touches Italy, the world's leading manufacturer of drugs derived from the deadly white powder.

In spite of Yugoslav and Italian frontier guards and British and American occupation security forces, the contraband is sneaked from the Yugoslav-occupied Zone B into the controversial Zone A, which was, until the fall of 1954, under Anglo-American control. The "professionals" went into action in this melting pot, to get the raw material across the border. It is smuggled by farmers or laborers who cross the so-called Morgan Line daily, going to and from work, as well as by fishing boats and coastal vessels plying between Trieste and neighboring Adriatic ports. And by thousands of other smugglers, mostly of amateur, or, at best, semipro rating.

Quite recently, American Military Police became curious about a truck loaded with lumber, which passed the frontier guards without trouble. Long unhewn logs were piled in rows on top, and underneath were shorter lengths. By chance, an MP picked up an ax and swung at one of the short pieces. The wood split apart as if it were cheese. The log was hollow—and inside lay a cake of pressed crude opium. When all the logs were broken open, the load yielded 880 pounds of raw opium!

Amid these appropriate goings on, the congenial, free-spending newcomer from Mulberry Bend proceeded to drop a discreet hint here and there.

"I'm in the market for 'horse,'" he whispered. "All I can get."

Matteo Carpinetti, one of the local characters, let it be known that he had eleven pounds of heroin and was willing to talk business. Carpinetti wanted the normal Trieste black market price of $2,170. This was more than twice the legal maximum, but the stranger could very likely wholesale it for five figures per pound, back in the States. He "made a meet" with Carpinetti to close the deal.

Each showed up with two sturdy pals. (From long experience, the thug simply feels it best not to take any unnecessary chances.) The parcel of heroin and a thick wad of bank notes changed hands. Then, all of a sudden, Carpinetti and his aides were staring into the business ends of three guns.

"I'm a United States Agent," announced the New York mobster (who actually was Henry Manfredi, now with Army Intelligence). "You're under arrest."

In recent years, U.S. Federal Narcotics Agents have been working closely with Italian authorities and INTERPOL investigators in the never ending war against the slow murder.

The World Health Organization and United Nations

have strived for complete suspension, by international agreement, of the manufacture of heroin. Italy, the world's leading producer, hung back. Italian authorities were criticized repeatedly for failure to prevent large-scale diversion into illegitimate markets. In July, 1952, the Rome government agreed to suspend production, at least temporarily. Italy herself produces no opium. But the extensive poppy plantations in the neighboring countries of Yugoslavia, Greece, and Turkey supply the Italian market.

Five pharmaceutical firms, mostly in northern Italy, are licensed to purchase specified amounts of the raw material from government stocks for conversion into the multiple derivatives. The leading manufacturer is Societa Anonima Stabilimenti Chimici Riuniti Schiaparelli, in the northern industrial metropolis of Turin. Schiaparelli accounts for about 90 per cent of all legal narcotics production in the nation.

Italian law prescribes that any time drugs change hands, a "Modulo H" (Form H) must accompany each lot. The purchaser fills out the form and turns it over to the seller, who enters the data in a special ledger and then forwards it to the Medico Provinciale, or Regional Board of Health.

On paper, the control seems airtight. But heroin is pure gold in illicit traffic. Forging or falsifying of the Modulo H has not been difficult or dangerous. Many drug manufacturers and wholesalers were woefully guilty of negligence. Some would accept forms insufficiently filled out; others failed to insist upon proper identification.

Professionals learn quickly of loopholes as inviting as these.

Investigators probing into the supply lines of dope were shocked at the enormity of the frauds. Licensed manufacturers had been turning out a total of some 330 to 360 pounds of legal heroin annually before 1952. But no more than eleven pounds of this legal output was consumed legally each year. The rest landed in the illicit traffic!

Nor is that all. It has been established that, year in and year out, more than four hundred pounds of heroin—all illegal—is shipped from Italy. Obviously, then, more has been available than the supply diverted from legal stocks. Besides the large-scale conversion from controlled stocks, a factory or factories somewhere must be producing hundreds of pounds of illegal heroin each year. But where?

The great chemical firms, legally licensed, would hardly be mixed up in anything like this. Some of the biggest names in business and science were in those firms. Professor Carlo Migliardi of the University of Turin was the General Manager of Schiaparelli Laboratories. Professor Guglielmo Bonomo was executive director of the influential SAIPOM Corporation of Milan. Egidio Calascibetta, a *commendatore*—the highest honorary title the king could bestow, in the days of the monarchy—owned SACI, a respected company licensed to sell to the medical profession. Men of standing, like these, were not likely to be mixed up in anything as evil as dope trafficking.

For years, the investigating agents groped in the dark, through a jungle of intrigue, collusion, and corruption. Every city was watched, from the tip of the boot to the Brenner Pass, from Genoa to Trieste.

It was this vigilance that enabled U.S. Agent Manfredi to catch Matteo Carpinetti red-handed in Trieste in the summer of 1950.

Carpinetti was put through the wringer, and one of the items he let drop was the fact that the source of some of his supply was RAMSA. This was a shocker. RAMSA was a large, important company in the wholesaling of legal narcotics, authorized to purchase drugs for export. As the check continued, it developed that the very eleven pounds that had trapped Carpinetti had been bought by RAMSA from the huge firm of Schiaparelli, principal manufacturers in all Italy—at the official legal price of $100 a pound. Instead of exporting the heroin, though, RAMSA had resold it to the dope racketeer.

RAMSA's records were immediately combed, and out came more sensations. A second consignment of twenty-two pounds, which the wholesale firm had recently purchased from Schiaparelli, had been turned over—without the necessary form—to Dr. Gheo Baccarani, a pharmaceutical chemist and joint owner of a firm bearing his name in Modena.

Back in February, 1946, Dr. Baccarani had been arrested on charges of lawless dealings in penicillin and cocaine. The following year, he had obtained, with a false Form H, five-hundred grams of cocaine from Dr. Riccardo Morganti, one of the heads of RAMSA! And twice, during the next year, Baccarani had obtained thirty-three pounds of heroin with forms made out in the names of licensed dealers. And here were both Baccarani and Morganti implicated again, in the Carpinetti affair.

Dr. Baccarani admitted that he had bought ten kilos from RAMSA, dealing directly with Dr. Morganti. Reminded that heroin could only be obtained through strict legal formalities, Baccarani revealed that he had not bought the drugs in his own name or on behalf of his own pharmaceutical firm. Rather, he had acted for the SACI Company, an organization of high commercial standing in Milan, licensed to sell to the medical profession. He obtained the heroin without the required form, Baccarani conceded, but said he expected to get it later from SACI to be forwarded to RAMSA. Eyebrows lifted at the claim that a firm of SACI's standing would pick a long-involved trafficker to represent it in dealing with RAMSA.

"Just a favor for a friend," Baccarani tossed off. "I have known *Commendatore* Egidio Calascibetta, who owns SACI, for some time."

No one who got around like Baccarani could have believed that a story as full of holes as this one would carry any weight, except with a naïve child. And the agents were anything but naïve. They soon trapped Baccarani by nailing Dr. Morganti, who admitted his part in the illegal transaction.

In all this intrigue, the really shocking disclosure had been Dr. Baccarani's claim that he—a known dope trafficker—was a buddy of Egidio Calascibetta, who was one of the most esteemed citizens and social leaders of Milan, and that Calascibetta had assigned him as SACI's representative. The *Commendatore* promptly threw the lie at the doctor and everything he said.

"I never instructed him to get any drugs for me," Calascibetta asserted angrily.

As between believing a man of Calascibetta's standing or the dubious Baccarani, there was no choice. Baccarani obviously was looking for a way out. Certainly, no blame could attach to SACI in the transaction, for apparently it had not received any of the heroin.

A tap was put on the telephones at Baccarani's home and business. One day, a week or two later, a long-distance call came in from Genoa. The caller identified himself as "Bracco," and inquired cautiously whether the "stuff" had arrived. He urged most earnestly that this "stuff" be delivered to no one but himself. Questioned once more, Baccarani said he had known this Bracco about a year, had met him several times—but never had any deals with him in heroin or any other drug. And the mysterious "stuff" that had been mentioned?

"Just a shipment of sulfonamide I promised to get Bracco from Rome," Dr. Baccarani tossed off.

Unfortunately for the guileless doctor, however, Genoa police had a voluminous dossier on Carlo Bracco. He is known as the Duchess, is a notorious dope trafficker, and has been reported to be an associate of Luciano in Italy!

Italian justice in narcotics matters moves slowly. It was November, 1952, before the principals in this pretzel-like negotiation went on trial. Morganti and Cesare Melli, the co-owners of RAMSA, were sentenced to three years, eight months and two years, five months, respectively, and fined 790,000 lire. Carpinetti, caught red-handed, was given five years. But Baccarani, as a resident of Italy, did not fall under the jurisdiction of Trieste and was tried *in absentia*. He is, no doubt, still chuckling over the sentence of two years and two months that is waiting in the free territory—if he ever goes back. One lesson derived from all this is that in Italy, long delays precede trials of dope violators, and convictions carry but light sentences.

Intricate and, in parts, still obscure, the case nevertheless afforded a classroom example of one of the tortuous ways in which illicit enterprises might obtain their supplies. Through the complicated and confused business involving manufacturer, wholesaler, middleman, front man, consignee, and on and on, one fact emerged:

From the dark reaches of the criminal underworld, a firmly constructed narcotics pipeline, reeking with corruption, seemed to rise well up into Italian society!

The priceless information from the Trieste transactions indicated clearly that Baccarani and Morganti were really small fry. There must be higher-ups of influence and resources who manipulated the flow of heroin at its source. But who were these wire-pullers?

In mid-1951, strange whispers began to be heard of a mysterious Club della Talpa, or Mole Club. Since then, the "Moles" have become infamous through a good part of Europe as an international outfit thriving on dope and white slavery, with headquarters in Milan and branch offices in many cities. The reports are that the bizarre club is hand and hand with, if not an actual arm of, Unione. Italy's Commissioner of Public Health, Giovanni Migliori has described the Moles as an international criminal cartel.

"Some members carry on their real activities behind a political front," he charged in 1951. "Others hold top-ranking positions in commerce."

Elaborating, he indicated that a number of important business firms in northern Italy, particularly legitimate drug manufacturers, had been forced into virtual partnership with racketeers through "a real economic blackmail system," and he felt that the Moles were doing the digging. "One of the principal ringleaders, a top-notch international businessman, is hiding behind a respectable trade," he said. "In all our inquiries, there always proved to be, somewhere along the line, a missing link in the chain of command. The masterminds take excellent care to maintain contact with the underlings only through a long and practically untraceable pipeline." It sounded almost as if he were describing a typical Luciano operation of the Boss's palmy racket days.

Among the early tourists from New York in the spring of 1952, was one Giuseppe Biondo. Giuseppe had a date with an old friend—Lucky Luciano. Back in the thirties, Joe and Charlie Lucky were close associates—close enough, in fact, so that they were picked up together in the lobby of one of Cleveland's leading hotels during a police investigation in July, 1931. They had been visiting the Ohio metropolis for a prize fight, and were caught in a police racket cleanup.

Joe Biondo had figured for many years in the "International List of Narcotics Violators"—a world-wide Who's Who of dope, compiled by the INTERPOL. As far back as 1919, he was nabbed for dope dealing. During the Murder, Inc., investigations in Brooklyn in the early forties, Kid Twist Reles, turning state's evidence, told of a thriving taxicab extortion racket and said that one Joe Biunde, or Biondo was mixed up in it, along with the powerfully connected Joey Adonis.

Apparently *Signor* Biondo was well aware of his standing in international narcotics circles. He took the most solicitous care to hide his tracks through the entire trip from New York to his date with Lucky in Naples, in 1952.

Once in Italy, he pointed like a bird dog straight for his old pal Lucky. They greeted each other most cordially. In a short time, the Boss and his henchman started on a trip through the Italian countryside, going all the way to Milan. And there, to the astonishment of the investigators, they proceeded directly to see *Commendatore* Egidio Calascibetta, head of the esteemed SACI Company!

It is difficult to understand the reasoning behind this

open, unconcealed visit. Lucky certainly knew he was under observation. He must certainly have expected, too, that a character with Joe Biondo's form chart would have an official eye on him. Yet, he escorted his chum to his meeting with the impeccable *Commendatore,* and even made the introductions, with no effort at keeping the visit a secret.

Milan police picked up both Biondo and Lucky. The transatlantic tourist could hardly deny meeting Calascibetta, or that he had been introduced by Lucky himself. He did, however, deny most strenuously that it had anything at all to do with narcotics.

"A sad misunderstanding," said Biondo sadly. He saw Calascibetta, he explained, merely for the harmless purpose of buying acetic acid for shipment to the United States.

Authorities helpfully pointed out a few facts to Biondo. Acetic acid is cheaper and available in much larger quantities in the United States than in Italy. The traveler could have saved himself a five-thousand-mile trip.

"I like to travel," Biondo explained, and stuck to his story.

There were, however, other details that did not quite fit. For one thing, acetic acid can be used in cutting opium to manufacture heroin. For another, Biondo claimed he was representing a number of well-known American firms. These business organizations were queried and quickly insisted that they had never heard of Biondo.

Lucky was just as emphatic. "I only brought Biondo and Calascibetta together to help arrange a nice clean deal," the Boss persisted. Nor was there a single contradictory word to dispute them; no evidence linking Calascibetta to the two thugs in anything except a legitimate business transaction.

Lucky and Biondo would have gotten away with it, too—if romance hadn't blossomed in the house of Calascibetta! A niece of the *Commendatore* got married, and the happy couple spent their honeymoon on the enchanted isle of lovers—Capri.

Curiosity got the better of an inquisitive—and unromantic—investigator. He took a close look and discovered that the newlyweds of the house of Calascibetta were honeymooning as the guests of Lucky Luciano! This was out-and-out, stand-up evidence that a close personal relationship must exist between the notorious Unione whoremaster and the respected social and business leader.

Not even the complete respectability and reputation, which had hitherto absolved the powerful SACI organization and its owner in the minds of the patient police, could weather this. The firm was promptly raided. And the books and records disclosed that Calascibetta—*Commendatore* of the king, social lion, business tycoon—had, through a long string of clever bookkeeping tricks, been covering up large-scale diversions of heroin into the illicit traffic for years! Calascibetta had tried to corner the entire heroin market, both legitimate and illicit. He had put pressure on other pharmaceutical firms to sell their entire output to him—under threat, on occasion, of running them out of business if they didn't!

The untouchable executive was hauled in and indicted. It was evident now who and what Health Commissioner Migliori had meant when he revealed the existence of the

294

Club della Talpa and an "economic blackmail system" by which legitimate firms were being forced out of business through the evil purveyors of dope. Nor could there be a shred of doubt any longer as to the identity of the "top-notch international businessman hiding behind a respectable trade."

It turned out, too, that Calascibetta's meeting with Lucky, when the Boss brought Joe Biondo up to buy "acetic acid," had not been an isolated occurrence. Lucky had visited the *Commendatore* any number of times before. This was definitely a long-established connection. Now, at long last, the light had broken through on Lucky's place, and it was far removed from among the hustlers and the peddlers where the Narcotics Agents generally put him. As usual, the Boss was right up close to the top!

In spite of the crushing evidence against him, Calascibetta was not arrested, but merely "denounced" to the public prosecutor. There are no indications that he will come up for trial any time in the near future. One victory was, however, achieved. SACI was closed down.

What is very apparent is the fact that Lucky still knows his way around. Through an unapproachable front, the master of the new Crime, International, had evidently gained access to legitimate heroin production. The various source springs had been channeled into one large pool, controlled by the esteemed Calascibetta. From this, supplies could be drained into the big transoceanic pipeline at will. But with the old Luciano touch, as usual, Lucky, himself, was in the clear. The entire burden of answering to the Law fell on the *Commendatore*. Lucky could not be touched for a violation of any kind. This was the old American-style cover-up.

An important depot along the concealed route of the White Road had been closed down by the SACI affair—but the road was not blocked, by any means.

Remember, the quantity of Italian heroin smuggled into the United States annually was known to be well over the grand total licensed output of Italy's factories. The only explanation was that some factory or factories were producing the "horse" under the table. SACI, a wholesaling house, was not the answer. Somewhere, in the unexplored shadows, other Moles—perhaps even bigger than the *Commendatore* —were burrowing.

The investigation continued across northern Italy. Various characters fell into the net—businessmen, legitimate wholesalers, and distributors and, sometimes, Lucky's pals— without very startling results.

One day, Armando Lodi, a drug wholesaler of Genoa, turned up in the catch. Armando was no stranger to the narcotics "Who's Who"—or to Lucky. Lodi had been a key man in organizing and streamlining the large-scale transatlantic traffic. It was he who developed the system of having seamen smuggle dope into the United States—a method that has been vital to the stepped-up traffic since 1947.

In 1949, Lodi had been convicted of shipping vast quantities of heroin to America. Now in 1952, he was still obtaining drugs from legal channels! After much prodding as to the source, Armando finally admitted, "I bought ninety pounds of heroin from ALFA."

ALFA was a chemical concern of some standing in Savonna. Its books were immediately checked and revealed black-market operations running into several hundred pounds. The name of SACI was prominently entered. In one transaction, ALFA had obtained from SACI close to ninety pounds of heroin on forged H forms. Another shipment of similar size had been made directly from SACI to Lodi.

This shaped up now as a major operation. The probers hammered hard at Lodi. Where did the very considerable amounts of contraband come from, besides ALFA, and where did they go?

"I resold seventy pounds in one transaction," he answered.

"To whom?"

The wholesaler named Professor Guglielmo Bonomo as the purchaser. The agents had been getting to the point where nothing surprised them any more in this incredible chain, but they were not yet sufficiently shockproof for this one. Professor Bonomo simply could not be suspect!

Executive director of the important SAIPOM Corporation of Milan, he was holder of three academic degrees. He taught chemistry at the University of Milan. And, like Calascibetta, the respected professor figured prominently in the Milan social register.

Nonetheless, the records of SAIPOM were nabbed. And they revealed that over a three-year period, Professor Bonomo alone had handled the fantastic total of nine hundred pounds of heroin. (Remember, legal production in the entire country was only some 330 pounds a year.)

What's more, Professor Bonomo had been closely associated with Calascibetta, already exposed as Luciano's buddy. Between them, these two pillars of society had siphoned into the pipeline well over one thousand, two hundred pounds of the deadly drug!

At first, Professor Bonomo resisted questioning. When he did start to talk, he was asked to tell the identity of the man to whom he had turned over these tremendous stockpiles. He named Giovanni Greco.

Once more, it was a stunner. Giovanni Greco and the esteemed professor? Incredible! Almost any time a hoodlum had been picked up with dope, he had insisted that he had purchased it from one Giovanni Greco of Palermo. Frank Callace, Joe Pici, Serafino Mancuso—all of them had pointed a finger at this sinister Sicilian.

The dragnet went out. For weeks and weeks, it came up with nothing. At last, Giovanni Greco was found—dead!

The exact circumstances of his demise remain shrouded in underworld archives. But if Giovanni Greco was not done in because he knew too much, then a better motive has yet to be found. It is standard operating procedure in gangdom.

And here was the professor confessing that he sold the huge stock of illicit dope he handled to the very nefarious—and extinct—dealer who turned it over to the mobsters.

Professor Bonomo, having delivered one choice titbit, now provided another. He suggested that a good long talk with his colleague in Turin, Professor Carlo Migliardi, might not be wasted.

This had to top all the shockers. The forty-one-year old Professor Migliardi loomed above all the others. He was a distinguished scholar and a teacher of biological chemistry at the University of Turin. And he was general manager and technical director of the Schiaparelli Laboratories, the largest manufacturer of heroin in Italy. At Schiaparelli, he enjoyed the complete confidence of the owners and unquestioned authority over his staff. Up to that moment, any and all previous reference to the great pharmaceutical concern in these nefarious dealings had been brushed away by investigators as fabrication.

The firm had been mentioned in the very first dope revelations, back in 1950, when the trafficking Dr. Baccarani had insisted that the ten kilograms which had brought him into the net had been manufactured by the huge firm. But Schiaparelli had filled that order for the RAMSA Company, ostensibly without knowing Baccarani had anything to do with it. If the drug was subsequently diverted into the illicit traffic, blame could hardly attach to the manufacturer.

However, the name of the professor and the great old chemical house had cropped up one time too many. For four years, the investigators had been trying to find a factory that was producing clandestine heroin behind its legal front. Now, for the first time, they were led to a factory of consequence.

In short order, Professor Migliardi was suspended by the directors of Schiaparelli. Three months later, the Regents of the University of Turin took similar action against him.

In November, 1952, the Guardia di Finanza's top narcotics expert, Captain Guillermo Oliva, and two aides arrived in Turin. All three were graduates in chemistry and trained in a special police school in narcotics manufacture and trade.

From the amount of residue left over after extractions, experts can determine, with minute mathematical accuracy, the percentages of derivatives obtainable from any given amount of opium. Under the law, all residue must be put into vats and preserved for authorities.

The calculations of the captain and his men showed

by formulas that the total of extracted drugs and the residue did not add up at Schiaparelli. In fact, over a period of four years, beginning in 1948, 770 pounds of heroin had been clandestinely produced at the mighty, untouchable laboratories.

At the official legal price, this output represented 105,-000,000 lire. On the Italian black market, the value jumped to 525,000,000 lire. That was chicken feed compared to the take in the United States. For 770 pounds of pure heroin, the U.S. wholesaler will pay $24,500,000—and on the retail market, after cutting, the return is a fabulous $175,000,000!

It developed now that in the years he was in charge, Professor Migliardi had spent many hours alone in the laboratory at night. Sometimes he even sent the night watchman away. Witnesses came forward to report that they had seen containers being removed from the plant in the dark hours. *Commendatore* Calascibetta had also been observed visiting the laboratory after it had shut down for the day.

Professor Migliardi, esteemed and respected scientist and executive, was indicted.

"Clandestine and fraudulent traffic in narcotics," the accusation read. There was charge after charge in the bill. It took a two-hundred-page dossier to list them all. Yet, for this lawlessness that would lead to the degradation and slow murder of many thousands, Italian law stipulates a penalty of only one to three years, plus a fine! For handling perhaps a billion lire worth of dope, mind you!

The professor was not placed under arrest. As this is written, no trial date has yet been set—although the indictment is a year old.

Naturally, Professor Migliardi vigorously denies all the accusations. He claims he is the victim of scientific error.

"The huge amount of missing drug simply evaporated in the manufacturing process," is his defense.

Italian police authorities reveal that Migliardi sold practically his entire clandestine output, falsely labeled "codeine," to Egidio Calascibetta, Lucky's long-standing acquaintance inside the drug industry.

The Italian High Commissioner for Hygiene and Public Health ordered Schiaparelli shut down in January, 1953. Astonishingly, the ban was lifted in just one month, on the grounds that no evidence showed the company was responsible for the professor's work. What's more, Schiaparelli was given the green light to go right on manufacturing opium derivatives!

The Italian police charged with enforcing Italy's antinarcotics laws were not happy. They insist Schiaparelli was granted the clean bill in the face of definitely contradictory evidence.

With the unmasking of Migliardi and Schiaparelli, the missing link in the long chain of complicity was found, at last, and the setup exposed to the naked eye. The discovery of this link will hardly stop the operations. The fact still remains, however, that a gigantic chain of command reaches from the lowest depths of the underworld into the highest strata of Italian society, and it is largely responsible for wrecking thousands of American schoolchildren year after year.

At the top of the ladder stood two eminent scientists. On the rung below was the equally respected *Commendatore* Calascibetta, captain of industry—and friend of Charlie Lucky, the whoremaster. Another rung down, are the doctors, Baccarani and Morganti, and still others—men of breeding and learning—acting as figureheads, brokers, mid-

dlemen, and fronts for this incredibly profitable department of Crime International.

As for Lucky himself, there is, naturally, no visible rung
where he may be seen. The gang lord who was a founding
father of the National Crime Syndicate stands apart from
the ladder, surveying, manipulating, directing—and untouched.

He knows everybody, from the Turkish and Iranian
exporter to the Yugoslav official who can be bribed to let a
shipment over the border, to the North Italian processor,
to the smuggler, to the distributor.

He puts X in touch with Y; has Y meet Z. He may be
exiled and watched and guarded, but he still manipulates.
He is the Boss.

13 LUCKY TALKS

Picture of a poor persecuted mobster, beset by gambling and women.... Cousins galore, looking for a touch. ...Lunch with the Boss: philosophy, mob style.... The cabaret wiggler and the Neapolitan penthouse.... Is Lucky indispensable?

WHEN THIS BOOK was undertaken, it was considered imperative to locate and interview the general manager of international crime. There were so many conflicting stories and indiscriminate charges against Lucky, that it was impossible for all to be true.

For example, within the space of a few weeks in 1951, the following contradictory diagnoses were made:

The Kefauver Senate Crime Committee said there were two major syndicates in organized crime, and that Lucky was the "umpire" or "arbiter" between them.

The Federal Narcotics Bureau unequivocally tabbed Lucky as the big boss of everything.

The Internal Revenue Bureau insisted Luciano was not the big boss, but only second in command to Frank Costello or some other high-ranking Unione officer.

Naturally, Lucky could not be counted on to co-operate on subjects such as these. A notorious criminal is not likely to gush forth his innermost secrets. Besides, the Boss's relations with the press have seldom been happy ones. He will, to be sure, put on an occasional sugar coating, to create a good impression. But he is more likely to burst out in a stormy rage, complete with thunder and high winds.

There was that news conference in Naples, a couple of years ago, at which he gave the press a thorough spanking for connecting him with any and all illegitimacy.

"The name of Lucky Luciano has been associated for some time with all the acts of American gangsters," he pronounced irately, "and I was said to be the mastermind of them all. I feel indignant about that. They are defaming me, and spoiling my reputation."

(At that one, a number of the newsmen found it necessary to bury their faces in their handkerchiefs.)

When Lucky really gets angry, he is not above letting a fist fly. Once, after being held in Regina Coeli Prison in Rome for one of his numerous questionings, he came out storming.

"No pictures," he snarled at the waiting photographers.

One persistent cameraman dogged him all the way home. At the entrance to his apartment, the excitable exile made for the picture snapper, grabbed him roughly, and fired a couple of punches at him.

Just the same, the spotlight is never off him—and not only in Italy. In newspaper offices from New York to New South Wales, he is copy—far better copy as the exile in Italy than he was as the vice czar in Manhattan. In almost every country you visit, including those far outside his sphere of interest, people talk about Luciano.

And in spite of his dislike for newsmen, the Boss keeps himself well informed on what they are saying about him. For some years he has been keeping tabs on his "press" in every language by subscribing to a world-wide clipping service. The references in the daily batch of clippings are, naturally, anything but complimentary. The unwelcome notoriety worries Lucky. He has not forgotten that the mob lord who remains covered up gets along; the one whose name is in the papers doesn't.

Consequently, the chances of a writer getting to Lucky (and then getting anything out of him) were not very bright. The outlook became even less encouraging when some sources reported that he had slipped out of Italy. There are more pleasant ways to spend a month in Europe than hunting an international hoodlum.

Actually, meeting crimeland's number-one celebrity turned out to be hardly more difficult than locating a pizzeria in Italy!

(One of the authors—Joachim Joesten—undertook the assignment, in 1953. The personal pronoun in this chapter is his.)

In Rome, Ed Hill, executive editor of the *Daily American,* and former Associated Press staff writer, as well as night city editor of the New York *World Telegram,* was especially helpful. He obtained from his Italian advertising manager a letter of introduction to *Signore* Fantoccio, manager of the Hotel Turistico in Naples.

This large and luxurious hostelry is the most popular in Naples among American tourists and military personnel. Luciano is said to be either the outright owner or holder of the controlling interest in it. He still maintains business headquarters there—for receiving mail, anyway.

I took a room at the Turistico, then asked to see *Signore* Fantoccio on a personal matter. A small, spare man came forward in the lobby, with a most pleasant greeting.

"I want to meet Lucky Luciano," I announced, point-blank. "Can you set up the interview?"

The smile went blank, the affability vanished.

"I'll see what I can do," mumbled *Signore* Fantoccio after some hesitation.

He summoned a reception clerk, a dark, burly character with none too reassuring looks, and inquired how *Signore* Lucania could be reached. From the ensuing rapid-fire conversation in Italian, it appeared that the Boss had been out of town for a couple of days, and that it was not certain whether he had returned.

"*Signore* Lucania has no telephone," both men quickly explained. (Untrue, of course, as Lucky himself was to reveal inadvertently later.)

It was arranged for the clerk to send a special delivery letter, asking *Signore* Lucania to call the hotel as soon as possible. It took all of one night to get an answer.

"*Signore* Lucania is down in the lobby," was the telephone message, bright and early the next morning.

You are struck at once by an appearance almost of dignity in this international hoodlum with the heavy eyebrows, fleshy nose, hard lips and thick hair barely touched with gray. At fifty-five plus, Lucky looks like someone's uncle. The rather low forehead wrinkles in deep horizontal furrows when he is puzzled or thoughtful. When he laughs or smiles—which he does frequently—he bares strong white teeth. His complexion is rather remarkable—swarthy and yet ruddy, in a leathery sort of way, with tiny pockmarks and blemishes about the jaw and neck. He peers warily through rimless glasses, and replies to questions with the utmost caution and hesitation.

That morning his dark blue worsted was extremely con-

servative. His white shirt was soft-collared; the tie a subdued blue and white pattern, held by a gold clasp bearing
the initials "ELS." Whose they were, never came out. His
small feet were encased in dark blue socks and well-polished
brown shoes.

There was about Lucky the diffidence and watchfulness
of the hunted—or the observant gang man. Whenever a
newcomer entered the lobby or someone passed in the adjoining hallway, his intent but furtive eyes shifted to the
movement. All that morning, he didn't miss a single trick
that went on in the hotel's public area.

Frequently, he exchanged mute signals with various attendants hovering in the immediate background—never in
the way, but always at hand. Twice he got up and went to
the telephone—once to make a call, again to answer one.

In view of Luciano's strained relations with, and undis-
guised scorn for, the press, it was surprising that he con-
sented to the interview at all. Even more astonishing was
his freedom and willingness to be drawn out on points
about which he is supposed to be notoriously sensitive.

Perhaps it was because, in this instance, he was seeing
not a newspaperman or magazine writer, but the author of
a prospective book about him.

"The American press is disgraceful," he blurted out
shortly after we met. "There is too much freedom of the
press in America."

He proceeded to make it clear, however, that he was
not overenthusiastic about this biography. It seems the Boss
has literary aspirations of his own.

"Someday, I'm gonna write my own memories," he said.
"Then the real story is gonna come out."

He has also been toying with the idea of a motion picture

on the same subject. The theory behind both film and book is to prove that society alone was to blame for his life of crime.

"I'm gonna write about my side of it," he explained. "But the time ain't right yet."

He blasts motion-picture producers who have approached him as greedy entrepreneurs out to milk him.

"They want me to foot all the expenses!" he snorted in outrage. "They figure it'll be about $300,000. It's nuthin' but a straight deal to get dough outa me. Them guys must think I'm swimmin' in an ocean of money.

"I don't have to put up a dime for a picture," he went on. "I got a lotta offers—offers to pay me good, too. I'm not puttin' up a nickel of my own for it."

It stands to reason no picture of Lucky could possibly be a true-to-life presentation—and still get by the Johnson Office. This story of one of the most lawless, scandalous lives ever lived would have to be loaded with prostitution and dope and the devil knows what else that is revolting and distasteful. But can you imagine the scrambling among some of the hustling Hollywood belles for the role of Nancy Presser!

Mention of the film got Lucky talking about his finances. Like practically everyone else these days, the gang lord with his fingers in all kinds of illicit pies voiced that most common of all complaints—lack of money! He claimed he's pretty nearly broke.

"I got no millions," he insisted. "I need dough bad. I lose a bundle here to a lotta people—just give it to them not to harm the foim."

The cryptic remark apparently was Lucky's disclosure of his investments in "legitimate business." He claimed that his *pasticceria* (bakeshop) in Sicily cost him $10,000 alone, in the short time it operated. He makes no bones about operating through dummies, rather than as an active partner in a "foim," because of his record and reputation.

"Let's say I'm a partner in a cannery, for instance," he elucidated. "If it gets around that I am, it ruins the foim. Like if the cannery does business in the United States. If they know Lucky's in it, they probably open every single can we ship, to look for dope."

What of the millions he extorted and collected in one way or another, in the years he was living high off the hog in the United States? "I like gamblin'; I like women," he candidly told Miss Llewellyn Miller, when she interviewed him for *American Weekly* Magazine. "Those are the two things that make money go fast. It came and it went."

Luciano is deeply disappointed in his Italian business associates. He indicated that they had either squandered his money, bungled business, or defrauded him outright.

Still, he proudly admits that he has lots of friends—and no enemies that he knows of. He gets very upset over any mention of a bodyguard.

"That's all newspaper stuff. Baloney!" he exploded. "Whenever a guy walks into a room where I am, somebody says 'That's one of Lucky's lieutenants.' I got no lieutenants—and no captains, either!"

As for bodyguards, he simply doesn't need them, he says, and for a very good reason. "The police watch me close," he pointed out. "It gives me trouble, sure. But with all them cops on my tail, at least my shoulders are pertected."

The reference was, unmistakably, to the Mob's old handy homicide habit of leaving a knife handle protruding squarely between a victim's shoulder blades. It was an incongruous admission from a fellow who had just broadcast that everyone loves him, and he hasn't an enemy in the world!

Rumor-spreaders in the States hinted not long ago that all may not be sweetness and love between Lucky and his old underworld *"paisan,"* Frank Costello. They have whispered that Costello's dislike has gone so far as to provide information to the Narcotics Bureau. Even if the code of the society didn't make that claim asinine, word about Lucky in dope was hardly needed from Frank C., who has not been in Italy for many years.

In September, 1951, a reporter for the newspaper *Milano Sera* wrote of Lucky's insistence that Washington alone, and not Costello, was responsible for the accusations against him.

"Costello once shined my shoes, and was glad to do it," he was quoted as adding.

In our interview, Luciano was even more positive. "Costello? Why shouldn't he be a friend of mine?" he commented curtly when the subject came up.

"What about that statement that he once shined your shoes?"

"That? That's an invention," he asserted.

If Lucky has no enemies and no lieutenants—he says—he has more "cousins" than he can handle. The number of people claiming kinship with the Boss, if collected in one spot, would make the world's largest family reunion. These relatives, however, have only one thing in common: lack of money.

"You don't know what I go through since I been in Italy," Lucky shook his head in misery. "In this country, everybody who got money, got a lotta cousins; when he's poor, he got no cousins. Things are very bad in this country."

Lucky has never made a secret of his low opinion of his fellow countrymen. His dislike, for some reason, is only toward the unadulterated Italian. He has no prejudice against Italian blood, so long as it has been mixed with Americanism—or Lucky's perverted idea of Americanism. His closest friends and associates are Italo-American like himself. And the very closest are of Sicilian extraction.

The Italian folk, on the other hand, seem to be attached to him. One publication recently devoted three pages to an especially sympathetic article, playing up his philanthropy as the major contributor, if not sole sponsor, of a 120-bed hospital in the village of San Sebastian, on Vesuvius' slopes.

One of Lucky's chief complaints is directed against Italian jurisprudence. When he was held for eight days for questioning in a narcotics investigation, with no charges against him, he mourned: "It couldn't happen in the good old days in New York. My lawyer woulda had me out on bail inside forty-eight hours. These people don't know what the word bail means."

Luciano's speech is undistinguished and common. He has never lost the old Mulberry Bend huskiness of voice and the downtown pronunciation and colloquialism. It is still "foim" for "firm" or—a word he frequently uses—"soitenly" for "certainly." The "g" is forever lost from his participial endings. He swears occasionally and uses much bad slang. But he never fails to apologize when a lady is present.

Just as he is an easy mark for a cash touch, Lucky also is a sucker for a hard-luck story, and some newsmen know it. Not too long ago, two young newsreel cameramen were sent to Naples to shoot some film of the Boss at work and play. They caught him in one of his uglier moods and got only a gruff refusal to every plea to pose.

One of the photographers dreamed up a sob story and sang it to Lucky. He told how they were working their way through college, and that they would have to pay the expenses for this Naples trip out of their own pockets, if they came back without pictures. The other took it from there.

"My wife is expecting a baby," he revealed, his voice touched with just the right tremble. "If we blow this assignment, I'm stuck for the trip, I don't know what I'll do for dough."

Lucky fell for it. He posed for all the pictures they wanted. And to top it off, took both of them to the races for the afternoon!

Lucky, of course, vociferously disclaimed any connection with, knowledge of, or dealing in dope, cigarette smuggling, or any other lawlessness. He made a sweeping denial of all incriminating allegations, official, quasi-official, or just plain gossip. To all, he had the same answer—his pet word, "Baloney!"

"They talk about me and never come up with evidence," he charged. And again: "It's all politics, and I'm the victim. It's about time to stop rapping me for all the bad things that happen in the United States and Europe. They even blamed an illegal Venezuela diamond racket on me!"

He did admit, at long last, that he had broken the law once since he reached Italy in 1946. That was when someone brought $57,000 into the country to him without bothering to inform authorities—and the authorities found out. It marked the only occasion when Lucky was threatened with really serious trouble, for the officials discovered he also had "abusively smuggled" in an American automobile, along with the $57,000.

Actually, they stumbled on it quite by accident, at the time of Callace's arrest with the suitcase full of heroin at Ciampino Airport in 1951. In the ensuing investigation, up popped Lucky's contraband money and car!

The car should not have been a surprise to authorities, inasmuch as they insist so vociferously that they have their eyes closely on him. At that time, he had already been riding it around the countryside for three years or more. The car is a 1948 green Oldsmobile, and you can't miss it in Naples. He wheels it through the city's crazy traffic daily. If Lucky is in the Turistico or any other of his daily hangouts, it is generally parked right outside. Police certainly had to spot it long before, for the smart sedan is almost as familiar in Naples as the Central Station.

It was brought in from the United States, brand-new, by Pasquale Mastranga, a Brooklyn olive oil and cheese dealer and lathe company operator. Mastranga's story is that when he was preparing for a trip to Italy to see his aged parents in 1948, one Tony Sabio, a friend of Lucky, asked him to take the automobile along as a favor. Lucky met the obliging Brooklynite at the dock in Naples, and drove the car away. Investigation discloses, however, that the vehicle was very likely a gift from Willie Moretti, the underworld's well-liked *"gumbari"* and New Jersey gambling impresario, who was so popular that he was shot dead a couple of years ago.

"What kind of registration have you got on the car?" I asked Lucky.

"American," he replied without hesitation. "New York plates."

Actually, the car bears 1948 plates—of New Jersey!

Lucky also owns an old Fiat. Frequently, he shifts from one to the other, trying to cloak his movements. For example, he will drive the Olds right up to the *Questura* (police headquarters), leave it parked there conspicuously, and walk into the building. A few moments later, he will emerge through another door and jump into the Fiat, which he has waiting. This little maneuver no longer fools any but the most obtuse policeman in Naples. It is, however, supposed to have lent Lucky an occasional alibi in the past. Moreover, it is well known that nowadays Luciano transacts nearly all of his business from one or the other of his cars. They cannot contain concealed spies—or be wired for sound.

It is remarkable that a gangster under surveillance—and an Italian citizen, to boot—is permitted to go on, year after year, driving an American car, imported in violation of the law and bearing plates that have been illegal for five years or more. Lucky insists he has tried for years to have the car, as he puts it, "nationalized." Under Italian law, however, registration of illegally imported cars is prevented. There are thousands of American cars in Italy under similar circumstances—imported illegally, and because of the statutes, not registerable by Italian citizens.

Treasury agents put Lucky through an intense twenty-hour grilling over both the smuggled $57,000 and the car. At the time, police announced that he faced fines of up to five times the value of the currency, or close to $300,000. Then it was reported he would have to pay $60,000. Actually, the penalty wound up as a fine of exactly $4,000!

"And I'm paying the four grand in installments," he disclosed.

He must have given the Italian Treasury Department quite a sales talk to get away with this pat on the wrist. As long ago as May, 1952, in fact, the Department threatened him with imprisonment unless he paid up the fine in ten days.

Even while admitting his guilt, Lucky tried to make it appear as though he had been the innocent victim of unfortunate circumstances and the evils of the times.

"I didn't know the laws of the country, and that's all that happened," he explained sanctimoniously during our conversation. "I just changed the money for a better rate on the black market, just like most Americans do here, and most of the tourists too," he declared. "That's all I did."

Lucky is neither American nor tourist, but his whole air is that of a man who feels that as long as the black market is doing business, what's the harm in trading in it?

"What would you do," Lucky continued, "if you knew you could get 675 lire to the dollar on the black market, and only 620 on the official rate?"

Although Lucky goes into hiding from time to time, I soon learned that he is really quite accessible to anyone who wishes to catch a glimpse of him at work or play.

Whenever the fleet is in, sailors queue up like a chow line in front of one or another of Lucky's well-known haunts, just to get his autograph. Visiting firemen seldom fail to inquire about him, and enterprising sight-seeing guides make a regular business of barking the Luciano sights to tourists.

These days the Boss adheres to a daily routine almost as rigid as he followed at Dannemora. His schedule begins with a morning appointment at his barber, near the Central Station. He lunches every noon at the same table at Da Giacomino's, an old favorite among Naples' better-heeled gourmets, with gleaming white walls and flower vases, and the motto, "Here Eats Lucullus."

When the horses are running, he heads for the Agnano Hippodrome promptly at three each afternoon. Then there is dinner at the widely famed Zi Teresa, in the Santa Lucia water-front district. In between, the Boss can be found going through his mail at the Turistico or putting in an occasional appearance at the even swankier Excelsiore Hotel. And afterward, as a celebrated man about town, he hovers at certain favorite cafés and bars.

Some time after the Turistico interview, I went to Da Giacomino's for lunch. He was there, as usual, seated at a table at the far end of the restaurant. He gave no sign of recognition, so I figured there was no reason for me to acknowledge him either.

But, just as in the Turistico, no one enters Da Giacomino's unnoticed by the mobster in exile. A moment after I sat down, a waiter stopped at my table.

"Would you care to join *Signore* Lucania at his table?" he invited. He spoke Italian, and when it did not register immediately, he repeated, in English. Only, this time he said, "*Signore* Lucky Luciano."

Local folks tell you this sort of thing is not unusual for Lucky. Not infrequently, he strikes up conversation with tourists in one or another of his haunts, sometimes to talk only of the weather back in the States, or other subjects similarly prosaic. Italian police who have noted this custom suggest that it is nothing but lonesomeness and nostalgia for America. In his conversation, too, he leaves the strong impression that he feels a real exile.

Lunching with Lucky, you notice first that he pays close attention to the business of eating. His opening course was a heaping platter of spaghetti.

"I really go for it—never get tired of it," he smiled. He is, however, no more adept than the next man at manipulating the slippery serpentines from plate to mouth.

Next on his menu was a plate of fried fish, which he did little more than toy with. He wound up with a piece of provolone, the dry tasty cheese so popular on the Italian table, and, for dessert, a *crême* caramel. During the meal, we drank a bottle of sweet Verona wine.

Between fish and cheese, came a puzzling order for a dish of boiled beef. Not until he cut it entirely into small pieces did it become apparent that the plate was for Bello, a giant German shepherd stretched out at his feet throughout the meal.

Most of the patrons seemed to know him. Virtually all nodded in his direction, and one tall, distinguished gentleman, catching sight of Luciano as he entered, tipped his hat and bowed deferentially, as if to a big-shot politician. The Boss knows all the waiters and orders them around in a personal, friendly manner. At one point, he mentioned that Naples' population is two million. The figure seemed too high. Lucky summoned a waiter to ask the correct total. It turned out to be a million and a half.

At another point during the meal, a girl approached selling tickets in the National Lottery. This gave the Boss an opportunity to let off steam about American laws against gambling.

"If this were the States," he snorted, "she'd be arrested right away."

He was hilarious over a report by the Kefauver Senate Committee estimating the bookmaking total in the United States at between three and five billion dollars a year.

"Tell them I'd like to get only one per cent of that take," he chortled. "How cockeyed can they get?"

Over lunch, Lucky seemed considerably more relaxed than at the Turistico. He chatted nonchalantly about every subject from spaghetti to Stalin, from pinschers to politics, from Senator Taft to taxes. He impresses one as being several cuts above the garden variety "dese-dem-dose" hoodlum, made so familiar by the movies. He has, though, a basic quality of smothered violence that is the gangster peeping out from under the polish.

No matter how many other subjects he discusses, he returns compulsively to the "persecution" he feels has been visited on him, and to protest that he is not bad—just misunderstood.

Lucky's resentment is aimed primarily at U.S. Narcotics Commissioner Henry Anslinger. If Old Nick himself were to appear before Luciano, he would very likely have the form of the stocky official who heads the organization charged with the job of cleaning dope out of America.

"Hitler was an angel in comparison to what Esslinger is," Lucky maintained. (He persists in calling him Esslinger, perhaps feeling that in this way he is placing a stamp of nonentity on the government man.)

"For six years, I have no peace at all," he cried. "It is a nonstop persecution. I don't know what Esslinger wants from me. No charge against me about dope will ever stand up. If there was evidence—just an inch of proof—I'd be in jail in less than an hour."

"I'm here, I'm not escaping, I'm not running away," he contended. "I stay here, and I don't have a worry, except racing horses."

He found considerable wrong with Anslinger's investigative methods. "Have you ever heard of a cop telling the public what he's going to do when he suspects somebody of a crime?" Lucky pointed out. "I'm waiting for Esslinger to put me in jail, just to see what comes next."

Oddly enough, he feels no such antagonism for J. Edgar Hoover, head of the Federal Bureau of Investigation. "Hoover's no friend of the hoodlums or the underworld," he was quoted by New York columnist Leonard Lyons in an article in Esquire Magazine. "I like him because he never makes an announcement about what he's gonna do. He never says a guy is tied up in a racket, and he's gonna grab him for it. None of that yakity-yak. A guy does somethin', Hoover grabs him. No announcements. He don't shoot his mouth off. He's got efficiency!

"But this other guy, this Esslinger," Lucky went on. "Yakity-yakity-yak. He makes announcements about me, but what does he do. Nuthin', absolutely nuthin'!"

The Boss even had a suggestion to prove his contention. "Why don't they file proceedings with the U.S. Government to get my deportation back to America, and let me defend myself personally?" he asked.

"I am barred from Rome, but I can go anywhere else in Italy," he stormed. "There's no reason why—only to oblige Mr. Esslinger in America.

"I'm an Italian citizen," he continued. "But Mr. Esslinger tells 'em take my passport away—and they take it.

That's how far things go. And this is only one of the things the man done to harm me. And it is all lies!"

Whether the loss of his passport has harmed Lucky is a very moot point. When he came back from his sneak to Cuba, the Government demanded his papers. However, it was no trick at all for him to get the permit back in a short time, when he wanted to go to Germany. He didn't make that trip, because he couldn't get a German visa. But he held the second passport a year and a half. Then it, too, was withdrawn on explicit orders of the Ministry of Interior.

Any number of observers will bet that Lucky still travels abroad, papers or no papers. Reliable authorities in Naples insist he has been to both France and Austria since the document was picked up. It is perfectly possible that, as with his cars, Lucky is equipped with a spare. Remember, when he was discovered in Cuba, two passports were found on him.

Late in 1952, the Associated Press reported him in the Vienna area, en route to Spa for the baths. The A. P.'s Naples correspondent countered with the dispatch that he had dined, as usual, at Zi Teresa the night before. The Naples man subsequently sent a correction. The Vienna report was true; when Lucky showed up at Zi Teresa, he had just returned from Austria by car.

Also in 1952, there was a report that he flew from Rome to Paris in a French plane. During our interview, however, he feelingly deplored the prospect that he would never see Paris.

"I never been there," he related. "Now that my passport is gone, I am barred from the world."

A few observations about Luciano's nationality status

might be in order here. Lucky lived in the United States
nearly thirty years as a free man—forty, counting his stay
in prison. It would have been easy for him to have become
a citizen at any time, even in his earlier hoodlum days
when naturalization requirements were less strict. Nevertheless, he remained an Italian citizen—although to this
day, he has no particular affection for his native land.
All his life, Lucky has considered himself "an American."
He still does—except when it is convenient not to.

"Why on earth didn't you ever take out naturalization
papers?" I asked him.

He shrugged his shoulders. In effect, he laid it to laziness.
He just would not be bothered going to the Naturalization
Office to apply for citizenship!

"Spend two hours in that office?" he said. "Nix."

Lucky is indignant at the Department of Justice's recent
stepped-up drive to rid the United States of so many of
his old mobster pals through deportation. He feels this
proves that he was right in his lackadaisical failure to seek
citizenship.

"What difference would it make now if I got my papers?"
he ranted. "Look at Frank Costello and those other guys
who got them. Didn't Frank get to be a citizen long ago?
What good is it doing him now, with the Government
starting deportation against him—and a lot more?"

In his usually biased approach, Lucky is completely
blind to the fact that if his mobster buddies had behaved
themselves—as so many tens of thousands of decent immigrants do, who consider American citizenship the privilege
it is—they would not now be in danger of losing it. And
that none loses it without full and fair hearing.

(Oddly enough, the policy by which the Justice Depart-

321

ment is catching up with Lucky's gangland cronies only now has been on the books for years.)

"Five years ago, this kinda thing would not be possible," was Lucky's comment on the new enforcement tactics. It was an enlightening observation on the cuteness of the thugs who roamed their criminal way, in full knowledge that because of an apparently dormant attitude, the Justice Department did not use the weapons it had to fight organized crime!

Lucky denied ever having voted in an American election—which, of course, would have been illegal, since he is not a citizen.

"And I sure coulda thrown a lotta votes the way I wanted, them days," he added, not without pride. "But I got no real interest in politics." There was no sign of a tongue in cheek as he said it. Lucky's memory must have dimmed badly over the years, to forget an old friend named Marinelli.

To the direct question whether he had paid anything for his release from prison in New York, Lucky entered a flat denial.

"I got my pardon because of the service I rendered the United States," he persisted. He thought that over a moment. "I guess," he added, "they also realized that fifty years was too much for a crime like that."

This must be, beyond question, the clearest confession of guilt ever to come from the man who had heretofore—and has since—never stopped protesting his complete innocence of any complicity in the prostitution ring. A man who was truly innocent would certainly not be discussing degrees of guilt or label his actions a "crime"—ever.

Lucky is quite secretive about his new penthouse address.

"If it weren't for the cops here and the laws that make everybody register," he said, "not even Christ would know where I live. I'd go somewhere into a mountain!"

Lucky expects a raft of all kinds of crank letters if and when his address becomes generally known.

"I get letters with all kinds of propositions," he admitted.

"Threatening ones too?"

"No!" The contempt with which he said this seemed to add, "How silly can you get?"

The address, however, is no more difficult to learn than to step into a taxi and ask the driver to take you to Luciano's place. It is No. 464 Via Tasso, high on the famed Vomero. There are reports that he owns the entire brand-new ten-family building, and paid $150,000 for it.

As Lucky has his thick black morning coffee on the terrace of his six-room aerie, one of the most glorious views in the world is spread at his feet. Far below, the breathtaking blue harbor, dotted with tiny white sails, rolls to the horizon. Off to the left, mysterious Mount Vesuvius rises, its eternal finger of smoke reaching for the sky. And in the distance across the bay, enchanting Capri sparkles in a setting of blue water.

The only writer, so far as is known, able to wangle an entry to Lucky's lofty nest, is Miss Llewellyn Miller. She described it in *American Weekly* Magazine:

Its six rooms are on the small, cozy side. So is the furniture. The living room has chairs upholstered in white, with design of pink flowers. Next is the study, with green velvet chairs and drapes, and an upright piano. The dining table is covered with an old-fashioned damask cloth, and set for two in pink china. In the master bedroom, a painting of Madonna and Child hangs over the bed. The maid's room I did not see, because it was occupied. Lucky looked in, because the girl had been sick, and he inquired if she needed anything. The bath is done in shocking pink and black tile. The kitchen sports a big, American-make refrigerator.

The floors are marble, which is less impressive than it sounds, since that is the cheapest and most common flooring in Italy. The real luxury is the addition of hardwood floor in three of the rooms, to cover that ordinary old marble. Also not standard equipment are two ominously heavy-duty bars on the front door. They would look better on a warehouse.

Lucky's snug hide-out, sitting on a terraced ridge amid pine, palm, and oleander, mimosa shrubs, and cactus hedge, is guarded by nothing more ferocious than a black-haired and rather slovenly concierge, who challenges all comers to state their business. No one is allowed to ascend to the inner sanctum without having been granted the sesame over the house phone.

Blissfully sharing this aerie with the mob lord in exile is a shapely Italian show girl, night club entertainer, and ballet dancer, Igea Lissoni. Igea is in her early thirties and has been Lucky's mistress since 1947. She is obviously very much in love with the gangland gorilla, whom she calls "My Sharlie."

The girl has no police record and generally creates a good impression upon those who have met her. Luciano makes no secret of the liaison, which has lasted more than six years, and so may be regarded as reasonably permanent. They met in Naples, where she was wiggling in a water-front cabaret. It was love at first sight. Igea followed the racketeer to Rome. He set her up in his apartment.

Llewellyn Miller described Lucky's light o' love in her article:

She was blonde when they met. Now her hair is soft brown, smartly short. She has clear blue eyes and a low voice. There is nothing about her, at first meeting, of the wised-up show girl or the hard moll. In a sense, she, too, is an exile, for her family disowned her when she took up with Luciano.

She . . . is laboring under the vast misapprehension that "he is good and generous." I was grateful that my Italian and her English were both too poor to pursue this subject. Let someone else tell her.

If you are wondering why a young, fresh-looking girl would throw in her lot with the aging and evil hoodlum, remember that Igea did play the rough-and-ready Italian night-club circuit. Back in the late thirties, moreover, she is supposed to have done her stepping in the hot spots of Cairo—which are very, very hot indeed. The reasonable assumption, then, is that Igea knew her way around by the time she ran into Lucky.

Luciano has several times formally denied rumors that he had gone so far as to marry her. As a matter of fact the "Terms and Conditions of Parole," which he signed on his release from prison and deportation, forbids his ever entering matrimony. Igea does wear a wedding ring on her left hand. Which, of course, proves nothing.

They frequently go off, for week ends or longer, to Capri, to the placid Sorrento peninsula, to the Riviera, or wherever else their hearts—and Lucky's business—dictate.

There is much curiosity, of course, about Lucky's girl friend. The mere fact that Igea has kept him constant longer than any of the long list of previous dalliances makes this converted blonde something special in the way of charmers. Any honey who could beat out the gorgeous Gay Orlova (who is also on the Continent, remember) must have considerably more to offer than interesting conversation.

Lucky promised to have me meet his light o' love, but he welched on it. When I found his apartment house, through a cab driver, and called the penthouse on the house phone, Igea answered. But that was as close as I could get. She was sorry, but she had company. (A shiny black Buick with 1952 Oregon license plates was parked outside the building.)

"The *signore* is out," she reported. She didn't have to add that as long as "Sharlie" was absent, no writer was going to be asked up.

Organized crime in the United States has long since proved that loss of personnel leaves no permanent hole in the National Syndicate. Lepke went . . . and Buggsy Siegel . . . and Lucky. Their vacancies were soon filled by competent, cunning successors. The business—the rackets—go on unimpaired and, in many ways, unhampered.

Only one man, up to now, has proved himself to be, if not indispensable, at least the one consistent founder and developer of new and expanded enterprises. And that man is Lucky Luciano.

It was Lucky who, year after year, campaigned for the co-operation that eventually resulted in the National Syndicate, which was the underworld's means of survival after repeal. (He even wiped out Mafia to accomplish it.)

It was Lucky who, ever alert to the business truth that crime cannot stand still and survive—that it must progress or go back—founded and developed Crime, International, now hooked in so closely with the National Syndicate.

Lucky explored the territory, made the contacts in high places, and opened up the trade routes.

More than Lepke, more than Costello or the Fischettis or Adonis or any of them, Lucky can take bows for organized crime. To him, the National Syndicate—and the International one—can stand as monuments. No label ever fitted the contents of the package more appropriately than the tag they pinned on Lucky: the Boss.

Little Salvatore from Fourteenth Street grew up into a lot of things. But, by his own reckoning, he escaped the one fate he dreaded most—winding up "a crum."

Or could he be wrong?